KU-101-303

KEY MANAGEMENT
IDEAS

Thinking that changed the management world

STUART CRAINER

FT
PITMAN
PUBLISHING

PITMAN PUBLISHING
128 Long Acre, London WC2E 9AN

A Division of Pearson Professional Limited

First published in Great Britain 1996

© Pearson Professional 1996

British Library Cataloguing in Publication Data
A CIP catalogue record for this book can be obtained
from the British Library.

ISBN 0 273 62195 5

10 9 8 7 6 5 4 3

Typeset by Pantek Arts, Maidstone, Kent.
Printed and bound in Great Britain by
Bell and Bain Ltd., Glasgow

*The Publishers' policy is to use paper manufactured
from sustainable forests.*

The Author

Stuart Crainer is a management and business writer. He is editor of *The Financial Times Handbook of Management* and author of numerous books including *The Real Power of Brands* and *How to Have a Brilliant Career*. Stuart contributes to a wide variety of publications on business and management issues including *Business Life*, *Management Today*, and various newspapers.

Contents

Acknowledgments

Grateful acknowledgment is given to the *Harvard Business Review* for permission to include extracts from the following:

B. Shapiro, "What the hell is market oriented?," *Harvard Business Review*, November–December 1988. Copyright 1988 © By the President and Fellows of Harvard College; all rights reserved.

P Drucker, "The new productivity challenge," *Harvard Business Review*, November–December 1991. Copyright 1991 © By the President and Fellows of Harvard College; all rights reserved.

L Hirschhorn and T Gilmore, "The new boundaries of the boundaryless company," *Harvard Business Review*, May–June 1992. Copyright 1992 © By the President and Fellows of Harvard College; all rights reserved.

R Pascale, A Athos, and T Goss, "The reinvention rollercoaster," *Harvard Business Review*, November–December 1993. Copyright 1993 © By the President and Fellows of Harvard College; all rights reserved.

W Taylor, "The logic of global business: an interview with Percy Barnevik," *Harvard Business Review*, March–April 1991. Copyright 1991 © By the President and Fellows of Harvard College; all rights reserved.

And to the following individuals, companies and organizations for permission to quote from their works.

McGraw Hill Inc for permission to quote an extract from Kenichi Ohmae's *The Mind of the Strategist*, 1982.

Edgar H Schein for permission to quote extracts from *Career Anchors: Discovering Your Real Values*, Pfeiffer, San Diego, CA, 1990.

Introduction

To the vast majority of managers, management is about action rather than ideas. They are motivated by the sense of achievement when they raise profits, successfully introduce new products into the marketplace, record a sale, or bring in a new customer. Their language is direct, snappy, and peppered with talk of the bottom line. To them management is not a passive, studious, desk-based art, but something which is immediate and active. Management lives in the here and now.

Theory is what MBA students amass at business schools. The MBA covers ideals and dry case studies which invariably lack the direct immediacy of real management. It is theory without substance. It is one thing obtaining an MBA but, it is argued, quite another to convert what you have learned about a concept, such as strategic management, into constant practice across an organization.

The managers are right. Management is active, not theoretical. It is about changing behavior and making things happen. It is about developing people, working with them, reaching objectives, and achieving results. Indeed, all the research into how managers spend their time reveals that they are creatures of the moment, perpetually immersed in the nitty-gritty of making things happen.

But, management is nothing without ideas. "There's nothing so practical as a good theory," George Bain, principal of London Business School has observed.[1] Ideas drive management as surely as the immediate problems which land on manager's desks or which arrive via their e-mail. Decisions have to be based on ideas, as well as instinct. Without ideas managers flit desperately from crisis to crisis. They cannot know where they are going, why they are doing something or what they will achieve without the vital fuel of ideas.

This observation of the economist Keynes holds true for management: "Practical men, who believe themselves to be quite exempt from any intellectual influences, are usually the slaves of some defunct economist. Madmen in authority, who hear voices in the air, are distilling their frenzy from some academic scribbler of a few years back."

Ideas count. Look at the postwar resurgence of Japanese industry. Its growth was based on the precept of quality – this was largely based on the ideas and research of two Americans, W Edwards Deming and Joseph Juran. While the duo were listened to in Japan their ideas were all but ignored in the West until the 1980s. By then it was almost too late. The Japanese converted theory into practice and became a huge industrial power thanks, in part, to their highly effective implementation of the ideas of Deming and Juran.

The Japanese have a tradition of revering ideas and being able to translate them into dynamic practice. Early management thinkers, such as Frederick Taylor and Mary Parker Follett, were widely acknowledged in Japan while receiving only tepid reactions in their home country. In contrast, ideas in the West tend to be seen as distractions and are categorized as instant solutions or as simply impractical. There is often an unwillingness to try to understand or to try and make them work. The requirements of the moment take precedence in a world beset by ever-increasing demands on time, energy, and money.

Paradoxically, though managers appear to be bogged down in the minutiae of the moment, they are hungry for ideas, new perspectives and fresh approaches. Management books sell in their millions. Managers want to know and learn more. The problem is that they simply don't have the time. Research by the Management Training Partnership found that three quarters of personnel directors buy at least four management books a year. However, only one in five are actually read.[2]

Beyond the quest for one best way

That management books tend to be decorative is not the only problem. The key ideas which have shaped and continue to drive management are often regarded as inflexible. They concentrate on the "one right way" to carry out a task or achieve an objective. In reality, managers know that it is unlikely that one particular approach will solve all their problems. Reengineering, the latest in a long line of corporate saviors, has been the idea of the 1990s. Yet, even its most enthusiastic adherents would admit that reengineering cannot cure all known organizational ills.

Ideas count, but they are not ready-made solutions. No matter what consultants might suggest, there is no panacea. Faced with a crisis a manager cannot reach across for the file on "How to implement strategy" and hope for instant results. Achieving success in the 1990s and beyond involves a multitude of ideas, approaches, and skills.

The trouble is that managers appear addicted to the idea of the quick fix. There is still an air of desperation in the way that managers cling to new ideas. Fads and fashions emerge in a fanfare of superlatives only to disappear almost as quickly.

The learning organization was one of the fads of the early 1990s. Peter Senge's *The Fifth Discipline* led the way. An international bestseller, it propelled the Massachusetts Institute of Technology (MIT) professor to international renown. By 1995 Senge was receiving a less enthusiastic response. "It's part of the fad cycle," he told the *Financial Times*. "People consume then drop fads and ideas all the time and corporations are no different."[3]

Indeed, research at MIT suggests that management fads follow a regular life cycle. This starts with academic discovery. The new idea is then formulated into a technique and published in an academic publication. It is then more widely promoted as a means of increasing productivity, reducing costs or whatever is currently exercising managerial minds. Consultants then pick the idea up and treat it as the universal panacea. After practical attempts fail to deliver the promised impressive results, there is realization of how difficult it is to convert the bright idea into sustainable practice. Finally, there follows committed exploitation by a small number of companies.

Ironically, blame for this obsession with the latest trend can be partly attributed to the professionalization of management. Once management became regarded as a profession, it was assumed that there were a number of skills and ideas which needed to be mastered before someone could proclaim themselves a professional manager. The skills of management were regarded like a bag of golf clubs. When the occasion demanded a particular skill it was extracted from the bag and put to work. New skills could occasionally be added to the managerial bag of tricks when, and if, required.

> "Management has always been beset by fads and fashions, gurus and demagogues. But never before has there been such a sheer volume of new approaches."
> EDWARD LAWLER

Unfortunately, managerial life is no longer so straightforward. Typically, work by the UK's Management Charter Initiative to identify standard competencies for all middle managers emerged with several hundred. Simplifying the complex is never easy.

Despite this, the faddishness of managers continues as they seek out new skills and new solutions to perennial problems. "It has become professionally legitimate in the United States to accept and utilize ideas without an in-depth grasp of their underlying foundation, and without the commitment necessary to sustain them," observes Richard Pascale in *Managing on the Edge*.[4]

The fad industry has emerged and the chief beneficiaries are management consultants and business schools. The global management consultancy industry is worth $18 billion. In 1993 AT&T, like many other large companies, spent a massive amount on consultants – a total of $347 million, an amount so large it was calculated by one newspaper as being equivalent to paying 1,150 full-time managers.[5]

The search for the secret of management has taken managers and organizations through bewildering loops and has spawned an entirely new vocabulary. Managers have embraced brainstorming as a useful tool; they have explored Douglas MacGregor's Theory X and Theory Y; negotiated Blake and Mouton's "Managerial Grid"; been driven on by "Management by Objectives"; discovered strategic management through Igor Ansoff in the late 1960s; been converted by Tom Peters and Robert Waterman's *In Search of Excellence*; and have, no doubt, also tried their hand with quality circles and various forms of Total Quality Management. And yet, there is no single best way to manage – simply a ragbag of shared experiences, short-lived best practice and high expectations.

It is not that these various ideas are poor concepts. Many do work, but they are not set in tablets of stone. They have to be flexible, and used when needed, rather than as all encompassing "solutions." "Management has always been beset by fads and fashions, gurus and demagogues. But never before has there been such a sheer volume of new approaches," says Edward Lawler of the Center for Effective Organizations. "This has led many managers to reach one of two incorrect conclusions: that the new approaches are all hype with no substance, or that a particular program is the answer. The reality is more complex and challenging."[6]

Using this book

So, where does this leave managers? Often, the answer is confused and cynical. They have heard the fanfares so often that it is hardly surprising that their pulses don't race with excitement when they hear the next big idea.

Yet, they remain hungry for knowledge. This book aims to satisfy their hunger. It provides a potpourri of the ideas and the pioneers who have shaped management and which affect the behavior, expectations, and aspirations of managers every day of their managerial lives. The ideas are not quick fixes. But, if they are understood and applied at the right time in the right environment, they can bridge the gap between theory and practice.

The principal ideas covered in *Key Management Ideas* are organized under nine headings:

- **The new world of management**
- **The new world of organizations**
- **Creating and implementing strategy**
- **New ways of managing people**

- The quality revolution
- Reinventing marketing
- Leadership
- Learning and development
- Global management.

The wide ranging nature of modern management means that managers need constantly to bring in concepts from among the plethora of leading edge ideas now at their disposal. This book aims to make these ideas more accessible, fitting them into place amid the pantheon of management pioneers and thinkers. For quick reference, the glossary includes an A to Z of the key management thinkers with details of their key ideas and publications.

Management is a great challenge. This book will not lessen the challenge, but may help to make the trends, influences and people behind them, more intelligible. The acid test is action. Can managers translate the ideas in this book into activities and initiatives which change the way they do business? In the hypercompetitive 1990s there is no choice. Concepts must be made to work. To be the best, managers and their organizations must learn from the best.

Stuart Crainer

References

1 Quoted in "Research into research," *The Observer*, Feb. 27, 1994.
2 *Financial Times*, Sept. 12, 1994.
3 Quoted in Griffith, V, "Corporate fashion victim," *Financial Times*, April 12, 1995.
4 Pascale, R, *Managing on the Edge*, Penguin, London, 1991.
5 Thackray, J, "All aboard the consulting gravy train," *The Observer*, Nov. 6, 1994.
6 Lawler, E, "New logic is here to stay," *Financial Times*, Jan. 28, 1994.

Key for symbols

The following icons and the concepts they represent have been used throughout this book.

 Thinkers

 Checklist

 Example

 Key idea

 Definition

 Further reading

 Action/taking note

The new world of management

"The directors of such companies ... being the managers of other people's money rather than of their own, it cannot be well expected that they should watch over it with the same anxious vigilance with which the partners in a copartnery frequently watch over their own ... Negligence and profusion, therefore, must always prevail, more or less, in the management of the affairs of such a company."
ADAM SMITH

"The old organizational life which may be comfortable and predictable is disappearing rapidly. The new logic is not like the fads and fashions that have have gripped management over the decades. Instead it represents fundamental change in the way organizations will operate. People who develop the skills to be effective in organizations which follow the new logic will thrive. Those who do not will be just as obsolete as poorly skilled production workers in a high-technology manufacturing facility."
EDWARD LAWLER[1]

FROM THE MACHINE AGE TO THE INFORMATION AGE

The roots of modern management lie in the "machine age" of the nineteenth century, though the practice of management has far more historical antecedents. Commentators repeatedly observe that the machine age is fast being replaced by what is called the "information age." In the words of futurist Alvin Toffler, the "brute force economy" is being superseded by a "brain force economy."

This new era presents revolutionary challenges to the way managers manage and how they think about those they manage. "The closer we get to the information age, the more questionable become the traditional practices and precepts of Management. (In most companies management still comes with a capital 'M')," says Gary Hamel, coauthor of *Competing for the Future*. "In the machine age a manager was a professional.... Managers were given credentials.... A manager was an analyst (value chain analysis, segmentation analysis, cost structure analysis). The act of management took place within the boundaries of industry convention, company tradition, vested authority, national context, functional specialization, the demonstrably feasible, and the here and now. Management was by the rules, by the numbers and by the book. That was then, this is now. The boundaries are gone. The game has changed. The rule book is out of date."[2]

Of course, there was never an actual "rule book" of management. But, like an unwritten constitution, there were ways of doing things and expectations which shaped every single aspect of managerial activity.

THE MACHINE-AGE RULE BOOK

There was no hallowed ring-binder, but the "rule book" of machine age management was based on a number of precepts:

- **command and control** – management was exercised on people through a kind of benign dictatorship. Inspired by military role models, the manager told people what to do and then supervised them.

- **one right way** – the instructions of management were assumed to be right. The role of those who were managed was not to question or suggest alternative approaches. There was a belief in one right way to undertake tasks.

- **subjugation not subversion** – the machine age was built around subjugation. Contrast this with the positive encouragement of what would once have been regarded as plain subversion in some of today's more innovative companies.

- **labor not human resources** – the workforce was "labor," hired hands with no stake in the organization. Labour was generally in plentiful supply and the company did not owe them anything, though they were expected to demonstrate loyalty to the company.

- **national not global** – perspectives were generally national, sometimes regional, and rarely international.

- **security not insecurity** – while employees were not offered recognition or responsibility, there was an unspoken contract built around security. Companies had a feel of permanence, dominating towns and their markets. The future seemed predictable and their place in the future even more predictable.

F W Taylor and Henri Fayol
Management as science

If there was any one creator of the machine-age rule book, FREDERICK WINSLOW TAYLOR (1856–1917) should probably take the credit. Today, the name of the American inventor and engineer is now known by only a few practicing managers. And yet, his work forms the cornerstone of much of the management practice of the twentieth century. The man may be forgotten, but his legacy lives determinedly on and, once described, would be instantly recognized by most managers.

TAYLORISM

Taylor was the originator of what became known as "scientific management." To the eyes of the late twentieth-century observer, scientific management would be considered anything but scientific. Taylor's science was built around minute observation of the best way a task could be undertaken and completed. Having found the best way, people could then be made to follow it, to the second, in the prescribed manner.

▶

Taylorism was based on the notion that there was a single "best way" to fulfill a particular job; and that then it was a matter of matching people to the task and supervising, rewarding, and punishing them according to their performance. The job of management was to plan and control the work.

"Hardly a competent workman can be found who does not devote a considerable amount of time to studying first how slowly he can work and still convince his employer that he is going at a good pace. Under our system a worker is just told what he is to do and how he is to do it. Any improvement he makes upon the orders given to him is fatal to his success," observed Taylor.

In effect, Taylor sought to dehumanize work. In doing so, he laid the ground for the mass production techniques which speedily emerged after his death. "His unforgivable sin was his assertion that there is no such thing as 'skill' in making and moving things. All such work was the same, Taylor asserted. And all could be analyzed step-by-step, as a series of unskilled operations that could them be combined into any kind of job. Anyone willing to learn these operations would be a 'first-class man,' deserving 'first class pay.' He could do the most advanced work and do it to perfection," Peter Drucker has accurately observed.[3]

A more indirect, but equally correct, critique comes from Kurt Vonnegut's novel, *Player Piano*: "If only it weren't for the people, the goddamned people," said Finnerty, "always getting tangled up in the machinery. If it weren't for them, earth would be an engineer's paradise." Taylor sought to create such a paradise.

Since the rise and fall of labor intensive, highly functionalized, mass production, Taylor's ideas have been routinely derided – treating workers as unthinking robots able to carry out carefully prescribed tasks *ad infinitum*. Similarly, in Taylor's philosophy the role of managers and supervisors appears to go little beyond holding the stop-watch and admonishing – or speedily sacking – malingerers or poor performers. Taylor also emphasized quantity rather than quality, something which is increasingly out of line with today's management practice.

While there is a great deal of truth in these interpretations, they underestimate the era in which Taylor lived and worked; the significance (and continuing impact of his ideas in many businesses) and they tend to gloss over some of his insights which do genuinely translate into the modern environment. In *Scientific Management*, for example, Taylor writes: "It becomes the duty of those on the management's side to deliberately study the character, the nature and the performance of each workman with a view to finding out his limitations on the one hand, but even more important, his possibilities for development on the

4

THE ROUTE TO SCIENTIFIC MANAGEMENT

Taylor's theories were first published in 1911 when he detailed how to improve work in a factory in five basic stages:

1. Find, say 10 or 15 different men (preferably in as many separate establishments and different parts of the country) who are especially skillful in doing the particular work to be analyzed.

2. Study the exact series of elementary operations or motions which each of these men use in doing the work being investigated, as well as the implements each man uses.

3. Study with a stop-watch the time required to make each of these elementary movements and then select the quickest way of doing each element of the work.

4. Eliminate all false movements, slow movements, and useless movements.

5. After doing away with all unnecessary movements, collect into one series the quickest and best movements as well as the best implements.

other hand." This idea is continually echoed in much of today's management literature.

Similarly, comparisons can be made between the 1990s' fascination with reengineering – which breaks down organizational processes into their constituent parts – and Taylor's attempts at analyzing each and every aspect of the production process.

As Peter Drucker has observed, Taylor's concepts may appear to be inhumane and limited to the modern manager, but he was the first person to really begin to think about the actual act of work rather than taking it for granted. For all his addiction to the stop-watch, Taylor was a truly remarkable man. He patented numerous inventions, excelled at tennis and (perhaps his most significant legacy) persuaded baseball pitchers to throw overarm rather than underarm because, typically enough, it was more efficient.

**Fayol – unlike Taylor – recognized that *esprit de corps* is a vital ingredient in any organization.
To Taylor any identification with fellow workers was a distraction rather than a motivation.**

In Europe the first steps towards identifying what management entails were taken by the Frenchman HENRI FAYOL (1841–1925), a still underestimated figure in the fledgling years of management theorizing. While Taylor gained attention (and later notoriety) for his "scientific management," Fayol's work is generally forgotten. Yet, Fayol pursued a much broader path than Taylor and his codification of what he thought management involved remains valuable.

FAYOL'S 14 PRINCIPLES OF MANAGEMENT

In his *General and Industrial Management*, published in 1916, Fayol laid down 14 principles of management. These were:

1. **Division of work:** tasks should be divided up and employees should specialize in a limited set of tasks so that expertise is developed and productivity increased.

2. **Authority and responsibility:** authority is the right to give orders and entails the responsibility for enforcing them with rewards and penalties; authority should be matched with corresponding responsibility.

3. **Discipline:** is essential for the smooth running of business and is dependent on good leadership, clear and fair arguments, and the judicious application of penalties.

4. **Unity of command:** for any action whatsoever, an employee should receive orders from one superior only; otherwise authority, discipline, order and stability are threatened.

5. **Unity of direction:** a group of activities concerned with a single objective should be coordinated by a single plan under one head.

6. **Subordination of individual interest to general interest:** individual or group goals must not be allowed to override those of the business.

7. **Remuneration of personnel:** may be achieved by various methods and the choice is important; it should be fair, encourage effort, and not lead to overpayment.

8. **Centralization:** the extent to which orders should be issued only from the top of the organization is a problem which should take into account its characteristics, such as size and the capabilities of the personnel.

9. **Scalar chain (line of authority):** communications should normally flow up and down the line of authority running from the top to the bottom of the organization, but sideways communication between those of equivalent rank in different departments can be desirable so long as superiors are kept informed.

10. **Order:** both materials and personnel must always be in their proper place; people must be suited to their posts so there must be careful organization of work and selection of personnel.

11. **Equity:** personnel must be treated with kindliness and justice.

12. **Stability of tenure of personnel:** rapid turnover of personnel should be avoided because of the time required for the development of expertise.

13. **Initiative:** all employees should be encouraged to exercise initiative within the limits imposed by the requirements of authority and discipline.

14. *Esprit de corps*: efforts must be made to promote harmony within the organization and prevent dissension and divisiveness.

Fayol – unlike Taylor – recognized that *esprit de corps* is a vital ingredient in any organization. To Taylor any identification with fellow workers was a distraction rather than a motivation.

Fayol also divided a commercial organization's activities into six basic elements: technical, commercial, financial, security, accounting, and management. The management function, Fayol believed, consisted of planning, organizing, commanding, coordinating, and controlling. It is likely that many practicing managers, even today, would identify similar elements as the core of their activities.

F W Taylor and Henri Fayol

TAYLOR, F W, *The Principles of Scientific Management*, Harper & Row, New York, 1913

FAYOL, H, *General and Industrial Management*, Pitman, London, 1949

Beyond scientific management

Scientific management spawned a number of corollaries. One of the most influential is the work of MAX WEBER (1864–1920). Weber took

Taylor's highly practical supervisory form of management and sought to apply it to the organization as a whole – if there is a best way to do a job, there must also be a best way of running an organization.

Weber's conclusion was that the most efficient form of organization was mechanical. He labeled the ideal organizational form "rational–legal" in contrast to the less reliable "charismatic" and "traditional" organizations. Weber's long-lasting legacy is the image of the organization as machine – a mechanical and bureaucratic institution driven rationally and inexorably forward. According to Weber, the bureaucratic organization worked because of its "precision, speed, unambiguity, knowledge of files, continuity, discretion, unity, strict subordination, reduction of friction and of material and personal costs."

While it is easy to ridicule the bureaucratic organization envisaged by Weber, his analysis was probably right for the time. The charismatic type of organization, led by an outstanding individual, has always proved problematical – though the need for charismatic leaders to provide persuasive visions of the future is now widely acknowledged – and the traditional family company, where management was by hereditary right, had outgrown its usefulness even then.

PARKINSON'S LAW

Scientific management could also be said to have led to one of the most enduring rules of management: Parkinson's Law. Created by a British academic, NORTHCOTE PARKINSON (1910–93), the law takes an ironic slant on Taylor's conclusions. Parkinson's Law observes that work expands to fill the time available for its completion – something which Taylor well appreciated. Parkinson took the thinking a stage further observing that organizations have an inbuilt drive to grow regardless of their productive output. Even if nothing results, the number of staff increases, creating unnecessary work for each other so that everyone becomes even busier. This brings in Parkinson's second law – expenditure rises to overtake income. Parkinson's ironic genius was to identify management and the business world as irrational. Applying rationality to the irrational produced humorous results – unfortunately, this is not something widely appreciated by management writers.

Parkinson's observations were part of the slow process of humanizing the more extreme thinking of the machine age (a process which has conspicuously failed in many organizations). But, in the decades since the Second World War, the key ideas have become more humanized as management thinkers have turned their attention to what motivates people and how managers can transform their roles from ones of supervision to leadership.

Even so, the virility of machine age thinking can be seen in the conclusions reached by LOUIS ALLEN in his 1973 book *Professional Management*. Allen's research began in 1953 and aimed to establish which management methods were most effective and what companies should do to manage more effectively.

> "With your bosses doing the thinking while the workers wield the screwdrivers, you're convinced deep down that this is the way to run a business."
> KONOSUKE MATSUSHITA

ALLEN'S MANAGEMENT ACTIVITIES

Professional Management put forward four functions of management based on a belief that managers think and act rationally – planning, organizing, leading, and controlling.[4] Allen broke these functions down into 19 management activities:

1. **planning function** – forecasting, developing objectives, programing, scheduling, budgeting, developing procedures, and developing policies

2. **organizing function** – developing organization structure, delegating, and developing relationships

3. **leading function** – decision-making, communicating, motivating, selecting, and developing people

4. **controlling function** – developing performance standards, measuring, evaluating and correcting performance.

The echoes of Taylorism are there, though they are refined and developed. Indeed, in the eyes of many, Taylor's legacy lives on. More recently than Louis Allen, Konosuke Matsushita, founder of the Japanese electronics giant which carries his name, has observed that Western firms remain "built on the Taylor model. Even worse, so are your heads. With your bosses doing the thinking while the workers wield the screwdrivers, you're convinced deep down that this is the way to run a business ... We [Japanese] are beyond the Taylor model. Business, we know, is now so complex and difficult, the survival of the firm so hazardous in an environment increasingly unpredictable, competitive and fraught with danger, that its continued existence depends on the day-today mobilization of every ounce of intelligence."[5] The truth of Matsushita's damning observation is only now being fully explored and uncovered – but only by those brave enough to do so.

Breaking the managerial myth

Scientific management was not interested in mobilizing every ounce of intelligence, simply every ounce of *necessary* intelligence and energy to complete a particular task. It also nurtured a myth of management which usually bore little relation to reality. Managers are not always right. Nor do they think and act rationally all of the time. HENRY MINTZBERG'S book, *The Nature of Managerial Work*, also published in 1973, proved a significant step forward in that he cast aside many long-held, but idealistic views.

MINTZBERG'S MODEL OF MANAGERIAL WORK

Mintzberg found:

1. a similarity in managerial work, whether carried out by the company president, the health service administrator, or the general foreman. He categorized it into 10 basic roles and six sets of work characteristics.
2. while differences exist arising from functional or hierarchical level they can be described largely in common roles and characteristics
3. the managerial job is made up of regular and programed duties as well as nonprogramed activities
4. the manager is both a generalist and a specialist
5. the manager is reliant on information particularly that which has been verbally received
6. work activities are characterized by brevity, variety, and fragmentation
7. management work is more an art than a science, reliant on intuitive and nonexplicit processes
8. management work is increasingly complex.[6]

Mintzberg's model of managerial work identified three overall categories and specific roles within each:

1. **Interpersonal category**
   a. the figurehead role where the manager performs symbolic duties as head of the organization
   b. the leader role where he/she establishes the work atmosphere and motivates subordinates to achieve organizational goals

    c. the liaison role where the manager develops and maintains webs of contacts outside the organization.

2. **Informational category**
   a. the monitor role where the manager collects all types of information relevant and useful to the organization
   b. the disseminator role where the manager transmits information from the outside to members in the organization
   c. the spokesman role where he/she transmits information from inside the organization to outsiders.

3. **Decisional category**
   a. the entrepreneur role where the manager initiates controlled change in his/her organization to adapt to the changing environment
   b. the disturbance handler role where the manager deals with unexpected changes
   c. the resource allocator role where he/she makes decisions on the use of organizational resources
   d. the negotiator role where the manager deals with other organizations and individuals.

Mintzberg found managers flitting from subject to subject, crisis to crisis, unable to concentrate for any length of time without the phone ringing or a colleague knocking at the door.

Revealed to be human after all, later analyses of managers' behavior have tended to highlight the softer side of management. It is much more than dictatorial supervision.

For example, over 700 managers – in a variety of organizations and at all levels of management – were surveyed at the Singapore Institute of Management at the beginning of the 1990s. From factor analysis five "mega-components" of management work were identified:

> **Management by the rules is redundant when the rules are in a constant state of irrational flux.**

1. Goal setting and review
2. Creating a conducive working environment
3. Managing quality
4. Relating to and managing the external environment
5. Managing performance.[7]

Only the first of these components could be said to be consistent with machine-age management. The others belong firmly in the new world.

The rule book is out of date. This is not to say that there is a need for a new rule book. "What's so wonderful about the Body Shop is that we still don't know the rules," says Anita Roddick.[8] Management by the rules is redundant when the rules are in a constant state of irrational flux.

New skills for the new world

What is the job of the manager in the information age? "Increasingly, managers at all levels will be required to do much more than just implement the plans put in place at higher levels," says David Birchall of the UK's Henley Management College. "They will be expected to define the problems facing their organizations in the rapidly changing and increasingly complex world in which their businesses operate and communicate this to the executive level. Information search and interpretation will be key skills."[9]

The management competences identified by the National Westminster Bank as crucial are representative:

- **information search:** environmental scanning
- **conceptual flexibility:** considers alternatives simultaneously
- **interpersonal search:** explores and understands others' viewpoints
- **managing interaction:** involves others, builds teams
- **developmental orientation:** helps others develop.[10]

In the new world the skills required of managers are diverse and continuously expanding. Some of the basics remain. These have been summed up in the unspeakable acronym, **POSDCORB**, which stands for:

- Planning
- Organizing
- Staffing
- Directing
- Coordinating
- Reporting
- Budgeting.

Many, if not all, these activities remain central to many managerial jobs. But, in addition, new managers are expected to:

- manage on an international scale
- manage cultural diversity
- respond to multiple sources of authority
- combine a variety of leadership and team roles
- act strategically
- utilize technology
- communicate internally

- communicate externally
- establish, reinforce, and develop values
- act responsibly
- distill complex flows of information
- manage across functions
- manage their own careers, as well as personal and professional development.

MANAGING CHANGE

The list of skills and competences now required of managers is daunting. It is made even more so by the fact that they must manage in an environment beset by radical change. It is a truism to observe that managing change is the great managerial challenge of our times. But, for all its repetition, it is nevertheless true.

"The greatest personal skill needed for this decade will be to manage radical change. There is unlikely to be any business or institution which will escape radical change in the nineties and the choices before us are to manage it ourselves or to have change forced upon us," says Sir John Harvey-Jones.[11]

Change is now endemic in the business world. "If you want to be content you should be a dog," acerbically advises one corporate executive. No organization is immune. Almost 40 percent of the companies which comprised the *Fortune 500* a decade ago no longer exist. Of the 1970 *Fortune* list, 60 percent have disappeared – either acquired or out of business. And of the 12 companies which comprised the Dow Jones Industrial index in 1900, only General Electric survives as a giant.

It is not an American phenomenon. Change is a worldwide issue. "There's a transition going on, from hierarchical corporate structures to more empowered structures. A generation of chief executives is moving into place, who are more receptive to these concepts," says Peter Sheldrake, executive director of the Australian Institute of Management.[12]

The changes now facing managers are more significant, broad-ranging and apparently endless than ever before. The many manifestations of change affect:

- **technology** – the information technology (IT) revolution continues to make jobs quicker and less labor intensive than they were even five years ago.
- **organizations** – new organizational structures are emerging, emphasizing and enabling speed of response

- **individuals** – people have to learn new skills and adapt to an uncertain environment
- **society** – the role of employment and organizations in society is increasingly debated.
- **consumers and markets** – these are becoming more demanding and quicker changing.

Richard Pascale
From change to transformation

While recognizing that change is happening there is still a widespread temptation for organizations and managers to believe that it does not affect them or perhaps that it can be managed through small incremental improvements rather than major shifts in attitude and behavior. Leading the call for the latter approach is American thinker, Richard Pascale.

Pascale urges management to invest the intellectual energy necessary to make an informed choice between **change** (incremental improvement) or **transformation** (discontinuous shifts in capability). He believes a mental muddle surrounds these choices with many change efforts masquerading as "transformation." An impassioned critic of management fads, Pascale advocates that organizations commit themselves to relentless self-questioning and reinvention.

Pascale has been described as the "scourge of the complacent and prodder of the timid."[13] Undoubtedly, his views and advice have made increasingly uncomfortable reading and listening for managers. He believes that gurus, writers, speakers, and the ultimate consumers – managers – are caught up in a game of sound bites and simplistic remedies.

"It's like the practice of medicine in the Middle Ages," he states. "A leech under the armpit and one to the groin." With no understanding of bacteria, viruses or how the body worked, there were lots of prescriptions by the physicians of the Middle Ages – but cures were largely the product of random chance. A parallel holds today. Lots of remedies but very few successful examples of authentic transformation. Organizations churn through one technique after another and at

> **"Organizations churn through one technique after another and at best get incremental improvement on top of business-as-usual. At worst, these efforts waste resources and evoke cynicism and resignation."**
> **RICHARD PASCALE**

best get incremental improvement on top of business-as-usual. At worst, these efforts waste resources and evoke cynicism and resignation.

"What is needed is a much deeper inquiry into first, a business's unfolding competitive situation and second, an understanding of the largely invisible patterns of thinking and behavior which define the 'box' inside which a company operates. Once revealed, it becomes clear whether the organization (improving at a predictable pace given past performance) can successfully meet the demands of competition. If not, there is a need for transformation. This is a difficult but manageable journey."

On a personal level he is a somewhat reluctant revolutionary. "I would describe my life as backing away from what didn't work toward a better fit with my gifts and capabilities," he says. But, Pascale – like other leading management thinkers – has pursued a single-minded path once the course became clear. "As I was finishing my MBA at Harvard, my colleagues were frantically searching for the 'perfect' job. I found myself troubled by the process and unable to engage in it with enthusiasm," he recalls. "Then, one day I had an epiphany – what I really wanted to do was spend a quarter of my life teaching; a quarter consulting (to test the relevance of theory in practice); a quarter writing (something I enjoy – and when you put your ideas on paper you discover the holes in the logic); and, finally, a quarter of my life on holiday (to re-create). I have endeavored to achieve that balance ever since."[14]

With the first 25 percent of his time, as a teacher, Pascale spent 20 years at Stanford's Graduate School of Business – his course on organizational survival was the most popular on the MBA program. As a consultant, his clients include many of the world's largest corporations.

"Over time, I have focused increasingly on the challenge of renewing large organizations," he observes. "I regard my clients as learning partners. Clearly, I am expected to add value and I endeavor to do so. But I am consistently learning from those I work with and confronted with how much further we have to go to enable corporations to revitalize themselves with a higher likelihood of success."

As a writer, Pascale's ideas first reached a mass audience through the 1981 book, *The Art of Japanese Management* (coauthored with Anthony Athos). The inspiration for the book was derived from Pascale's work with the National Commission on Productivity (a White House task force of *Fortune 50* chief executives and national union leaders). "I had spent a year in Japan in the late 1960s," he states. "While deeply impressed, I doubted we could learn much from the Japanese as their culture is so different from ours. One night on a flight back from Washington DC, it hit me: why not study Japanese companies in the United States? How would they adapt their ideas to American managers and an American workforce? This became the cornerstone of the study."

RICHARD PASCALE	born 1938; educator & consultant

Education: Harvard Business School

Career: Member of the faculty, Stanford's Graduate School of Business; White House Fellow, Special Assistant to the Secretary of Labor, and Senior Staff of a White House Task Force reorganizing the President's executive office; consultant to many *Fortune 500* companies including AT&T, General Electric, Intel, Shell, 3M, British Petroleum, and Coca Cola.

The Art of Japanese Management was a bestseller, eventually published in 20 languages. It drew lessons from archetypal Japanese success stories – such as Honda in the US. Japanese successes, like their best managed American counterparts, derived from a relentless commitment to learning and meticulous attention to the factors that motivate people, reinforce core values and fine-tune the interconnected elements of an organization. Pascale and Athos were the first to coin the term "**Managing by Walking About**" (**MBWA**) and to call attention to the singular importance of **shared values**.

THE SEVEN S FRAMEWORK

Another contribution of *The Art of Japanese Management* derives from the 1970s when Pascale worked with Tom Peters and Robert Waterman (then at the McKinsey consulting firm) and Anthony Athos (a professor at Harvard Business School). Pascale had a hand in developing the Seven S framework. "It's nothing more than seven important categories that managers use to make an organization work," he states.

"The seven Ss are **Strategy, Structure, Systems, Style, Shared values, Skills** (an organization's distinctive competence), and people (to maintain the alliteration we called the people category "**Staff**")."

Despite the book's success Pascale was anxious not to become typecast as a Japan expert. "I don't define myself as a Japan scholar – what I am interested in is making Western organizations more productive." Under pressure to come up with a sequel, Pascale wrote a three-page outline on what he believed was the next horizon for improving competitiveness: the importance of constructive contention as the fuel of self-renewal in organizations. "I thought I could write the book in six months," he says. "But all the data and interviews I had in my files only skimmed the surface. People conceal their conflicts; organizations suppress it. The most important contention is often an undiscussable. Yet it is precisely these hidden tensions within an organization that can be a source of vitality if they are channeled effectively."

Managing on the Edge: How the Smartest Companies use Conflict to Stay Ahead further cemented Pascale's reputation. The book is densely packed with anecdotes and ideas. At their root is Pascale's observation that many of the "excellent" companies which Peters and Waterman had celebrated in *In Search of Excellence* had fallen from grace within the short span of a few years. At the heart of their vulnerability were the very qualities that historically had enabled them to excel. Paradoxically, internal coherence (an asset during stable times) rendered them ill-equipped to deal with radical shifts in the environment. "They couldn't get out of their own way," says Pascale, "like weight-lifters with tremendous upper body strength suddenly asked to compete in the high hurdles."

THE LAW OF REQUISITE VARIETY

Coincidentally Pascale had also "stumbled" upon a law of cybernetics known as the Law of Requisite Variety. The law states that for any organism to adapt to its external environment, it must incorporate "variety." If you reduce "variety" internally you are less able to deal with it when it comes at you externally. "But how does variety show up in a social system?" asked Pascale. "It shows up as deviance from the norm – in other words, as conflict. The problem is that most companies are conflict averse. For many it is associated with wounded egos, harmed relationships and turf wars. Contention is often mistaken as an indicator of mismanagement. The trick is to learn to disagree without being disagreeable and channel this contention as a means of self questioning and keeping an organization on its toes."

In practice, Pascale believes 50 percent of the time when contention arises it is smoothed over and avoided. Another 30 percent of the time it leads to nonproductive fighting and no resolution. Only in 20 percent of the cases is contention truly confronted and resolved. "It's ironic," observes Pascale. "A threat that everyone perceives but no-one talks about is far more debilitating than a threat that is clearly revealed and resources mobilized to address it. Companies, like people, tend to be as sick as their secrets," says Pascale – who prescribes revealing the "undiscussables" and suggests that "breakdowns" be regarded as a source of learning.

His increasingly broad-ranging and holistic world view remains influenced by Japanese thinking. In particular, Pascale argues that Western managers need to become more attuned to the difference between *doing*

17

and *being*. "My exposure to the Japanese language made me aware of two words, *Ki* and *Kokoro*, which refer to the core essence of a person (in other words, who they are being). These terms are as commonplace to the Japanese language as 'me,' 'self,' 'I' and 'my' are to most Western languages. What this means is that a Japanese, regardless of educational attainment, is constantly cued by his language to pay attention to who they are being while in the process of doing something. (We see this in their seemingly ritualistic approach to the tea ceremony, flower arranging or sumo wrestling.) The way in which this comes to root in business is that it would not occur to the Japanese just to 'do' a management technique – such as Total Quality Management. Of course, they

> "Contention is often mistaken as an indicator of mismanagement. The trick is to learn to disagree without being disagreeable and channel this contention as a means of self questioning and keeping an organization on its toes."
> RICHARD PASCALE

would also 'be' quality. By contrast, they view their Western counterparts as precocious children – always chasing after the latest management technique and striving to distil it down to a recipe for doing. Organizations that churn through a succession of 'doings' (such as TQM and reengineering) without altering their underlying being often end up older, maybe slimmer, but rarely wiser. Transformation entails a shift in being – at the personal and organizational level."

To transform itself an organization needs to tackle its very core – its context – the underlying assumptions and invisible premises on which its decisions and actions are based. This sounds arcane but is no more complicated than assembling a critical mass of key stakeholders (perhaps the 100 to 200 people who really make things happen in a company) and

> "A butterfly is not more caterpillar or a better or improved caterpillar; a butterfly is a different creature."
> RICHARD PASCALE

conducting an organizational audit that reveals the invisible box inside which the company operates. Once revealed, it is easy to have a straightforward discussion about whether the organization, operating at its current level (i.e. doing what is predictable), can respond to the unfolding competitive threats. If not, a dramatic shift in organizational capability (i.e. transformation) is required.

Pascale points to a number of leading US companies such as Motorola, General Electric and even the department store chain, Nordstrum, as examples of successful ongoing transformation (or reinvention).

Transformation and **reinvention** are Pascale's coda for the future. "Many companies need to reinvent themselves," he says. "And reinvention is not changing what is, but creating what isn't. A butterfly is not more caterpillar or a better or improved caterpillar; a butterfly is a different creature. Reinvention entails a series of continuous metamorphoses of this magnitude over time."[15]

Pascale plays down his reputation. "I don't think of myself as a guru or as a repository of ultimate knowledge. That's the kiss of death as far as your own continuous learning is concerned. You can witness the undesirable impact of celebrity that accompanies guru-hood. When you become a persona rather than a person, it consumes your energy at the expense of the underlying inquiry upon which your reputation was built in the first place."

Richard Pascale

The Art of Japanese Management (with ANTHONY ATHOS), Penguin Books, London, 1981

Managing on the Edge, Viking, London, 1990

The people challenge

Change, if it is to work, must involve and alter the perceptions and behavior of people. The lengthy catalog of failed change and quality programs is testament to the general neglect of the people side of such initiatives and, when it is identified, of the failure of organizations to come to terms with it. Change has to carry people along with it. Less than wholehearted support will stop any change program in its tracks. A program which looks good in the boardroom can remain a theoretical ideal if people do not commit themselves to the change process.

ACCEPTING CHANGE

A survey by KPMG Management Consulting of top executives in 250 UK companies found that only 31 percent believed their change programs were "very effective."[16] "Identifying the need for change is relatively straightforward, what really causes problems is making change happen successfully," the KPMG survey reports.

The people-related issues are here to stay. Between 1992 and 1993 the US economy grew by 2.6 percent, but over 500,000 clerical and

▶

technical positions disappeared, probably for good.[17] A survey by *3i* in the UK found that early in 1994 – after the worst of recession was supposedly over – two thirds of companies expected a further reduction in middle management numbers.[18] Dealing with the ramifications of such a massive displacement of people is fundamental to the success or failure of any change program. Not only do managers often have to deal sympathetically with redundancies, but they have to convince those that remain in the organization of the logic for, and the necessity of, the change.

Most of the extensive theorizing and practice in the field of managing change pays scant attention to the concerns and fears of the people involved in making it happen. Talk of turbulence and the relentless progress of change through global business is easy. Talk of the effects of upheaval and change on individual managers and employees is less straightforward, fraught as it is with fears and disappointment.

There is an ongoing debate over whether behavioral and cultural change – through empowerment, teamworking etc – is an inherent result of a change program, or whether it needs to be launched before the program begins. At the center of this discussion is the common belief that a

A PREFERENCE FOR THE FAMILIAR

Centuries ago, the challenge was described by NICCOLÒ MACHIAVELLI (a man increasingly referred to in these traumatic times): "It should be borne in mind that there is nothing more difficult to arrange, more doubtful of success and more dangerous to carry through than initiating changes in a state's constitution. The innovator makes enemies of all those who prospered under the old order and only lukewarm support is forthcoming from those who would prosper under the new."

A more recent perspective comes from John Hagel of McKinsey & Co: "There are many reasons why people avoid change. Change is threatening. It means doing things differently, perhaps in ways that an individual will not be able to master. Change is difficult. It is always easier to continue doing things the same comfortable way rather than trying something new. Change is risky. If the new methods don't work, or if people lose sight of immediate needs while trying to master them, near-term performance may suffer, perhaps disastrously. Change is often illusory. Too many organizations have grown cynical as senior management announces yet another change initiative that will fall by the wayside three or four months later when some new issue diverts attention elsewhere."[19]

changed organizational structure or more radical reorganization naturally leads to a change in corporate culture. Though this may be the case, changing organizational cultures is a lengthy, time-consuming, and delicate process.

It is unlikely that successful cultural change can be made in a wholesale way. The past is not easily dismissed – nor should you want to totally dispense with some of the more positive and established ways of thinking and working. Marrying the old and new cultures is a formidable balancing act.

> **"The innovator makes enemies of all those who prospered under the old order and only lukewarm support is forthcoming from those who would prosper under the new."**
> NICCOLÒ MACHIAVELLI

How do people view change?

While the bookshelves of managers may bulge with advice on how to manage change, there remains a refusal to accept its necessity among many managers. Instead of being proactive, change is often reactive, the last resort.

Companies tend to commit themselves to change because of market pressure, plummeting profitability, or even the prospect of imminent bankruptcy. In such circumstances, the directors are prepared to take drastic steps to turn the company around. The trouble is that many more companies need to take radical action earlier to prevent themselves reaching this situation.

Managers, it seems, are at heart conservative and cautious. They regard change as logical and short-term, a small step rather than a quantum leap into the unknown.

CATEGORIZING THE UNKNOWN

Fear of change is understandable. It creates a new sense of ambiguity. People are uncertain about their roles and unsure what they should be doing and with who. This ambiguity covers a number of areas:

- **job definitions** – changes in the scope and nature of job definitions are, for many, deeply unsettling and remove a prime reference point

- **responsibilities** – people are unsure what they are responsible for and to who

- **expectations** – people are uncertain about what colleagues and the organization expects from them.

21

An obvious adjunct to the process of ambiguity is the disappearance of career ladders. Organizations shorn of their vertical hierarchy can appear to offer little opportunity for progression. IBM UK chairman, Sir Anthony Cleaver, announced that his organization was reducing its number of management tiers to a mere four. This, said Cleaver, "means a maximum of one promotion every ten years and even this is for the one man who makes it to the top."[20]

> **"As the pace of change accelerates, the idea of a progressive career within stable organizational structures is increasingly threatened."**
> IM REPORT

THE IMPACT ON MANAGERIAL CAREERS

Those who plan to join the upwardly mobile and still believe in neat and well-ordered career structures are increasingly likely to be disappointed. The Institute of Management (IM) tracked the career development of over 800 UK managers from 1980 to 1992. IM found that sideways or downwards moves among managers more than doubled during the period from seven per 100 managers in 1980–82 to nearly 15 per 100 in 1992.[21]

"As the pace of change accelerates, the idea of a progressive career within stable organizational structures is increasingly threatened," says the IM report on the research. "The structures which have traditionally supported rational long-term careers are being gradually replaced with more fluid organizations." And it is people who are the most fluid of corporate resources.

The impression of instability is emphasized by the IM's findings that managers are changing jobs more often. They are job hopping, often not on their own terms, in search of better jobs, but increasingly because of corporate restructuring. Managers tended to change jobs in the 1980s for proactive reasons – personal and career development – in the 1990s they are often reacting to change which has been imposed on them, whether redundancy or relocation. Among the 800 managers included in the survey, 25 percent of those who changed jobs in 1992 did so because of reorganization – in the early 1980s the figure was eight percent.

These dramatic changes in the way managerial careers develop pose questions which strike at the heart of Western managerial culture. "Young managers were once shown career structures stretching ten or even 15 years ahead. Stay with us and this is where you can go, they were told. Companies simply can't say that now," says Bill Hudson, one of the managers in the report.

For managers at the sharp end, the changing structure of careers is not easily understood. "In the 1980s you could plan your career. There were a lot of opportunities. Now, you have to accept that the only way is not always up," says a redundant manager who recently applied for a job working for someone he once managed.

> **"Stay with us and this is where you can go, they were told. Companies simply can't say that now."**
> **BILL HUDSON**

Strangely, the insecurity has not yet transmitted itself to some managers. Trudy Coe, coauthor of the survey, says: "Managers have to be prepared and, at the moment, many appear complacent. They think their careers are safe."

Research carried out by the IM in 1992 found that 40 percent of managers anticipated that their next career move would be upward. "Managers need to look at their careers differently," says Coe. "They have to see sideways moves as an opportunity to develop the broad portfolio of skills they now need. In the past managers looked to organizations to shape their careers and skills for them, now the onus is on them. They need to be prepared for change and to recognize its potential benefits rather than regarding it as a threat."

Research repeatedly shows that it is managers who are the chief stumbling block to making change happen. Changing organizational structures and managerial thinking challenges and undercuts traditional power bases. The future is nightmarish, elusively intangible. Functions are broken apart, some disappear from the organization, subcontracted to external suppliers. For the manager reared on the old functional certainties the new world organization is very difficult to manage. Indeed, the vast majority of managers are not trained or equipped to manage in such an environment. Nor can they attend a short course to be converted from a functional to a process manager. Changing the way you work and think about your work is a process which is more likely to take months and possibly years than weeks and months.

> **Unfortunately and inaccurately, change programs can be regarded as euphemisms for redundancy.**

Managers often feel threatened by the change, a reaction that is reasonable given the fact that many initiatives involve management delayering (BT, for example, has shed over 5,000 managers during its reengineering program, and a European oil manufacturing company esti-mates that it will lose 50 percent of its middle managers during a similar program over the next few years). Unfortunately and inaccurately, change programs can be regarded as euphemisms for redundancy.

Managers are caught between the twin nightmares of redundancy and of radically altering the way they work. There are no easy options. Research suggests that while companies have developed a wide range of supportive packages to help people who have been made redundant they – perhaps not surprisingly – often forget the worries and concerns of those who remain with the organization. In a survey of 50 top UK com-panies in 1993, recruitment company Cedar International found that a massive 86 percent had implemented redundancies in the previous year and, in addition, 36 percent were operating rolling programs spanning a number of years involving a significant proportion of the workforce.

Skills to manage change

Caught in this maelstrom of change, what new skills do managers need? From being functional specialists, managers are becoming sophisticated generalists, able to manage a potpourri of projects, people, resources, and issues. In the new world, managers are enablers rather than doers. For most managers to make the transition from a doer to an enabler involves the development of a number of central new skills:

Managing conflict

Managers are unused to the rigorous and ceaseless questioning which true change brings. Often they are extremely uncomfortable with the idea of their work being analyzed in anything other than a superficial way. The potential for dissension and conflict is high. If, for example, a team is made up of an engineer, a customer development manager and a company accountant, some sort of conflict is inevitable – and often healthy. There are and will be basic misunderstandings. The manager might ask the engineer why he is doing something in a certain way. Reared on a diet of functional division, the engineer may well say that he has always done it that way and he knows more about engineering than the manager. To make teams work, however, mutual respect must exist or be developed. Managers have to learn to accept objective input from people they regard as outsiders.

RICHARD PASCALE estimates that 50 percent of the time contentious issues are smoothed over and avoided. Around 30 percent lead to non-productive fighting and no resolution while only 20 percent are truly confronted and resolved.[22]

Harvard's CHRIS ARGYRIS has examined in great depth the debilitating machinations of a firm of consultants. He found that the consultants, despite their learning and expertise were adept at masking their errors and misjudgements. Problems were routinely bypassed and covered up, one cover-up led to another and so on. Board meetings were spent discussing peripheral issues while major issues were routinely glossed over. Argyris' conclusion is that the more threatening a problem is to those responsible for solving it the deeper it will be ingrained under layers of corporate camouflage. Argyris' cure is for organizations to start learning from the top down.

If change is to be managed, managers, no matter how senior they are, must candidly and clearly take responsibility for their errors of judgement as well as their triumphs.

Interpersonal skills

Managers change from supervisors to coaches. They are there to provide resources, answer questions and look out for the long-term career development of the individual. How they deal with people is key to their day-to-day success and to the progression of their career within the organization.

Project management skills[23]

Many aspects of change can be managed as discrete projects. Project management is no longer the sole preserve of the the construction industry. Change management expert Eddie Obeng suggests that today's project manager (more accurately referred to as a project leader) needs training in four key areas:

1. **Planning and controlling** – project leaders need to be able to use a variety of methods to ensure they are keeping on schedule and within budget. Even more important, they need to be able to decide priorities for their objectives.

2. **Learning skills** – as most project leaders are working in an unfamiliar context it is crucial that they assimilate knowledge as rapidly as possible. This will enable them to adjust their plans and objectives and save valuable time and money. To do this, project leaders need to keep learning, planning, reviewing, and changing.

3. **People skills** – project leaders need to be able to negotiate for vital resources; be able to influence people to gain their commitment; be able to listen to coordinate and control the project; and be able to manage stakeholders from throughout the business.

25

4. **Organizational skills** – project leaders need to be politically astute and aware of the potential impact of wider organizational issues. They should be adept at networking with senior employees, should understand how the organization works, and should have a larger picture of the organization's goals and necessary conditions.

Leadership and flexibility

In organizations where the emerging emphasis is on horizontal cross-functional and team-based management, managers need to coach employees and empower them to feel ownership of the various processes. This demands a flexible style of managing, with the manager sometimes giving firm directions in order to ensure that the process output conforms to customer expectations, while at other times stepping back and allowing team members to take decisions.

Managing processes

Functional orientation is now being replaced by process orientation. In the majority of process-based companies, managers are required to improve their business processes on an ongoing basis. They need to be able to use the tools of process simplification and redesign, which include benchmarking, process mapping tools (such as systems dynamics, flowcharting, and activity diagrams) and require understanding of the potential business benefits of IT applications.

Managing strategy

Process ownership is not solely concerned with the nitty-gritty of direct implementation. Managers need also to understand how their process aligns with strategic goals and performance measures. They have, for example, to have an understanding of the company's mission, competitive capabilities, and core constituencies, as well as some of the basic principles of activity-based costing. This enables the process owner to fully understand and communicate the full benefits of corporate change – the elimination of non-value adding activities, the enhancement of value-adding activities, substantial gains in productivity and far greater market responsiveness.

Managing their own development

To meet the new challenge requires managers to think beyond position and develop comprehensive general skills which will allow them to respond flexibly to organizational needs. It is not surprising, therefore, that people at all levels in organizations are seeing the opportunities for personal development. Indeed, it is increasingly regarded as a major part of what was once called the remuneration package.

Making change work

Senior management commitment

In discussing and carrying through any program of change a crucial dilemma soon surfaces. Who should be involved in the planning and implementation? Involving the most powerful senior managers at the planning stage invites them to protect their own patch. Ignoring them in the implementation phase risks their blocking plans they don't like. The existing structure guarantees their power through their control over the largest and best resources currently available.

The fact is that despite the protestations of annual reports, senior managers are often the strongest and most persuasive corporate force against the process of change. They are, after all, creatures of the organization – some will have spent their entire careers working within a particular culture in a particular way. As a result, they are protective of their own sphere of influence, often unwilling to upset the corporate equilibrium and unlikely to become passionate advocates of any one idea. They are in favor of stability and more of the same – it has elevated them to the corporate heights.

In the 1990s, such conservatism or plain stagnation is a guarantee of failure. "If the top is committed deeply to maintaining the status quo, there's no hope," says P Ranganath Nayak, senior vice president of consultants Arthur D Little.[24]

Dr Ian Cunningham, author and change management consultant, says: "The old planning models are no longer enough. You cannot plan for a revolution. Instead, companies and managers need to prepare; managers need to be quicker, more able and feel confident enough to buck trends and be different. While it is difficult for many managers to develop this ability, they have to remember that you make money by not going along with the market. When it comes to change management, managers no longer have the luxury of being able to learn from their mistakes. They have to get it right."[25]

Managers obsessed with corporate strategy, which juggles assets, buys and sells businesses, thinks more about leveraged buyouts than about basic changes in the work they actually do, can have little if any place in achieving true changes in their organization.

According to Dan Valentino, chief executive of Gemini Consulting, restructuring involves the chief executive becoming "a tyrant, sacrificing people on the altar of shareholder value." But it has to be done. "All working processes, and their associated systems, must be under constant review."[26] The trouble is that acting tyranically, however noble the objectives, is a sure route to eventual unemployment.

LEADING CHANGE

Harvard Business School's John Kotter has identified eight steps in the process of leading change:

1. a leader with a good track record is appointed,

2. one with an outsider's openness to new ideas,

3. who creates a sense of crisis,

4. who creates and communicates a new vision and new strategies,

5. who then behaves accordingly, acting as a role model,

6. and thus involves others in key jobs in the drive for change;

7. these others then use thousands of opportunities to influence behavior throughout the organization,

8. producing tangible results within two years, thus reinforcing the drive to persevere without the change program.

Vision

"Most people think of the future as the ends and the present as the means, whereas, in fact, the present is the ends and the future the means," observed organizational behaviorist Fritz Roethlisberger in an unfortunately neglected aphorism.[27]

If change is to be achieved the way people think about their businesses must be transformed. Failure to achieve this is a common cause of senior executive failure. It is a major challenge to shake a company away from its past obsession. Organizations are cautious slow-moving creatures. Tire companies, for example, are still likely to believe that success is reliant on how many tires they produce and coal mines may assume that tonnage automatically equates with profitability. There is a growing catalog of senior and well-respected managers who have lost their jobs as they have wrestled with reshaping the outlook of a large corporation. Recent years have seen John Akers at IBM; Bob Stempel at General Motors; Bob Horton at BP and a number of others succumb.

They failed, not because they are poor managers – their track records are impressive – but because implementing major change requires much more than the attention and commitment of a single executive. The entire organization needs to be carried forward with them.

The problem encountered by Akers and the like was that though their vision of the future was ambitious, credible, and possibly achievable, it did not seem so to their colleagues or subordinates. Instead, all that their colleagues could see was a long line of obstacles and impediments to achieving the distant goal.

Creating a destination is the easy part – all the research and papers on the trouble companies have in making strategy happen are evidence of the prime difficulty in converting theory into practice. To work, change programs must address how widespread change affects the policy of a business, its values, and its beliefs. This requires the vision to be able to motivate people through a radical rethink of their roles and tasks and sustain them through its implementation. This also results in new roles and changes in organization development, rewards resource allocation and management systems.

Managers must become visionaries – creating and implementing strong and clear visions of the corporate future. In General Electric's 1990 annual report, chief executive Jack Welch mapped out the company's vision: "Our dream for the 1990s is a boundaryless company ... where we knock down the walls that separate us from each other on the inside and from our key constituents on the outside."

After initial enthusiasm for corporate visions in the 1980s, recent years have seen mounting scepticism about their real value. Often they appear overly ambitious, entirely unrelated to the current situation of the business. Senior managers must bridge the gap between the vision and the day-to-day reality.

Communication

Communication and vision are intertwined – or should be. Visionary business leaders who achieve their objectives, communicate automatically and continually.

As an example, look at the program of radical change achieved by British Airways. After the arrival of new chief executive, Colin (now Sir Colin) Marshall, BA developed a set of corporate objectives which pinned the company's future on the development of service excellence throughout its operations.

The opportunity was clear. Research showed that two thirds of recent airline passengers thought that BA was neither better or worse than other airlines. This presented an opportunity for BA to achieve a vital competitive edge through service. Neutral responses could be turned into positive experiences and support.

BA's SEVEN CENTRAL OBJECTIVES

1. to provide the highest levels of service to all customers, passengers, shippers, travel agents, and freight agents

2. to preserve high professional and technical standards in order to achieve the highest levels of safety

3. to provide a uniform image worldwide and to maintain a specific set of standards for each clearly defined market segment

4. to respond quickly and sensitively to the changing needs of our present and potential customers

5. to maintain and, where opportunity occurs, expand our present route structure

6. to manage, operate, and market the airline in the most efficient manner

7. to create a service and people-oriented work environment, assuring all employees of fair pay and working conditions and continuing concern for their career.

BA's PROGRAMS FOR CHANGE

The first step was the staff awareness program, "Putting People First." This program, launched at the end of 1983, was initially aimed at the 15,000 people in direct contact with customers. Its success was such that it was extended throughout the airline. Initially it was criticised by some as being too American – though in fact it was developed in the UK by a Danish company. The program lasted two days and the groups were up to 180 strong. Colin Marshall made a point of closing as many of the program's seminars as possible. They ran for two and a half years and he closed 40 percent of them.

"I was conscious when we embarked on the program that it couldn't be a one-off," recalls Marshall. "It had to re-focus the organization, changing it from a company focused on operations to one which was led by the marketplace and one which recognized the needs of customers. I thought it would take at least five years, but more likely a decade to really carry it through. To achieve genuine culture change takes time, effort and the overriding concern to get at the values involved. The reason so many companies seem to achieve a useful change in culture and then slowly disintegrate over the passage of even short spans of time is that one suspects they confuse the appearance of culture change, the presence of the symbols, with the needed solid change in values and their acceptance."

"Putting People First" was only the beginning for BA. It was accompanied by "Managing People First" which focussed on how to lead, to be willing to take risks and raise your head above the parapet. This one-week training program aimed to help managers deal with the transition and to manage their people through the process of change.

BA has now completed the fourth of the total employee programs. The second, entitled "A Day in the Life," focused on what the company actually does in its day-to-day operations. The third program, "To be the Best," focussed on the competition in world and the fourth, "Winners," on quality and customer service. A fifth is now being developed to be launched in 1996.

BA's success is built around communication. Sir Colin Marshall explains: "Crucial to the entire process is a breaking down of barriers and an opening of lines of communication. People are invited to write down questions during the seminars and at the end we answer them. People at the top of the organizational hierarchy must have access to people in the workplace. If they don't they quickly become cut off."

> "A threat that everyone perceives but no one talks about is far more debilitating to a company than a threat that has been clearly revealed."
> RICHARD PASCALE

Communication makes business sense. "A threat that everyone perceives but no one talks about is far more debilitating to a company than a threat that has been clearly revealed," Richard Pascale has observed.

The trouble is that managers are notoriously poor communicators. Brought up to defend their territory and regard information as power, they are often not attuned to sharing information or communicating it effectively. "For all the millions spent on internal communication over the last 20 years employee satisfaction with it has barely improved," observes Bill Quirke in *Communicating Change*.[28] Quirke found that in most companies half the employees have no idea where the organization is going; 75 percent get no feedback on performance and 100 percent believe management has a hidden agenda. Managers always rate themselves at least 20 percent better at communicating than their staff do.

Research by the consulting firm, Ingersoll Engineers, cited the communication problems faced in change programs. Communication both upward and downward is considered crucial. "Frequently the downward is there, but the upward falls on deaf ears," commented one manager in the survey of top UK directors. "Attempts [to change] without communicating ... lead to the suspicion of a hidden agenda," said another. "Communicating a clear plan superlatively well is central to creating the confidence for successful change," says Brian Small, managing director of Ingersoll.[29]

Forums for communication need to be established at an early stage in any change program – and maintained and enhanced as the process unfolds. The UK savings and loan company, N&P, for example, introduced fortnightly meetings, "team events" at which all area staff receive updates from top management to gain their commitment to the entire process. If people have no role to play in the formulation of ideas and the design of new processes it is unlikely they will implement them consistently or convincingly.

QUESTIONING CHANGE

Managers clearly need to prepare themselves to provide satisfactory answers to wide-ranging and fundamental questions from people who work for them. Typically, these will include:

- *Will my job description change?*

- *Will I lose my job?*

- *What is the project about?*

- *How long will it take?*

- *Who is in the project team?*

- *What exactly are you doing?*

- *Will it affect the way I do my job?*

- *Why are you doing it?*

- *Will it save the company money?*

- *What's in it for me?*

- *Who has asked for the project to be done?*

- *Why do we need all this documentation?*

- *Does this mean I am not doing my job correctly?*

- *Are you checking up on me?*

- *What do I have to do?*
- *How does the project fit in with the computer department?*
- *What is a business process?*
- *Does this mean I am going to end up with more work?*

Identifying stakeholders

There is a sure way to fail in any change program: appoint managers who have little credibility to drive the process forward. This is surprisingly common. Companies may accept the potential merits of change, but are unwilling or unable to bring their best minds in to run the revolution. If managers lack credibility or simply lack the right communication or leadership skills, a change program will not get off the ground.

US giant EDS picked 150 people to begin a process of corporate change. They were selected for what the chairman and chief executive Les Alberthal called "their ability to think outside the box." In selecting them the emphasis was on having a spread of ages, from throughout the world, different levels with different ways of thinking. They were then broken into five "waves" of 30 to focus on different issues.[30]

STAKEHOLDER CATEGORIES

The stakeholders in any change program are many and varied. All have their own motivations and agenda – both hidden and open. Managing a change program you can divide stakeholders into several categories:

- **People who you need as resources.** These may, for example, include the IT department.

- **People who you need to take along.** Those in the company who need to be persuaded and talked round as their role is potentially vital.

- **People who are going to be affected by the change.**

- **People on the sidelines who are watching the progress of the change.** These may include institutional investors, shareholders, and customers.

Only if the needs, expectations and fears of all stakeholders are considered, and acted on, can progress be made. Programs of change are stopped in the blocks by:

- lack of trust
- lack of communication upward, downward, sideways, externally, and internally
- poor motivation
- lack of entrepreneurial skills among managers
- slow decision-making
- lack of collaboration between functions, teams, and individuals
- lack of emphasis on learning.

Managing change

BENNIS, W; BENNE KD; & CHIN, R, *The Planning of Change* (2nd edition), Holt, Rinehart & Winston, 1970

CUNNINGHAM, I, *The Wisdom of Strategic Learning*, McGraw Hill, Maidenhead, 1994

KANTER, RM; STEIN, B; & JICK, TD, *The Challenge of Organizational Change*, Free Press, New York, 1992

VAILL, P, *Managing as a Performing Art*, Jossey-Bass, San Francisco, 1990

WATZLAWICK, P; WEAKLAND, JH; & FISCH, R, *Change: Principles of Problem Formation and Problem Resolution*, Norton, New York, 1974

Peter Drucker
The prophet of change

No discussion of the new world of management would be complete without inclusion of the century's most influential management thinker, Peter Drucker. The bare bones of Drucker's career give little insight to the profound effect and influence he has had – and continues to have – on management thinking. Born in Austria, he became an investment banker in London in 1933. In 1937 he emigrated to the United States and worked in newspapers. In 1942 he became a Professor of Philosophy and Politics at Bennington College in Vermont and later a Professor of Management at New York University. During his career he has also been a consultant to many large organizations. Now, Drucker is the Clarke Professor of Social Science and Management at the Claremont Graduate School in Claremont, California (he is also lectures on oriental art at the same institution).

Behind these scant details lies a career as a writer and thinker on virtually every aspect of management. Drucker's books are as diverse in content as they are numerous. His first book appeared in 1939, *The End of Economic Man*. A succession of others has followed. In the 1940s Drucker wrote *The Future of Industrial Man* and *The Concept of the Corporation*; in the 1950s, his output included *The Practice of Management*; in the 1960s, came *Managing for Results, The Effective Executive, The Age of Discontinuity*; the 1970s brought the encyclopaedic *Management: Tasks, Responsibilities, Practices*; the 1980s included, *Managing in Turbulent Times* and *The Frontiers of Management*; and in the 1990s, *Managing the Nonprofit Organization* and *Managing for the Future*. By any stretch of the imagination, this is a phenomenal output. In addition, Drucker has written novels and the autobiographical *Adventures of a Bystander*.

PETER DRUCKER   born 1909; writer

Education: Doctorate in international and public law, Frankfurt University, 1931

Career: Journalist in Germany and the UK where he also advised banks; went to the US in 1937 to teach; 1939, *The End of Economic Man*, published;1942, Professor of Philosophy and Politics at Bennington College, Vermont; Professor of Management at New York University; since 1971 Clarke Professor of Social Science and Management at the Claremont Graduate School in Claremont, California.

Drucker has deliberately set himself apart from the mainstream of management education – not for nothing is the greatest management thinker of the century a professor at a relatively obscure institution. He has roundly condemned Harvard Business School and the business school system and, during his lengthy career, has studiously avoided becoming part of any one organization. The theorist has studiously retained an objective distance from organizational practice.

What is notable about Drucker's work is his uncanny ability to spot trends and describe them in an almost downbeat manner drawing wisdom from an array of sources (though Jane Austen and Trollope remain consistent inspirations to him). Later they are almost always picked up by others and become the height of managerial fashion. Often, their roots can be traced back to Drucker's work a decade previously. His 1969 book, *The Age of Discontinuity*, for example, is now much referred to as writers and managers attempt to come to terms with managing change. In this book he observed that America was "a knowledge economy" – a theme he later returned to in *Managing for the Future* (1992) in which he observed: "From now on the key is knowledge." Twenty-five years on from his original observation, the concept

35

of knowledge-workers and knowledge-intensive organizations is gaining widespread attention (not least from Drucker himself).

Other of his works have ignited interest long after their publication. In the 1973 book, *People and Performance*, he discussed the broader social responsibilities of managers and organizations – once again, this is something organizations are slowly coming to terms with. Drucker called for less hierarchical structures and leaner organizations in the 1960s and again in the 1980s before they became fashionable in the 1990s.

Drucker predicted what is now labeled postindustrialism and examined how this would impact on managerial best practice. Indeed, his recent writings have reaffirmed the radical challenges facing managers: "The single greatest challenge facing managers in the developed countries of the world is to raise the productivity of knowledge and service workers. This challenge, which will dominate the management agenda for the next several decades, will ultimately determine the competitive performance of companies. Even more important, it will determine the very fabric of society and the quality of life in every industrialized nation."[31]

> "The single greatest challenge facing managers in the developed countries of the world is to raise the productivity of knowledge and service workers."
> PETER DRUCKER

Perhaps his greatest achievements are *The Practice of Management* (1954) and *Management: Tasks, Responsibilities, Practices* (1973). In the latter, a massive work, he identifies five "basic operations in the work of the manager." These are: setting objectives, organizing, motivating and communicating, measuring, and developing people (including him or herself).

The length of his career and his level of book production has enabled him to extol a company's virtues and then, later, to point out how and when its virtues became liabilities. Most famously, his book *Concept of the Corporation* analyzed and celebrated GM's divisional structure – in 1991 he recognized that what had once made the company successful, its long established management practices, were what was now holding it back.

Undoubtedly, Drucker's ideas have evolved – his fascination with corporations, for example, has given way to an interest in small firms and nonprofit organizations. His broad brush brings in history, sociology, and anthropology and, by its very nature, courts disappointment and failure. The *Economist* observed that Drucker has "a burning sense of the importance of management. He believes that poor management helped to plunge the Europe of his youth into disaster, and he fears that the scope for poor management is growing larger, as organizations become ever more complicated and interdependent."[32]

Despite such concerns, Drucker is encouraged that the emphasis is now on changing organizations to become more efficient – rather than on dragging every ounce of energy out of tired managers and employees. He also believes that globalization will produce managers who are more in-tune with the needs of the global environment than politicians. Only then will managers be able to take what Drucker regards as their rightful place as the driving forces behind the great economies.

Peter Drucker

Concept of the Corporation, John Day, New York, 1946

The New Society, Heinemann, London, 1951

The Practice of Management, Harper & Row, New York, 1954

Managing for Results, Heinemann, London, 1964

The Age of Discontinuity, Heinemann, London, 1969

Management: Tasks, Responsibilities, Practices, Heinemann, London, 1974

Innovation and Entrepreneurship, Heinemann, London, 1985

The New Realities, Heinemann, London, 1989

Managing the Nonprofit Organization, Harper Collins, New York, 1990

References: The new world of management

1 LAWLER, E, "New logic is here to stay," *Financial Times*, Jan. 28, 1994.

2 HAMEL, G, *Foreword* to *Financial Times Handbook of Management*, FT/Pitman, London, 1995.

3 DRUCKER, P, "The New Productivity Challenge," *Harvard Business Review*, Nov.–Dec. 1991.

4 ALLEN, LA, *Professional Management: new concepts and proven practices*, McGraw Hill, Maidenhead, 1973.

5 Quoted in CAULKIN, S, "The boy from Brazil," *The Observer*, Oct. 17, 1993.

6 MINTZBERG, H, *The Nature of Managerial Work*, Prentice-Hall, Englewood Cliffs, NJ, 1973.

7 TAN, JH, "Management work in Singapore: developing a factor model," Henley Management College/Brunel University, 1994.

8 Quoted in *The Observer*, Nov. 6, 1994.

9 BIRCHALL, D, "The changing nature of management," *Financial Times Handbook of Management*, FT/Pitman, London, 1995.

10 COCKERILL, AP, "The kind of competence for rapid change," *Personnel Management*, 21, 1989.

11 HARVEY JONES, J, *Managing to Survive*, Heinemann, London, 1993.
12 Quoted in TAIT, N, "Hungry for gurus," *Financial Times*, Aug. 11, 1995.
13 LORENZ, C, "Change is not enough," *Financial Times*, Jan. 12, 1994.
14 Interview with Stuart Crainer, April 22, 1994.
15 PASCALE, R, ATHOS, A, & GOSS, T, "The reinvention roller coaster," *Harvard Business Review*, Nov./Dec. 1993.
16 KPMG, *Change Management*, KPMG, 1993.
17 "The technology pay-off," *Business Week*, June 14, 1993.
18 "Outsource boom for in-house services," *Financial Times*, Jan. 11, 1994.
19 HAGEL, J, "Keeping CPR on track," *McKinsey Quarterly*, May 1993.
20 DIXON, M, "The benefits of a switchable personality," *Financial Times*, Jan. 26, 1994.
21 Institute of Management, *Are career ladders disappearing?*, IM, Corby, 1993.
22 PASCALE, R, "The benefit of a clash of opinions," *Personnel Management*, Oct. 1993.
23 OBENG, EDA, "Avoiding the fast-track pitfalls," *Sunday Times*, March 11, 1990.
24 LORENZ, C, "Struggling with the curse of success," *Financial Times*, Oct. 22, 1993.
25 CRAINER, S, "Better for the change," *The Times*, Sept. 30, 1993.
26 TRAPP, R, "How to ride the winds of change," *Independent on Sunday*, Dec. 12, 1993.
27 ROETHLISBERGER, F, *Training for Human Relations*, Harvard University, Boston, MA, 1954.
28 QUIRKE, W, *Communicating Change*, McGraw Hill, Maidenhead, 1995.
29 "Putting over the message," *Financial Times*, Sept. 3, 1993.
30 LORENZ, C, "Avoiding the IBM Trap," *Financial Times*, Oct. 15, 1993.
31 DRUCKER, PF, "The new productivity challenge," *Harvard Business Review*, Nov.–Dec. 1991.
32 "Peter Drucker, salvationist," *Economist*, Oct. 1, 1994.

The new world of organizations

"It is not necessary for any one department to know what any other department is doing. It is the business of those who plan the entire work to see that all of the departments are working ... towards the same end."
HENRY FORD

"Any company that cannot imagine the future won't be around to enjoy it."
GARY HAMEL and C K PRAHALAD[1]

THE RISE AND FALL OF THE FUNCTIONAL ORGANIZATION

Organizations are traditionally seen as vertical structures. This has been the critical ingredient of the conventional recipe for organizational success. Though organizations have tried many different ways of representing their structure most, if not all, end up with some sort of vertical axis from top to bottom. It is a striking truth that today's organizations remain modeled on the principles described by Adam Smith in 1776.

Smith's fundamentals were later developed by Frederick Taylor. Practical use of Taylor's "scientific management," built around specialization and the division of labor, reached a high point with the advent of the mass production line with workers performing repetitious tasks on a mammoth scale. Management followed similar structures with different functions – such as marketing, sales, R&D, and production – being ruthlessly separated.

Henry Ford
A genius for mass production

Mass production techniques reaped impressive early dividends. HENRY FORD (1863–1947), the arch exponent of the art, generated a huge fortune built on the increased productivity brought by mass production. Ford believed that managers should work in isolation, unencumbered by the problems of their colleagues, simply concentrating on what they are employed to do.

While Ford is routinely lauded as the man who brought the world mass production lines, his idiosyncratic career (from boy racer to multimillionaire antiwar campaigner), as well as his many barbed observations, tend to be forgotten. There was, however, more to Ford than flow lines, workers doing mindlessly repetitive tasks and the ubiquitous Model T.

> **"I have no use for a motor car which has more spark plugs than a cow has teats."**
> **HENRY FORD**

Marketing guru, Ted Levitt has argued that Ford's genius actually lay in marketing, not manufacturing. Ford first decided that the world was ready for an affordable car; and then that mass production techniques

were the only way of providing it. Instead of controlling costs to produce lower prices, Ford set the price and challenged the organization to
ensure costs were low enough to meet the figure.

Ford's masterly piece of marketing lay in his intuitive realization that
the middle-class car market existed – it just remained for him to provide
the products the market wanted. In management jargon, Ford stuck to
the knitting. Model Ts were black, straightforward and affordable. "I
have no use for a motor car which has more spark plugs than a cow has
teats," said Ford. The trouble was that when other manufacturers added
extras, Ford kept it simple and dramatically lost ground. The man with a
genius for marketing lost touch with the aspirations of customers.

Even now, Ford's achievements remain impressive. He built his first car
in 1896; started his own company in 1903; and between 1908 and 1927
produced 15 million Model Ts. In 1920 Ford was making a car a minute.

Compare this with the approach of
Ford's predecessors. The first car
makers, such as France's Panhard et
Levassor, employed a small number of
skilled craftsmen. The cars they produced were unique – almost prototypes
– with parts being filed and cut to make
them fit. As the parts were of varying
sizes, craftsmanship was required.

> **"Time waste differs from material waste in that there can be no salvage."**
> **HENRY FORD**

Ford brought in uniform and interchangeable parts. Skill departed
and, instead, production was based round strict functional divides –
demarcations. Ford believed in people getting on with their jobs and
not raising their heads above functional parapets. He didn't want engineers talking to salespeople, or people making decisions without his say
so. Management and managers he dismissed as largely unnecessary.

Ford did not invent the production line. He was actually inspired by
what he had seen in the slaughterhouses of Chicago. Others – such as
musket-maker Eli Whitney in the nineteenth century – had also made
tentative steps towards the production line. But, Ford transformed it
into a means of previously unimagined mass production.

At the center of Ford's thinking was the aim of standardization –
something continually emphasized by the car makers of today though
they talk in terms of quality, and Ford in quantity.

While Ford will never be celebrated for his people management skills,
he had an international perspective which was ahead of his time. His
plant at Highland Park, Detroit, produced and the world – not just the
US – bought. Also, Ford was acutely aware that time was an important
competitive weapon – "Time waste differs from material waste in that
there can be no salvage," he observed.

"In some respects Ford remains a good role model," says Ray Wild, principal of Henley Management College. "He was an improviser and innovator, he borrowed ideas and then adapted and synthesized them. He developed flow lines that involved people; now, we have flow lines without people, but no one questions their relevance or importance. Though he is seen as having de-humanized work, it shouldn't be forgotten that he provided a level of wealth for workers and products for consumers which weren't previously available."

Down the functional tunnel

In fact, it was Adam Smith who identified the potential problem of mass production. "A man who spends his life carrying out a small number of very simple operations with perhaps the same effects has no room to develop his intelligence or to stretch his imagination so as to look for ways of overcoming difficulties which never occur. He thereby loses quite naturally the habit of using these faculties and, in general, he becomes as stupid and ignorant as it is possible for a human being to become."

The downside of such "scientific" management is now well known and accepted. Ruthlessly satirized by Charlie Chaplin in *Modern Times*, such "science" brought with it worker alienation, a lack of coordination between different functions and a complete absence of flexibility. Any sense of individual responsibility was sucked away by the system. Imaginations were never stretched; intelligence was not developed.

Though the production line model of Henry Ford is disappearing and arguments over demarcation no longer fill

> "With new technology diffusing information widely, many feel that the issue isn't who you are in the structure but what you get accomplished."
> D QUINN MILLS

the headlines, its legacy persists. Even in the fashionably downsized, lean, and flat organization of the 1990s, there are likely to be an unhealthy quota of controllers, overseers, and supervisors. Middle managers, planners, and accountants have established themselves as middle men between technology and implementation. Technology, brought in to reduce complexity, has more often than not brought with it teams of managers each intent on finding or creating their own place in the corporate order.

"The hierarchy is under siege because it's increasingly inefficient and many of the most effective workers in our companies are sick of it. They're tired of the rituals, the lack of real communication, the delays in making decisions and taking actions. With new technology diffusing information widely, many feel that the issue isn't who you are in the structure but what you get accomplished," observes Harvard Business School's D Quinn Mills.[2]

HIERARCHIES LOSING SIGHT OF THE CUSTOMER

Hierarchies have expanded and new layers have been added with each technological step forward – note the growth of IT departments, strategy departments and so on. Companies have preoccupied themselves with bridging the gap between management and workers or organizing the workforce to perform more efficiently. Little attention has been paid to the role of customers; the layers of management or the core processes which enable the business to attract and retain customers.

Over the last 20 years great strides have been made in eradicating Taylorism from the factory floor. Management demarcations have, however, usually emerged unscathed. The current fascination for reengineering may, perhaps, tackle white collar business processes in a way that has never before been convincingly attempted. It seeks to bridge the gap between management and employees to create a seamless organization geared around the needs of core constituencies rather than functions.

Skeptics may argue that the functional organization works. Undoubtedly, it does. Companies have been organized along functional lines throughout the twentieth century. They have not failed, but they have worked inefficiently. The functional system isn't broken, but it needs fixing.

THE CENTRAL PROBLEMS OF FUNCTIONAL ORGANIZATIONS

- Goal setting
- Senior to junior process steps
- Job definitions
- Responsibility
- Communications
- Corporate Bermuda Triangles
- Self-perpetuation

Goal setting

Functional organizations set goals that are functional rather than business oriented. This means that groups of people in different functions have their own alternative targets and *raison d'être*. There may be over-all corporate strategies and objectives, but they are effectively relegated in importance. A manager working in a functional organization first and foremost requires that his or her function succeeds. Performance bonuses are usually related to divisional performance and managers are well aware that functions which succeed attract resources and the most talented people.

The end result of this is that the performance of different functions within the same organization is often desperately uneven. This can be seen in companies which have developed excellence in one particular area of their business. They may well be financially brilliant but, overall, their organization is not achieving its full potential. A company with an excellent R&D department may well be unable to transform ideas into practice due to a poorly performing production function.

Senior to junior process steps

A business process often passes from one hierarchical level to another as it moves from one function to another. Frequently, a junior person needs input from a senior manager – perhaps a signature or some other task – and in most of these cases the senior manager fails to take the work seriously. They may delay the work in preference to other work, even if the customer needs it urgently, or may make errors which the junior person has to correct.

Job definitions

Harnessed by the restraints of their particular function, staff are overly specialized. The language used in one function may be unfamiliar or obscure to another. Usually the concepts they hold dear are at odds with the pragmatic demands of customers. Because of this they are unable to react to increasingly diverse customer needs. Instead of maxi-mizing the potential of people, a functional organization denies it. As a result, people become bored and frustrated, which leads to a higher staff turnover. Job definitions strongly reflect the functional nature of the organization. There are few jobs – apart from chief executive – which bridge the gap between different functions (and the chief executive may well have a specialized functional background). Job titles are unlikely to include the word "customer." Those that do are vested with little in the way of power or seniority.

Responsibility

In functional organizations customer service is not usually the responsibility of any one person. Any problems or customer queries spanning more than one department are passed on and on. Alternatively, problems are identified in purely functional terms – there is a problem with sales or an accounting problem. Identified in functional isolation they are solved in a similar style. Within one particular organization some salesmen personally looked after several hundred customers and an engineer typically handled around 100. Responsibility was effectively diluted until very little existed.

Communication

The functional organization is often characterized by Byzantine communication chains. Paper passes back and forth between departments. Delays are inevitable as in-trays become more full and customers more irate. The entire process is time consuming and inflexible.

You don't have to travel far to find bureaucracy alive and well. At Bell Atlantic a 15 to 30 day order-to-delivery cycle contained a mere 10 to 15 hours of actual work. The rest of the time was spent in waiting or was simply wasted as one department passed paperwork on to another. (Having identified the problem the company began to sort it out.) Similarly, at AT&T a design cycle included 80 "hand-offs" from one department to another and 24 meetings. (This was later reduced to 17 and one respectively.)

Corporate Bermuda Triangles

In the Pacific Ocean there may well be no such thing as the Bermuda Triangle. In corporate *terra firma* its existence is more easily established. Functional organizations often have stages of the process where no one has been assigned responsibility. Because processes tend to move to and fro between functions they remain unmanaged.

One chief executive said that an important part of his job was identifying who has responsibility for what in his organization. He found that managers were in the habit of passing things on to him when they were unsure of whose domain they belonged. By abdicating responsibility the managers believed they had solved the problem. The chief executive then had to decide who should take responsibility for the particular issue. In effect he found himself in charge of the Bermuda Triangle.

The irony is that the functional organization appears to offer clarity of responsibility. In practice it often overlooks the grey areas between different functions where no one takes responsibility.

Self-perpetuation

As new functions and divisions are added to the basic functional structure, the old ones are never replaced. A company may have functional divisions as well as product divisions and, quite possibly, geographic, national, strategic, and market-driven splits between different activities.

There is nothing new in revealing the inadequacies and limitations of vertical and functional structures. They have been recognized for a number of years, but attempts at breaking them down have tended to be isolated and short-term. Companies have turned to temporary project teams, task forces, and various alternative matrices at times of crisis or to tackle specific localized problems. Once the problem was solved, they resorted to their old ways, continuing to gloss over the fundamental problem.

Functional organizations inevitably produce functional solutions to their problems. Functional organizations produce functional managers. Managers become hidebound by managing things rather than getting them done.

If a company is patently struggling, different functional heads will advocate different functional-based solutions to the problem. The marketing director will argue that the company needs to increase its investment in marketing. If only it had more sales people making direct contact with customers it would be more able to give customers what they want. They might also suggest that the sales team would feel more confident if they had a new glossy brochure to distribute to prospective customers.

The finance director is liable to shake his or her head at this point. From their point of view, the company's troubles are cost-related. If the company reduced costs it would be leaner and fitter. The production director will, in turn, argue the case for investment in better quality, more modern machinery. The chief executive, beset by arguing factions who are

Functional organizations inevitably produce functional solutions to their problems.

unlikely to ever agree, is likely to strike a balance – giving a little bit more money to each function or coming up with a company-wide initiative which each function will interpret as they wish and then ignore.

In his book *Administrative Behavior*, Herbert Simon summed up this process and coined a phrase for it: "satisficing" – settling for adequate instead of optimal solutions.[3] This is an in-built characteristic of the conventional functional organization. Past strategy is fused with current organizational culture, so that people begin to believe that they know how things are done and stop questioning the assumptions behind their thoughts and actions. The recipe for success takes over and doubts about the company's ability to actually deliver success are automatically repressed. Success once bred success. Now, corporations are increasingly aware that success can breed complacency and then failure.

Alfred P Sloan
Antidotes to functional failure

While the deficiencies of the functional approach were soon apparent, solutions to the problems it raised have proved perennially elusive. The first concerted attempt at creating an antidote to straight functionalism was carried out by ALFRED P SLOAN (1875–1966) at General Motors. Sloan took what Ford had achieved on the factory floor and sought to apply it to managers and the organization as a whole.

Sloan's sole contribution to management literature is *My Years at General Motors*. Published in 1963, it is a one-paced, intricate account of how Sloan managed GM. Today, it appears dated – GM employees, for example, are generally conspicuous by their absence. Sloan was not an up-tempo evangelist with a pithy catch-phrase and a store of witty anecdotes and yet, the book is among the most important in management and Sloan one of the most influential managers of the century.

"His book is one thing, what he did at GM is quite another," says London Business School's Sumantra Ghoshal. "Sloan created a new organizational form – the multi-divisional form – which became a doctrine of management. Today, it is not ascribed to him, but Sloan was its instigator."

> **"Sloan created a new organizational form – the multi-divisional form – which became a doctrine of management. Today, it is not ascribed to him, but Sloan was its instigator."**
> **SUMANTRA GHOSHAL**

Sloan became president of GM in 1923, chairman in 1946 and honorary chairman from 1956 until his death. When he took over, GM was struggling to hold its own as Ford, with its Model T, swept all aside. He set about revitalizing and reorganizing GM along "federal" lines, the very antithesis of the way Ford organized itself. He replaced GM's messy, bureaucratic, centralized system with one based on divisions, each with its own clearly delineated responsibilities. Over 30 divisions, further divided into groups, emerged. Instead of fighting for dominance, separate functions were treated as equals. In the marketplace, GM's products – including Chevrolet and Cadillac – competed as separate divisions coming up with rapid model changes and added extras.

Much of the current debate about being both local and global can be traced back to Sloan's delicate balancing act between the twin forces of decentralization and centralization. Sloan's triumph was in achieving a balance over so many years.

The decentralized structure proved the making of GM. By the late 1970s its US market share was over 45 percent, compared to a relatively meagre 12 percent when Sloan took over in the 1920s. The federal structure meant that instead of concerning themselves with the nitty-gritty of production, executives could turn their energies to ensuring that divisions met their performance targets and to providing overall direction. GM's fortunes revived and Sloan began to meet his aim of providing a car for "every purse and every purpose."

Sloan believed senior managers had three functions: to decide on the company's strategy; to design its structure and select its control systems. The new GM became venerated as a model of management. Its admirers included Peter Drucker and the economic historian, Alfred Chandler. Chandler's important book, *Strategy and Structure* (1962) studied major US corporations between 1850 and 1920. At that time strategy was generally neglected – indeed, Chandler sparked interest in the subject. He argued that strategy came first and then organizations had to determine the most appropriate structure to deliver the strategy.

Chandler championed the multidivisional form – labeled the M-form – with senior managers overseeing a decentralized organization and concentrating on making "entrepreneurial decisions."

In practice, troubles emerged with the multidivisional system. It was built around a vast web of committees and groups which became bogged down in their own power struggles and bureaucracy. Stringent targets and narrow measures of success stultified initiative. Also, by the 1960s the delicate balance was lost – finance emerged as the dominant function – and GM became paralyzed by what had once made it great.

Sloan's approach is now regarded as too inflexible and cumbersome to work in the fast moving 1990s. "It was right for the 1970s, a growing handicap in the 1980s and it would have been a ticket to the bone-yard in the 1990s," caustically observes GE chairman Jack Welch.[4]

Even so, Sloan's legacy lives on – the multidivisional organization remains dominant; in the 1980s it was estimated that 85 percent of large corporations had adopted the multidivisional structure. Only now, says Sumantra Ghoshal, is a new, more entrepreneurial, organizational model emerging to replace the world according to Sloan.

The rise and fall of the functional organization

CHANDLER, A D, *Strategy and Structure*, MIT Press, Boston, MA, 1962

CHANDLER, A D, *The Visible Hand: The Managerial Revolution in American Business*, Harvard University Press, Cambridge, MA, 1977

CHANDLER, A D, and DEAMS, H (eds), *Managerial Hierarchies*, Harvard University Press, Cambridge, MA, 1980

The rise of corporate man

And, what kind of manager did the systems championed by Taylor, Ford, and Sloan produce? The answer is pithy: corporate man. Dedicated, loyal, unquestioning, hard working and clean-cut; corporate man was the paragon of rational management.

His first champion (corporate woman was yet to come) was CHESTER BARNARD (1886–1961), an executive with AT&T and then president of New Jersey Bell. "The most important single contribution required of an executive, certainly the most universal qualification, is loyalty, domination by the organization personality," wrote Barnard in his impenetrable *The Functions of the Executive*.[5]

Despite such sentiments, Barnard recognized the role of the individual and saw the executive's role as creating shared values within the organization. "I rejected the concept of organization as compromising a rather definitive group of people whose behavior is co-ordinated with reference to some explicit goal or goals. In a community all acts of individuals and of organizations are directly or indirectly interconnected and interdependent," he said.

These relationships remained largely unacknowledged in the first 50 years of the twentieth century. The employee–corporation relationship was narrowly defined and even more stringently practiced. Linking the two together in a more dynamic way has preoccupied a great many minds in recent decades.

THE IBM WAY: CULTURING CORPORATE MAN

One of the most successful creators of corporate man was (and, perhaps, is) IBM. Its growth was built on service excellence and clear company values, as well as products and manufacturing processes. Within companies like IBM, corporate culture and the individuality of managers became intertwined in a way never envisaged when the manager was a mere supervisor.

▶

The person largely responsible for the IBM culture was THOMAS WATSON SENIOR (1874–1956). Few business people create companies in their own image which then thrive after their departure. Most plummet after the final farewell from the great leader, unable or unwilling to carry on as before. Thomas Watson is one of the rare exceptions. Under Watson, IBM became the stuff of corporate and stock market legend, continuing to dominate long after Watson's death.

Watson created a corporate culture which lasted. IBM – "Big Blue" – became the archetypal modern corporation and its managers the ultimate stereotype – with their regulation sombre suits, white shirts, plain ties, zeal for selling, and company song. Beneath this, however, lay a belief in competing vigorously and providing quality service. Later, competitors complained that IBM's sheer size won it orders. This was only partly true. Its size masked a deeper commitment to managing customer accounts, providing service, and building relationships. These elements were established by the demanding perfectionist, Watson. "He emphasized people and service – obsessively," noted Tom Peters in *Liberation Management*. "IBM was a service star in an era of malperforming machines."

> **"IBM was a service star in an era of malperforming machines."**
> THOMAS WATSON SNR

IBM's origins lay in the semantically challenged Computing-Tabulating-Recording Company which Watson joined in 1914. Under Watson the company's revenues doubled from $4.2 million to $8.3 million by 1917. Initially making everything from butcher's scales to meat slicers, its activities gradually concentrated on tabulating machines which processed information mechanically on punched cards. Watson boldly renamed the company International Business Machines. This was, at the time, overstating the company's credentials though IBM Japan was established before the Second World War.

IBM's development was helped by the 1937 Wages-Hours Act which required US companies to record hours worked and wages paid. The existing machines couldn't cope and Watson instigated work on a solution. In 1944 the Mark 1 was launched, followed by the Selective Sequence Electronic Calculator in 1947. By then IBM's revenues were $119 million and it was set to make the great leap forward to become the world's largest computer company.

> **"The secret I learned early on from my father was to run scared and never think I had made it."**
> THOMAS WATSON JNR

While Thomas Watson Senior created IBM's culture, his son, THOMAS WATSON JUNIOR (1914–94) moved it from being an outstanding performer to world dominance. Watson Jr brought a vision of the future to the company which his father had lacked. Yet, the strength of the original culture remained intact. Indeed, Watson Jr fleshed it out, creating a framework of theories round the intuitive and hard-nosed business acumen of his father.

Typically, Watson Sr made sure his son served a brief apprenticeship – as an IBM salesman – and Watson Jr remained driven by his father's lessons throughout his career. "The secret I learned early on from my father was to run scared and never think I had made it," he said. And, sure enough, when IBM thought it had made it the ground slipped beneath its previously sure feet.

In his book, *A Business and Its Beliefs* – an extended IBM mission statement – Watson Jr tellingly observes: "'The beliefs that mold great organizations frequently grow out of the character, the experience and the convictions of a single person." In IBM's case that person was Thomas Watson Senior.

Corporate man existed confidently enough until the early 1980s. Indeed, his demise can be linked to the precipitous fall in IBM's own fortunes. The end of corporate man was – in media terms at least – brought about by the rise of the new breed of entrepreneurial, all-action, management heroes. In fiction they were embodied by Gordon Ghekko in Oliver Stone's film, *Wall Street*. In a typically colorful speech, Ghekko propounds:

> Now, in the days of the free market when our country was a top industrial power there was accountability. The Carnegies, the Mellons, the men that built this great industrial empire made sure it was, because it was their money at stake.
>
> Today management has no stake in the company. All together these men sitting up here own less than three percent of the company. And where does Mr Cromwell put his $M dollar salary? Not in Teldar stock. He owns less than one percent. You own the company, that's right, you, the stockholders and you are being royally screwed by these bureaucrats with their stock lunches, their hunting and fishing trips, their corporate jets and their golden parachutes.

Eschewing corporate loyalty, individual initiative was back in fashion. If the corporation couldn't give you what you wanted, why belong to the corporation? Management was seen as exciting and intuitive, built around deals, instant decisions and hard work. Corporate man gave into his machismo and allowed it full rein.

With the reinvention of the traditional manager, organizations struggled to keep pace. The 1980s saw a host of books on how to set the individual free in organizations – managers were, for example, encouraged to become "intrapreneurs," entrepreneurial within the constraints of the organization.

The trouble with managers reinventing themselves was that organizations failed to keep pace. Fed on a steady stream of corporate men – and increasingly corporate women – the great corporations weren't about to do a U-turn and relish the possibilities of individual inspiration. They liked the way Gordon Ghekko made money, but they didn't like how he did it and what he stood for.

THE NEW ORGANIZATIONAL MODEL

The changing aspirations of managers have clearly had an impact on the shape and structure of organizations. But, what has provided the important impetus for organizations to change their shape has been a potent combination of circumstances and trends – not the least of which has been increasing awareness that the functional model is too inflexible to meet the new demands of business.

The business agenda of the late 1980s and early 1990s was – and is – increasingly shaped by new facts of corporate life.

First, hierarchies have spawned greater costs rather than improved productivity or higher quality products and services. The vast numbers of middle and junior managers are recognized by a growing number of organizations as a costly indulgence.

The most obvious side-effect of the burdensome hierarchy is the slow speed of decision-making. If every decision has to be filtered through ten lines of hierarchy, no decision is likely to be quick. In the past this had not proved a significant impediment to commercial success. In the 1960s and 1970s companies did not have to move quickly – markets were there, usually national in nature, and evolving at a slow pace. Now, with emphasis on the speed of product development and delivery, it is crucial that decisions are immediate. For example, 3M requires that 30 percent of each of its unit's sales must be generated by products introduced in the last four years.

The obvious conclusion drawn by companies throughout the world, is that layers of management need to be eradicated. Instead of pyramids of middle managers rarely communicating with one another, the onus is on project teams and cross functional working.

Behind this is the inescapable impact of information technology (IT). IT enables managers to communicate more effectively than ever before.

It is not constrained by hierarchical structures. Instead, it allows managers to cut through hierarchy to communicate with the people they need to communicate with, no matter where they are positioned in the organization – geographically or hierarchically. As many middle management jobs had become ones of filtering and directing information, they are effectively redundant.

To all these factors in the early 1990s was added worldwide economic recession which simply served to highlight the need for change. Times are changing. But that does not mean that managers are necessarily moving as quickly as the trends which engulf them. "Most managers are still stuck with an outdated view of the nature of organizations, and of their own roles within them," observes the *Financial Times*' Christopher Lorenz.[6]

Creating the new organization

Though these trends and events brought things to a head, the new organizational model is not an overnight phenomenon. "Organizations are a system of co-operative activities – and their co-ordination requires something intangible and personal that is largely a matter of relationships," noted Chester Barnard.[7]

BURNS' AND STALKER'S ORGANIZATIONAL MODEL

Indeed, in the early 1960s the British sociologist TOM BURNS was one of the earliest thinkers to produce a coherent argument against the commonly accepted practices of mass production and organizations based around self-perpetuating bureaucracy. His 1961 book, *The Management of Innovation* (written with the psychologist, GM Stalker) concluded that the Weber-inspired bureaucratic machine was severely limited by the fact that it simply could not cope with changes in the internal or external environment. Burns and Stalker propounded an **organic organization**. Though it retains a ring of the 1960s, their organizational model contains many of the characteristics of the new model organization of the late 1990s. It emphasizes "networks," shared vision and values, teamworking which crosses functions and effective sharing of knowledge and expertise.

Burns and Stalker's book met with a general and resounding silence – though it has now been reissued. Its ideas are important and have, during the last decade, reemerged as the deficiencies of previous organizational models have become increasingly recognized.

"The emphasis on outputs, on tasks and costs has made organizations more diffuse bodies," says Shaun Tyson of Cranfield School of Management. "The present era has been described as 'post-Fordist' or 'post-modernist' – that is, organization managers have moved away from thinking of their operational activity as replicating a bureaucratic machine, a rational, non-human monolith which delivers standardized products or services with scant regard for customer choice or competitive rivalry. Instead, work is organized in a more organic way, susceptible to rapid change, and to adjustment albeit within a limited range of options. Banking services, for example, are designed as personal financial advisory services, with most routine withdrawals and regular payments handled by machines; car manufacturers have various specification mixes on offer; and airlines try to leverage sales through special packages, air miles schemes and the like."[8]

The problems and the challenges were potently mapped out by Larry Hirschhorn and Thomas Gilmore of the Wharton Center for Applied Research in a *Harvard Business Review* article:

> The problem is that this traditional organizational map describes a world that no longer exists. New technologies, fast-changing markets, and global competition are revolutionizing business relationships. As companies blur their traditional boundaries to respond to this more fluid business environment, the roles that people play at work and the tasks they perform become correspondingly blurred and ambiguous.
>
> However, just because work roles are no longer defined by the formal organizational structure doesn't mean that differences in authority, skill, talent and perspective simply disappear."[9]

What has excited attention in the 1990s is that organizational theory is being seen to be translated into dynamic business practice. Many accept that the age calls for radical responses, and now there are a growing number of radical role models.

GE's ORGANIZATIONAL REVOLUTION

In the US the modern blueprint for the organizational revolution can be seen at General Electric (GE). When chief executive Jack Welch arrived in 1981, the company was cumbersome and underperforming. Welch has since succeeded in overhauling and realigning it in a way which few thought possible. Between 1981 and 1990 GE cut the average number of management layers between Welch and the very front line from nine to four. Its headquarters was slashed from 2,100 people to fewer than 1,000. The number of senior executives across the company was cut, first from 700 to 500, and between 1990 and 1994 by another 100. The overall workforce was almost halved, from 404,000 to 220,000. Yet GE's revenues more than doubled through this period, from $27 billion to $60 billion.

Welch has stripped hierarchies away. When he arrived GE had an average of five or six people reporting to each manager. By the late 1980s this average had doubled and is now at about 14 – with some units reaching 25 or more. With more people to manage, managers have to manage in a different way using new skills and, increasingly, enabling others to do jobs once the sole preserve of management.

The matrix model: ABB

While Jack Welch and GE have grabbed the attention in the United States, Europe's benchmark of the new organizational model is the Swedish–Swiss conglomerate, Asea Brown Boveri (ABB). Under chief executive, Percy Barnevik, ABB has set unprecedented standards. Its ability to change itself continually impresses and concerns commentators – and ABB managers – in equal amounts.

The genesis of ABB began in 1987 when Barnevik, at the time chief executive of the Swedish engineering group, ASEA, announced what was then the world's largest cross-border merger between ASEA and the Swiss company, Brown Boveri. Since then ABB has acquired over 70 more companies, assembling a corporate monster worth $30 billion. Its engineering markets include electric power generation and transmission equipment, high speed trains, automation and robots, and environmental control systems.

Barnevik has rigorously rooted out and extinguished any vestiges of bureaucracy in ABB. His straightforward and much quoted rule is that 30 percent of central staff can be spun off into separate and independent profit centres, another 30 percent can be transferred to the operational companies as part of their overhead, another 30 percent can be eliminated as superfluous to requirements and the remaining 10 percent can be kept on as the minimum required. At ASEA, Barnevik reduced the number of employees at head office from 2,000 to 200.

Barnevik's revolution is based round a number of simple precepts (though their implementation is often highly complex):

● **identify the skills required of executives and identify a small number of key executives** (250 in ABB's case) to carry changes through. Barnevik sought out "people capable of becoming superstars – toughskinned individuals, who were fast on their feet, had good technical and commercial backgrounds and had demonstrated the ability to lead others."[10]

● **emphasize and practice open communication.** ABB continually states, communicates and evolves clear values. The ABB values – meeting customer needs, decentralization, taking action, respecting an ethic, and cooperating – are reinforced through intensive in-house programs of executive education, in which Barnevik and other members of the Konzernleitung invest a great deal of time. The prime values, from Barnevik's point of view, are meeting customer needs and decentralization. ABB emphasizes human contact. It is what its executive vice-president Goran Lindahl has labelled "human engineering."

> **"We want to be global and local, big and small, and radically decentralized with centralized reporting and control."**
> **PERCY BARNEVIK**

● **eliminate head office bureaucracy.** Barnevik reduced ABB's head office to a relatively meagre 150 people.

● **develop a matrix structure.** With its 250 top managers, ABB split itself into a federation of 5,000 profit centres with defined product segments. Alongside this is a Top Management Council (70 executives who meet three times a year) and the Konzernleitung (Barnevik and seven others).

The matrix seeks to utilize the company's global presence with local knowledge and speed. It confronts one of the great paradoxes of contemporary business. "ABB is an organization with three internal contradictions. We want to be global and local, big and small, and radically decentralized with centralized reporting and control. If we resolve these contradictions we create real organizational advantage,"[11] says Barnevik.

The final phrase – "organizational advantage" – sums up the aims of the merging new model organization. Instead of regarding structure as a means to an end – increased production – how a corporation organizes itself can have an impact on all aspects of its performance and its values. Interpreted in such a way, it becomes an infinitely more dynamic process than a pyramid-shaped chart on an office wall.

The new organization

The new organization is moving towards what WARREN BENNIS termed an **"adhocracy"**. This phrase, invented in the late 1960s and recently popularized by ALVIN TOFFLER, basically describes an organization which is the diametric opposite of Weber's bureaucracy. It disregards the accepted, classical principles of management under which each and every one has a carefully defined and permanent role.

- **The new organization is flexible and free flowing.** "Tomorrow's effective organization will be conjured up anew each day," says Tom Peters in *Liberation Management*.[12] Atkinson's well known model of the flexible firm describes a stable core of permanent employees in each firm, augmented by an array of other contractual arrangements including temporary, casual, part-time, and subcontractors as well as franchise and outsourcing arrangements. This provides the company with a pool of labor into which it may expand to satisfy surges in demand without committing itself to permanent employees. Such a strategy also permits withdrawal without heavy costs and, therefore, increases flexibility. Increasingly, the issue becomes one of what should be retained in the core and what should be put in the periphery. Changes of this kind also allow companies to better balance labor demand with supply.

- **The new organization is non-hierarchical.** Hierarchies have not disappeared and, indeed, they are unlikely to ever do so. But they have been reduced and orgnizations have become leaner and fitter. They will have to continue this process if they are to compete in the future.

- **The new organization is based on participation.** Managers don't have all the best ideas. The new organization recognizes this – and has managers who recognize it. It seeks out ideas and feedback from everyone – inside and outside the organization.

- **The new organization is creative and entrepreneurial.** "The entrepreneurial process drives the opportunity seeking, externally focused ability of the organization to create new businesses," say Sumantra Ghoshal and Christopher Bartlett.

- **The new organization is based round networks.** Andy Grove, chief executive of Intel, has compared his business "to the theatre business in New York, which has an itinerant workforce of actors, directors, writers and technicians as well as experienced financial backers ... By tapping into this network, you can quickly put a production together. It might be a smash hit ... or it might be panned by the critics. Inevitably the number of long-running plays is small, but new creative ideas keep bubbling up."

- **The new organization is driven by corporate goals – rather than narrowly-defined functional ones.**

- **The new organization utilizes IT as a key resource.** It brings IT into the mainstream.

The new organization

THOMPSON, JD, *Organizations in Action*, McGraw Hill, Maidenhead, 1967

BARKER, J, *Discovering the Future: The Business of Paradigms*, ILI Press, St Paul, MN, 1985

MARCH, JG, and SIMON, HA, *Organizations*, John Wiley, New York, 1958

PUGH, DS, (ed.) *Organization Theory, Selected Readings*, Penguin, London, 1990

WATERMAN, R, *The Frontiers of Excellence*, Nicholas Brealey, London, 1994

WEBER, M, *The Theory of Social and Economic Organization*, Oxford University Press, New York, 1947

Charles Handy
Shaping the future

Among the key thinkers shaping the new organization is Charles Handy, one of the few European management thinkers to have been elevated to the heady status of guru. The publication of *The Age of Unreason* (1989) and *The Empty Raincoat* (1994) have cemented his reputation, gaining worldwide attention. His work is increasingly philosophical rather than restricted to the confines of management or organizational behavior. It is marked by a humane disaffection with how organizations are run and managed. Handy argues that the very nature of organizations and of managerial work needs to be radically altered if organizations and people are to prosper and develop in the future.

Charles Handy's reputation has grown throughout a career which has taken him from Shell International to London Business School and now to being a freelance luminary, writing and thinking. "Most of the things I have learnt were not learned formally but through accidents and failure. I learned from small catastrophes," he says. Unlike other leading business and management thinkers, he is not a consultant. "A consultant solves other people's problems," he says, "I could never do that. I want to help other people solve their own problems."

After leaving university Handy became an oil executive for Shell International based in Malaysia. Returning to London he became disillusioned with corporate bureaucracy and, after a time working for Anglo-American, joined MIT's Sloan Management Program. Here, he came into contact with leading management thinkers such as Warren Bennis, Chris Argyris, and Ed Schein. This proved to be the turning point in Handy's career. He returned to the UK to play a leading role in the early days of London Business School and the creation of its Sloan Program.

Handy's first book was *Understanding Organizations* (1976), a densely packed potboiler which has become required reading for many managers. It is a comprehensive and thought-provoking exploration of organizations. For Handy it was, to a large extent, a process of self-education and discovery, putting down on paper the things he had learned and believed in. It remains

"I am more interested in the questions than the answers, but bystanders often see things more clearly."
CHARLES HANDY

a highly relevant and comprehensive text book. His other books, though radically different, all retain this impression of Handy developing his own ideas. "My books aren't based on an immense amount of statistics. I am struggling with the reality of organizational life as I see it and trying to make sense of it," he admits. "I am more interested in the questions than the answers, but bystanders often see things more clearly." He tests out his ideas on small groups of managers as he travels the world – "This helps me to crystalize my thinking. They don't have to agree with my solutions; I want them to agree with my diagnosis."

Perhaps the most idiosyncratic of Handy's books is his second, *Gods of Management* (1979), which explores corporate culture through an elaborate analogy. The four gods of the title are: Zeus (power and patriarchy), Apollo (order, reason and bureaucracy), Athena (expertise and meritocracy), and Dionysus (individualism). This creative approach signaled the beginning of a process of rigorous questioning which marks Handy's more recent work which has become progressively more personal. In *Gods of Management* he observes: "Management is more fun, more creative, more personal, more political and more intuitive than any textbook. Nevertheless, while every organization is different, there are patterns which can be discerned, models to be imitated and some guidelines which can be followed."

CHARLES HANDY   born 1932: educator and writer

Education: Oxford University (studied "Greats", a combination of classics, history, and philosophy); Massachusetts Institute of Technology

Career: Joined Shell International and became the company's South-East Asia economist; worked for a short time for the Anglo-American Corporation; MIT Sloan School of Management (graduated 1967); helped launch and then directed London Business School's Sloan Program; Professor at LBS; Warden of St George's House, Windsor Castle (a study centre for ethics and social policy) 1977–81; now Fellow of LBS.

PEOPLE: THE SINGLE MOST IMPORTANT ASSET

The cornerstones of Handy's thinking are laid out most powerfully in *The Age of Unreason* and *The Empty Raincoat*. (The latter is entitled *The Age of Paradox* in the US.) In both he argues that fundamental and revolutionary changes are required in our perceptions of organizations and managers within them. "The way we are doing things is not the best way," argues Handy, calling on organizations to recognize that their single most important asset is their people. "The micro-division of labour has fostered a basic distrust of human beings. People weren't allowed to put the whole puzzle together. Instead they were given small parts because companies feared what people would do if they knew and saw the whole puzzle," says Handy. "Human assets shouldn't be misused. Brains are becoming the core of organizations – other activities can be contracted out." He points to Singapore which has largely exported its manufacturing activities elsewhere, but retains managerial control. Such approaches are necessary, he argues, if organizations are to achieve the objectives summed up by one chief executive as half as many people being paid twice as much to do three times as much work.

Since it was published in 1989, *The Age of Unreason* has become one of the classics of management literature. Its elevation to this status is still something of a surprise. It is not a guru-style book with lots of answers to the problems facing managers. There are no neat, well-packaged solutions. Instead, it is a disturbing and unsettling challenge to the organizations of the world. *The Age of Unreason* dynamically overturns conventional orthodoxies of how we manage; how organizations structure themselves; our attitudes to work and, indeed, our attitudes to life. It is, as Tom Peters has said, "lucid exciting and shocking."

> "Human assets shouldn't be misused. Brains are becoming the core of organizations – other activities can be contracted out."
> CHARLES HANDY

Handy's argument is as simple as it is radical: "We are entering an age of unreason, a time when the future, in so many areas, it to be shaped by us and for us; a time when the only prediction that will hold true is that no prediction will hold true; a time, therefore, for bold imagining in private life as well as public; for thinking the unlikely and doing the unreasonable."

In unreasonable times, the traditional ways of thinking are no longer enough. Take strategy. When the future was predictable – or, at least, when we believed it to be predictable – companies could chart their strategies with confidence. Knowing where they wanted to go meant that they could implement activities and initiatives to get them there. The future was knowable. Take away that certainty (Handy's latest book is called *Beyond Certainty*) and the traditional means of formulating and generating strategy are all but redundant. In the new world order, companies must pursue a plethora of objectives.

Of course, organizations are adept at burying their heads in the corporate sand. They can refuse to acknowledge that things are changing. Handy provides a neat analogy to describe what will happen to those who resist the tides of change : "If you put a frog in cold water and slowly heat it, the frog will eventually let itself be boiled to death. We, too, will not survive if we don't respond to the radical way in which the world is changing. From now on, success and happiness will depend on an understanding of the boiled frog."

The fundamental changes which Handy believes are now underway, not only question our approach to strategy. The changes being experienced by organizations are "discontinuous." This means that they are discomforting and disturbing, outside of comfortable timescales, seismic, and continuous. The status quo is being rigorously shaken and, in many cases, overturned.

As the structures have changed so, too, has the language of management. Says Handy: "Organizations used to be perceived as gigantic pieces of engineering, with largely interchangeable human parts. We talked of their structures and their systems, of inputs and outputs, of control devices and of managing them, as if the whole was one large factory. Today the language is not that of engineering but of politics, with talk of cultures and networks, of teams and coalitions, of influence or power rather than control, of leadership not management."

Logically, Handy argues that in periods of great turbulence and upheaval our old ways of thinking are no longer appropriate and no longer useful. The rules of engagement have changed so it is little use pretending otherwise. This requires "discontinuous upside-down thinking ... even if both thinkers and thoughts appear absurd at first sight."

Handy contends that the way work is organized must take a quantum leap into this world of unreason and that "the way our work is organized ... will make the biggest differences to the way we will live." He also believes that it is changes in the little things of life which will have the most profound impact. We may hope for a cure for cancer, but in all likelihood more personal events and issues, such as having children, will have a greater impact on our lives. In the unreasonable world, ideals and aspirations come face-to-face with daily reality. The unreasonable world remains intensely personal, more personal than ever before.

In the personal world Handy challenges accepted wisdom on a wide range of issues. He allows ideas to fly while not necessarily bringing them down to ground with an answer. If the future is unknowable we can forget having faith in one best-way solutions and "answers." Instead of answers there are possibilities and endless permutations on what we could do, and how organizations could structure themselves. Equally, there has also to be acceptance that our personal choices can be wrong and that we exist not simply as individuals but as individuals within a society.

Handy adeptly points out the confines and limitations of the way people now work. Why do we work 40 hours spread over five days of the week? Why don't people take their 2,000 hours of work per year and organize them differently, in a way which suits themselves and their family and their company?

The shamrock organization

Behind the changes in the way we work and perceive work is the emergence of what Handy labels "the shamrock organization." There is, he admits, nothing revolutionary in this concept. Indeed, many organizations and businesses have used the shamrock organization for many decades. It is defined as "a form of organization based around a core of essential executives and workers supported by outside contractors and part-time help."

THE THREE LEAVES OF THE SHAMROCK ORGANIZATION

In describing the working of the shamrock, and the actualities of working life, Handy is at his most persuasive. The shamrock has three leaves. The first represents **the core workers** of an organization. These, in Handy's analogy, are likely to be highly trained professionals. They are the high achieving executives who demand impressive salaries and work every hour of the day. Comparisons can be drawn with the people at the heart of advertising companies or management consultancies.

The second leaf of the shamrock is made up of **the contractual fringe**. These may be individuals or organizations. Often they are people who once worked for the organization but now provide it with a service. They are self-employed with their own shamrocks.

The third leaf includes **the flexible labor force**. This, Handy makes clear, is not a band of casual cheap workers. They, too, are vital to the success of the organization they work for, even if they carry out relatively menial tasks on a part-time basis or irregularly. If they are treated as entirely peripheral they will have no motivation to provide ideas, develop or carry out their work to a high standard. It is here that the shamrock analogy confronts its hardest challenge. The flexible labor force can too easily be treated as hired hands with no vested interest in anything other than a wage packet. "If the flexible labor force is seen to be a valuable part of the organization then the organization will be prepared to invest in them, to provide training, even training leading to qualifications, to give them some status and some privileges (including paid holidays and sick leave entitlement). Then and only then, will the organization get the temporary or part-time help that it needs to the standard it requires."

As a continuation of the shamrock, Handy also points out that customers have effectively become subcontractors in a growing number of businesses. Customers do many of the jobs which were once carried out for them by organizations. Customers fill in forms and take their own money out of the bank; they fill their cars up with petrol and walk round supermarkets filling their trolleys. Compare this with the recent past when banks employed people in large numbers to carry out tasks now undertaken by computers; petrol stations employed people to fill our cars and shops got what we wanted from the shelves and filled our baskets. We are now part of the shamrock and are generally pleased to be so.

The shamrock in practice

The question must be: does the shamrock organization exist or is it a good idea which falls down in practice? Handy provides ample evidence that the shamrock works, and is working, for a growing number of organizations.

THE SHAMROCK WORKS

Handy cites the example of the UK company, FI Group (formerly known as F International). A total of 70 percent of FI's workers work from home and 90 percent are women. It is a large business with a turnover of nearly £20 million. The company has a small core staff and the staff are linked by computer networks to each other and to the company. The company is a network – and one whose virtues are now eulogized by Tom Peters.

The logic cannot be criticized. Research by Alvin Toffler among company presidents in the United States found that they believed that

25 to 75 percent of their work could be done equally effectively from home. The trouble is that though, practically speaking, people could work at home there are a number of barriers to this happening. Organizations remain built round a succession of meetings, face-to-face contacts and eagerly filled diaries. Filling your time at the office is part of the job – even if it isn't particularly effective use of your time. People are also strangely addicted to office life and, even, commuting.

Clearly for organizations the shamrock represents a sizeable challenge. It must, for example, first identify which are its core activities and, even harder, decide who it needs to make them work.

However, the basic attraction of this organization, as now practiced, is that it is cheaper. Utilizing the shamrock, organizations do not have to have as many full-time employees on their payroll. They outsource peripheral services and use them if and when they are needed.

Handy predicts that the shamrock organization is likely to develop further. This is because of a number of trends. First, the rise of what are now labeled "knowledge workers." Handy quotes research by the consultants McKinsey which estimated that 70 percent of jobs in Europe by the year 2000 would require cerebral rather than physical skills. This turns the past on its head. Managing a team of well-educated professionals clearly demands different skills than managing a team of people doing mainly physical work.

The shamrock organization is an effective means of organizing this growing band of cerebral workers who are more adept at working independently and more suited to the lifestyle of being a corporate resource, rather than a corporate number on the payroll.

As a corollary, if the world demands a more cerebral workforce this requires that education systems change to meet the emerging demand. Unfortunately, Handy sees little evidence that this is the case. He believes only Japan, the US, Taiwan, and South Korea have adequate university populations and, even then, there are concerns about the quality of the education received. If knowledge and information are key to success in the age of unreason we have to equip people with the skills to use, understand, disseminate, and generate information.

The second trend impacting on the shamrock organization is the growing number of older people within society. If people are living longer and the nature of the work being undertaken is changing, then a new balance needs to be struck. In the future, people in the core jobs will begin their jobs later in life – often in their mid-twenties armed with a post graduate qualification – and end them earlier.

There are more questions than answers. But, Handy would argue, that is the very nature of the new world we live in. We have to actively shape our own answers, invent them, and reinvent them continually.

To achieve this we must learn to learn. Change is, in Handy's world, another word for learning and learning is built round a continuous circle of: Question, Theory, Test, and Reflection.

To work, learning is a way of life. It is not a matter of acquiring skills, as simply as one might acquire a particular product. Learning is not measured by the number of letters after a person's name and nor is it the preserve of intellectuals. Learning is all embracing and highly personal. An intense learning experience for one individual will have less impact on someone else.

Again the power of the individual is highlighted. The individual takes responsibility, sets the agenda, identifies targets, and has to have an attitude which identifies learning as possible and essential. The individual makes learning happen. It is, what Handy labels, **"responsible selfishness"** – as opposed to the irresponsible selfishness he believes was engendered in the 1980s.

His recipe for making learning a reality involves **"re-framing"** (one of his few ventures into management-speak). "Re-framing is the ability to see things, problems, situations or people in other ways, to look at them sideways or upside down; to put them in another perspective or another context; to think of them as opportunities not problems, as hiccups rather than disasters."

Making learning happen also involves the ability to accept and learn from failure; to accept that the new rules of the unreasonable world are not set in tablets of stone. In an environment of doubt and uncertainty, intellectual certainty is as unhealthy as it is inappropriate. Beware of the person with the answers who cannot contemplate doubt, questioning or being wrong.

The very nature of the subject of learning involves Handy in a certain degree of wooliness. The bottom line is simply that individuals must take responsibility for their own development, must nurture learning from within themselves rather than waiting for their corporation to despatch them on a course.

HANDY's "RESPONSIBLE SELFISHNESS" AND ORGANIZATIONS

The idea of "a proper selfishness" can also be applied to organizations. All, says Handy, should ask themselves six basic questions:

1. What are the organization's strengths and talents?

2. Its weaknesses?

3. What sort of organization does it want to be?

4. What does it want to be known for?

5. How will its success be measured, by whom and when?

6. How does it plan to achieve it?

Organizations must match the pace of personal development which Handy believes is now necessary. If employees must learn and develop themselves, so, too, must organizations; if people must learn from mistakes, so should organizations; if people are expected to behave in a responsible, honest, and open manner, so must organizations.

The federal organization and the triple I organization

The shamrock organization is not the only organizational model identified by Handy. He also believes there is growing use and awareness of the federal organization.

THE FEDERAL ORGANIZATION

"Federalism implies a variety of individual groups allied together under a common flag with some shared identity. Federalism seeks to make it big by keeping it small, or at least independent, by combining autonomy with co-operation." It is, Handy admits, "the best of both worlds." And, when all the talk is of being global and local, a practical – though paradoxical – business solution.

The role of the centre is increasingly discussed – in most depth in *Corporate-Level Strategy* by Andrew Campbell, Michael Goold and Marcus Alexander – and it is central to the success or otherwise of the federal organization. Handy believes that federalism only works if there is **subsidiarity** – if the centre truly surrenders power to its units. This demands a level of trust which is often little in evidence in organizations. If true power if granted to subsidiaries, then it follows that managers in the central function must surrender some of their own power. As management and organizational life is dominated by the pursuit of power and the anxious protection of fiefdoms, this goes against the grain. Handy points to industries, such as television and journalism, where young people are given responsibility and are thrust into demanding situations which they thrive on.

To practice federalism demands a new generation of managers who regard the giving of power as more important than the acquisition of power; and of a new generation of business leaders. "Managers must think like leaders," he says. This involves changing attitudes to their career development. For example, they will need to become used to **horizontal tracking**. Instead, of concentrating their sights on progressing up the corporate hierarchy, managers will have to learn to regard sideways moves as an essential part of their development, rather than a disappointing alternative to promotion. Sideways moves present fresh opportunities for learning and expose managers to new environments, new people and new business situations.

Handy's third model is called the Triple I organization.

THE TRIPLE I ORGANIZATION

This model brings together the three Is of **intelligence, information,** and **ideas**. Handy provides the equation $I^3 = AV$, with AV standing for Added Value. The Triple I should be at the heart of the organization. Without its elements, any corporation is unlikely to thrive.

The 3Is are fueled by increased emphasis on quality and the growing application of IT. These trends encourage, says Handy, the effective utilization of the 3Is. But, to work, the 3Is demand intelligent people who are treated fairly and honestly by their employers. Herein, lies a paradox. The organization must do its utmost to recruit and retain the best possible people to run its business. But, it must do so at a time when the best people are increasingly unwilling to commit themselves to the organization. If employees regard the organization simply as a stepping stone why should the organization invest in them?

The solution – if it can be so called – is a combination of individual initiative and corporate support. Only by providing executives with the challenges and the development opportunities they require and expect will organizations retain them. The bottom line is that "Intelligent people prefer to agree rather than to obey."

The facts of living

If organizations, working patterns and the attitudes of people towards work are to change, so too must the rest of our lives, the world outside work.

With numbers of full-time workers decreasing, the onus will be on developing a **portfolio of work**. The skeptical might suggest that this is likely to be a portfolio of poorly paid part-time jobs. Handy, however, believes we have to embrace more positive possibilities. Portfolios of work include work which can be divided into five main categories: wage work and fee work (which earn money), homework, gift work, and study work (which do not).

To most people this sounds idealistic. Yet, it is simply a more flexible and better organized way of identifying the elements in many of our lives. It is the kind of flexibility that those who work for a large organization with its career progression, regular monthly salary and perks are ill-equipped to come to terms with. It does, however, fit in with the world of many self-employed people who are used to the pressure – and perhaps pleasure – of finding means of earning money to pay for particular things. If they want a new computer, they know they have to find an imaginative means of making the money to pay for it; rather than simply ringing the IT department for one to be despatched. The self-employed – as well as many in small businesses and professional partnerships – do not see bartering or selling their time and skills as unusual, but as facts of life. More full-time workers will have to embrace this approach if they are to develop their portfolios.

Handy's development of the concept of portfolios is a rejoinder to the idea of the leisure society. This, he argues, was simple idealism. Humankind is not made for a life of pure, unadulterated leisure. Instead, leisure needs to be seen as part of a balanced portfolio of interests and activities.

When he switches to contemplate the social and political fabric required to convert the trends he identifies into reality, Handy is at his most radical. He questions many of the basic economic assumptions – while not necessarily suggesting they are wrong and never suggesting that solutions are either immediate or easy. For example, he suggests that zero income tax may be a means of facilitating the creation of the shamrock organization. The growing numbers of people who are either self-employed or have a number of jobs mean that income tax is becoming more difficult to assess accurately and to collect. As numbers increase so, too, will the problems of collection. By increasing expenditure-based taxes, governments can recoup the lost income tax, allow people to save more and encourage far greater flexibility in employment practices.

Such ideas are unlikely to receive a warm welcome. But, it is precisely because they challenge traditional ways of thinking that Handy believes they deserve serious consideration – "A changing world needs new ideas. The more there are the more used we shall get to them. Thinking the unthinkable is a way of getting the wheel of learning moving, in society as much as in individuals." This is what Handy labels **"upside-down thinking,"** a kind of lateral thinking for the 1990s. Think differently and we may well emerge with a better understanding of the age of unreason; but, think the same, and we will surely fall behind as the pace of change accelerates.

Managing with paradox

In *The Empty Raincoat* Handy's world view is typically humane and liberal, though increasingly bleak. He argues that the organizational world is dominated by paradoxes – like the empty raincoat (inspired by a sculpture in Minneapolis). Perhaps the central paradox is the failure of technology to enhance the quality of our lives and work. Technology leads to greater efficiency which requires a smaller workforce; the company is then taxed to support those out of work through its increased efficiency.

"If economic progress means that we become anonymous cogs in some great machine, then progress is an empty promise. The challenge must be to show how paradox can be managed," says Handy, who saves his most vehement turns of phrase for "yellow-page economies of glitz and extras," where mass consumerism and consumption are out of control.

It is a message which, Handy recognizes, is unpalatable to many. Managers putting faith in people, for example, will lose some of their traditional power. "Managers have been brought up on a diet of power, divide and rule. They have been preoccupied with authority rather than making things happen," he says, adding a warning: "Since *The Age of Unreason* I have become more aware that you can't consider the professional class in isolation from the rest of society. Though the world is a good one for professional executives, they are a minority of the human race. If they only look after themselves they will run out of customers." They have to learn to manage paradoxes, surrender some of their power and take risks with people.

> "Managers have been brought up on a diet of power, divide and rule. They have been preoccupied with authority rather than making things happen."
> **CHARLES HANDY**

"Work is more than a job," says Handy. "In the past, business was the employer of all those who wanted to work. In the future there will be lots of customers, but not lots of jobs." He does not expect companies to become charitable institutions – "The job of any business is to be as effective as it can" – but for expectations and working practices to fundamentally alter. "The principal purpose of a company is not to make a profit, full stop. It is to make a profit in order to continue to do things or make things, and to do so ever better and more abundantly. Profit has to be a means to other ends rather an end in itself." Handy points to the need for organizations and people to develop senses of "continuity, connection and direction" – ever more important in a business world beset by disorientation.

His image of the organization of the future has evolved from the shamrock to the "doughnut principle" of *The Empty Raincoat* – "Organizations have their essential core of jobs and people surrounded by an open and flexible space which they fill with flexible workers and flexible supply contracts." Handy argues that organizations have neglected and misunderstood the core while expanding and developing the rest of the doughnut. He attaches the same image to people's personal development, suggesting that many need to sit down and return to first principles if they are to achieve a balance in their lives.

Increasingly, Handy seems to offer a dark view of the world of work, organizations and governments. But, he sees himself as articulating the fears of many in business and beyond. "A lot of people have similar concerns and questions as I have, but they don't know how to pursue them or articulate them so they are suppressed," says Handy. "In the end I have only suggestions. There is no formula or perfect solution. This is the tide of events. We can't turn the tide, but we can ride it."

Charles Handy

Understanding Organizations, Penguin Books, London, 1976

The Future of Work, Basil Blackwell, Oxford, 1984

Gods of Management, Business Books, London, 1986

The Making of Managers (with John Constable), Longman, London, 1988

The Age of Unreason, Business Books, London, 1989

Inside Organizations: 21 Ideas for Managers, BBC Books, London 1990

The Empty Raincoat, Hutchinson, London, 1994

Beyond Certainty, Century, London, 1995

Shapes and images: the virtues of virtuality

New organizations no longer fit into strict hierarchical pyramids, rising to a pinnacle where the all-knowing, all-seeing chief executive surveys the corporate domain. Instead, new shapes and images are emerging to describe the organization. The new organization is described in the terminology of the new science of chaos theory. An article in the *California Management Review* describes the organization of the future as one which is "dynamically stable," "capable of serving the widest range of customers and changing product demands (dynamic) while building on long-term process capabilities and the collective knowledge of the organization (stable)."[13] From the traditional images of machinery, the organization has become an elusive ever-changing amoeba.

THE ORGANIZATION OF THE FUTURE

The possibilities are endless. Says Cranfield's Shaun Tyson: "New, flatter organization shapes have come about as a consequence of delayering. In addition there are diamond shapes, where the top management is supported by technical experts, for example in mechanized production, but there are then only a few employees at the lowest level, as maintenance staff. Mushroom shapes reflect the organization structure in partnerships, for example in medical practice, consultancy, legal services and other professional activity. The smaller, partnership shapes may well be the organization structure most commonly found in the future."[14]

Describing the organization of the future, American writers William Davidow and Michael Malone say: "To the outside observer, it will appear almost edgeless, with permeable and continuously changing interfaces among company, supplier and customers. From inside the firm, the view will be no less amorphous with traditional offices, departments and operating divisions constantly re-forming according to need."[15]

The end-result is what is now known as the **virtual organization**.

Unfortunately the terminology of the virtual organization is inextricably linked to Californian IT companies or fashionable advertising corporations. These strong associations have tended to overshadow the genuine and sizeable opportunity which the virtual organization presents.

Though skeptics are already out in force the virtual organization is the epitome of the new form of organization. "In the past people had to be brought together because they couldn't do things for themselves," says Laurence Lyons, coauthor of *Creating Tomorrow's Organisation* and cofounder of Henley Management College's Future Work Forum. "Now, technology is giving more power to individuals. The implications for management development are phenomenal. Managers will have to organize, manage, motivate and develop themselves in a world where organizations and individuals become atomized. But, they will not do so in isolation. They need to be linked to the organization and to inter-act with the other people in it."[11]

MAKING VIRTUALITY WORK

Eddie Obeng, founder of Pentacle – The Virtual Business School, believes that the eponymous "v" word is misunderstood. "There is nothing grandiose about the concept. Managers are adept at using networks and, increasingly, at working in teams. It should never be forgotten that technology enables managers to work more effectively and to learn new skills cost-effectively. The virtual concept is a label, what matters is making it work."

One means of making virtuality work is the idea of **virtual teams**, first championed by telecommunications company, Mercury. The term is used to describe groups of people who are accountable for the achievement of transient or short-term objectives. The groups may be temporary – spe-

> **"In the 1990s and beyond, the smart organization is the one that survives."**
> LAWRENCE LYONS

cially assembled to complete a certain task or project – or permanent. The idea is that virtual teams enable a flexible and continuously evolving fit between skills, resources and immediate needs.

One of the attractions of such a pragmatic approach is that executives do not have to travel the world, flitting from one jet-lagged meeting to another. Instead, technology provides constant links, whether through e-mail, or computer noticeboards. This clearly places a premium on the communication and information platforms and groupware (software for groups on networks) selected.

The virtual organization remains a concept. Laurence Lyons believes the hype has been allowed to dominate the business message and that virtuality is a way of thinking, as much as anything else. Says Lyons: "The concept of the virtual organization as competitor, is nothing other than a zero-based method of thinking about the organization's architecture in the light of the new possibilities of *future work*. By using the ideal concept of a virtual organization – externally and then internally – senior managers can start to think with the interests of their organizations uppermost. They can enrich their strategy. And, most importantly, they can reduce risk by shifting their locus of approach from followers to become the intellectual leaders. In the 1990s and beyond, the smart organization is the one that survives."

Technology and the new organization

PRODUCTIVITY AND IT STRATEGY

The corporate resource which has the largest role to play in creating the new organization is IT. On the surface this is not a surprising claim. After all, the world IT market is expected to reach a massive $700 billion by 1997. Yet, IT has so far failed to yield the productivity and performance benefits anticipated by managers and organizations.

The reasons for this are many and varied. One central reason is that managers often have only a limited understanding of what IT can do for their organization. They have a broad sympathy with investing in high technology, but have a restricted view of its practical power and business advantage. For example, a survey by Henley Management College of more than 200 chief executives, directors, and other senior managers found that many top managers just did not understand the strategic importance of IT.

It is likely that, if asked, a great many managers would identify the benefits of IT in simple cost terms. IT reduces an organization's staff count, therefore it saves money. As Harvard's Shoshana Zuboff points out in her book, *In the Age of the Smart Machine*, companies have regarded IT as a means of reducing staff numbers through the automation of their jobs. The trouble is that the jobs which have been automated out of existence are often those which involve direct contact with customers. Zuboff argues that instead of automating tasks, IT's job should be to "informate" people – an ungainly, but apposite, word combining inform and educate. By regarding IT as a numbers and cost-cutting mechanism, organizations are failing to optimize its full potential which goes far beyond cost reduction.

While managers are comfortable with the concept of cost control and reduction, they find it difficult to come to terms with other implications of IT. With limited knowledge managers find that they are unable to bring the same reporting and measuring disciplines to bear when some new IT product is introduced. A large investment in a new machine on the production line inevitably means that every effort is made by the company to measure and monitor the performance and productivity increases which the machine brings. The machine's *raison d'être* is simple and well understood. If, however, managers invest in a costly new IT system not only is it likely that they cannot use it – even though it could help them in their work – but they have no idea how, and often little inclination, to accurately measure its productivity benefits. They may calculate direct cost savings but, in many cases, the more widespread advantages are assumed, with productivity gains neither monitored nor measured.

A UK survey carried out by Computervision Services, a support services company, shows that nine out of ten managers believe office networks contribute significantly to productivity – but only one in ten measures the gains. Organizations expect an average increase of 65 percent in the number of office network users during 1994. But 40 percent of companies and 80 percent of public sector bodies do not make any business case for network purchases.[16]

When it comes to IT, managers appear to suspend their disbelief and allow IT experts to get on with it. Managers also tend to have limited expertise in managing the obsessive enthusiasts who hone in on computer departments. It is not, perhaps, surprising that managers struggle to come to terms with IT – IT often unsettles their ways of working. IT may provide managers with information they have previously been starved of and sometimes never knew existed. Suddenly there is a deluge of statistical data and making a decision becomes ever more complex. As a result, there is the strong temptation to nod knowingly when the data falls onto your desk and carry on using the parameters and measurements you have always used as the basis for your decision-making. Managers remain fearful of falling into the trap described by Gertrude Stein: "Everybody gets so much information all day long that they lose their commonsense."

Using IT for the wrong jobs

A second factor in the failure of IT to boost productivity as significantly as it should, is the fact that it is often used for the wrong jobs. Quality programs, for example, have often exacerbated this situation to the extent that IT becomes marginalized. Instead of being regarded as a core tool by which quality and improved productivity can be achieved, IT has been treated simply as a means of collecting data and ensuring that quality processes are backed by sound statistics.

IT is a highly effective data-gathering device, but it is also much more. Unquestionably, IT is the best possible tool for organizations to gather a huge range of data about their business and its performance.

The crunch comes when data is turned into information – this requires that companies have the systems, processes and people in place to ask the right questions to convert data to information. Data remains data until you ask a question. Information is the answer to the question.

While IT has been used as a means of data-gathering, the emphasis of its practical use has also been on managing the links between different divisions, functions and activities rather than with customers. IT has traditionally looked at what departments do and then provided them with information. It has made an organization's internal life and system easier to handle rather than providing improved service to customers.

Often IT is backed by an individual department or function which identifies ways by which IT can make its work more efficient. These do not, however, necessarily apply across the entire organization. The end-result is a number of different systems emerge with little in the way of linkages between them or overall strategy.

> **Any IT strategy must embrace all the aims of the company rather than taking a parochial view.**

Any IT strategy must embrace all the aims of the company rather than taking a parochial view. The conventional approach to IT fails to see it in broader strategic terms. IT is regarded as a means of doing existing jobs faster. The obvious corollary of this is that organizations often make the same mistakes at twice the speed.

In many organizations IT has become yet another function when it should be a prime resource. Organizations are now, as a result, have to reengineer their IT function – according to research in the US, organizations are set to invest a massive $40 billion in reengineering their information systems in 1997. Acerbically, William Wheeler of Coopers & Lybrand, told *Fortune* magazine: "That's putting whipped cream on garbage."[17]

UTILIZING IT

- *How does IT link your organization to customers?*
- *How do you measure the productivity gains brought by IT?*
- *Is IT managed and controlled by a single function?*
- *Has IT provided you with data or information?*
- *How has IT helped you provide customers with better service?*

In the new organization, IT takes a central role as a key **enabler** of entirely new, cross-functional business processes. An example is in the use of relational databases which enable workers to relate data on what is happening in sales, marketing, operations and finance. This brings functional, horizontal, and vertical integration and asks fundamental questions as to what is the nature of the task to be performed and by whom. They view IT data on a functional basis, reflecting industrial organizational design and fail to exploit the relational nature of technology, acquired in the 1980s and now technologically mature. They forget that advances in technology mean that information can appear simultaneously in many places as it is needed – not just in one place at one time.

This ability to put information simultaneously in the hands of those who need to know – regardless of function or location – enables organizations to break the sequential nature of functional processes for radical improvements in productivity. "In most cases, the greatest practical strategic leverage of IT lies not in some IT-driven company overhaul from top-to-bottom, but in the ability of IT to support the re-design of a company's working practices – that is, its established routines, procedures, techniques and approaches for accomplishing core tasks and activities – as well as its organizational structures," say Richard Heygate and Greg Brebach of management consultants McKinsey.[18]

> **IT should be one of the key tools of any business which genuinely wishes to move closer to its customers.**

ORGANIZING IT

- *Have your organization's senior managers received IT training?*

- *Who makes IT buying decisions?*

- *Who has a say from outside the IT department?*

- *Does IT make your job easier?*

- *Does IT make you more effective?*

- *What performance does your organization measure through IT?*

- *Are you provided with data or information?*

- *Who measures the performance effectiveness of your IT systems?*

To convert IT from a blockage to an enabler requires that the organization clearly identifies the business benefits of IT. These can include: faster and more accurate communication of information; elimination of certain manual tasks; more informed decision-making; potential for increased teamworking; delegation of responsibility.

Clearly, IT should be one of the key tools of any business which genuinely wishes to move closer to its customers. Many organizations have already succeeded in using IT to provide imaginative solutions and create opportunities.

IT SOLUTIONS FOR GREATER CUSTOMER FOCUS

Responsiveness. Frank's Nursery and Crafts in Detroit can supply additional stock to its stores when the weekend weather forecast is good. It uses IT to anticipate demand.

US retailer Wal-Mart approached Procter and Gamble, pointing out that it should remind Wal-Mart when to reorder as P&G knows its business and customers better. As a result, P&G manages and finances the Pampers inventory thanks to direct links between Wal-Mart's check-out system and P&G's ordering system.

Customers of the Dutch PTT can sort out the installation of a new telephone with a single visit to one of the company's offices. This includes a contract, a new number, and the time of connection – now made within two days as opposed to the previous two weeks. Connections are now made on the spot. Dutch PTT achieved this level of responsiveness by taking the information from its huge mainframe computers and channeling them to individual terminals in sales offices. Instead of switching from one system to another to find all the relevant information – such as on debtors – operators can now locate it easily and quickly.

The IT system used by the Florida-based Home Shopping Network is such that its data is updated every ten seconds. This means that the presenters on TV who are selling the products can see how well each is doing. If the charming ceramic rhino is selling badly they can move on to the truly amazing electronic gadget. With this system, HSN can calculate its performance in "dollars per minute."

Flexibility. HSN answers customer orders with a recorded voice called "Tootie." The computerized system will take people's orders, sort out how they are going to pay and instruct the warehouse to despatch the product to their home address. Not all customers like the idea of speaking to a computer, even one called Tootie. But, if the customer does not speak to Tootie within five seconds, her dulcet tones are immediately replaced by a live operator.

Improving performance. The US's Federal National Mortgage Association (Fannie Mae) found that its huge computer system simply could not cope with the growth of its business. In response, it broke down time-consuming departmental divides and installed a network of 2,000 PCs with new easy-to-use software. Costing $10 million, it was a sizeable investment – it paid for itself in less than a year. Though volume doubled between 1991 and 1993, the company took on a mere 100 extra people to cope with the soaring demand. In 1993 Fannie Mae's profits reached $1.87 billion thanks to the company serving a record 3.3 million families through mortgage purchases and security guarantees.

Working with customers. "We know exactly where we want to go, because our customers will show us the way. Our customers know the solutions they need. It's our job to bring them solutions, through the application of technology," says Jerrie Stead, chief executive of AT&T Global Information Solutions.[19]

IT bridges gaps between organizations and their customers. DuPont no longer expects invoices from some of its vendors. Instead, it just processes bills electronically. With about five percent of its suppliers the company doesn't even bother with purchase orders. Outside suppliers are linked electronically with DuPont's internal inventory system. When suppliers see DuPont is running short on an item they deliver replacement goods.

"Most large organizations are now seeing IT as one of the most important bridges to enhancing customer service. They now rarely see customer service as having separate components, such as marketing, selling, after-sales service and invoicing, each with their own system," says Merlin Stone, visiting professor at Kingston University and a partner in Avanti Consultancy Services.[20]

Bringing people closer together. Expert systems enable nonspecialists to carry out what were once specialized tasks. IT should be a means of bringing people closer together and breaking down barriers.

References: The new world of organizations

1 HAMEL, G, AND PRAHALAD, CK, *Competing for the Future*, Harvard Business Schools Press, Boston, MA, 1994.
2 MILLS, DQ, *Rebirth of the Corporation*, John Wiley, Chichester, 1991.
3 SIMON, H, *Administrative Behavior*, Macmillan, New York, 1947.
4 Quoted in "The changing nature of leadership," *Economist*, June 10, 1995.
5 BARNARD, C, *The Functions of the Executive*, Harvard University Press, Cambridge, MA, 1938.
6 LORENZ, C, 'Time has come for a revolution in style', *Financial Times*, April 22, 1994.
7 BARNARD, C, *Functions of the Executive*, Harvard University Press, Cambridge, MA, 1938.
8 TYSON, S, Human Resource Management: Overview," *Financial Times Handbook of Management*, FT/Pitman, London, 1995.
9 HIRSCHHORN, L and GILMORE, T, "The new boundaries of the boundaryless company," *Harvard Business Review*, May–June, 1992.
10 ARBOSE, J, "ABB: the new industrial powerhouse," *International Management*, June 1988.
11 TAYLOR, W, "The logic of global business: an interview with Percy Barnevik," *Harvard Business Review*, March–April 1991.
12 PETERS, T, *Liberation Management*, Knopf, New York, 1992.
13 *California Management Review*, Winter 1993, Vol. 35, No.2.
14 TYSON, S, *Financial Times Handbook of Management*, FT/Pitman, London, 1995.
15 DAVIDOW, W and MALONE, M, *The Virtual Corporation*, Harper Business, New York, 1992.
16 KAVANAGH, J, "The fun starts when users switch on," *Financial Times Software at Work*, Winter 1993.
17 CARR, D, *et al*, *Breakpoint*, Coopers & Lybrand, Arlington, Virginia, 1992.
18 HEYGATE, R, & BREBACH, G, "Rethinking the corporation," *McKinsey Quarterly*, No.2 1991.
19 Advertisement in *Financial Times*, Jan. 27, 1994.
20 FISHER, A, "Speed is of the essence," *Financial Times*, Aug. 3, 1993.

Creating and implementing strategy

"In today's situation it should be acknowledged that there is no one best design, rather the design of such strategic management systems will probably have to be based on the particular strategic context of a firm."
PETER LORANGE[1]

"The strategist's method is very simply to challenge the prevailing assumptions with a single question: Why? and to put the same question relentlessly to those responsible for the current way of doing things until they are sick of it."
KENICHI OHMAE[2]

"Strategic management is a comprehensive procedure which starts with a strategic diagnosis and guides a firm through a series of additional steps which culminate in new products, markets and technologies, as well as new capabilities."
IGOR ANSOFF[3]

THE HOLY GRAIL OF STRATEGY

Igor Ansoff
Analysis and paralysis

In the 1960s the world discovered love, hallucinogenics, and Jimi Hendrix. Managers discovered their new holy grail, strategy. They did so, not in San Francisco or at Woodstock, but in Igor Ansoff's *Corporate Strategy*, published in 1965. "This book represented a kind of crescendo in the development of strategic planning theory, offering a degree of elaboration seldom attempted since," Henry Mintzberg later observed.[4]

A NEW PERSPECTIVE ON STRATEGY

Unstintingly serious, analytical and complex, *Corporate Strategy*, had a highly significant impact on the business world. It propelled consideration of strategy into a new dimension.

"The end product of strategic decisions is deceptively simple; a combination of products and markets is selected for the firm. This combination is arrived at by addition of new product-markets, divestment from some old ones, and expansion of the present position," writes Ansoff. While the end product was simple, the processes and decisions beforehand produced a labyrinth followed only by the most dedicated of managers. Ansoff's sub-title was "An Analytical Approach to Business Policy for Growth and Expansion." The book provided a highly complex "cascade of decisions." Analysis – and in particular **gap analysis** (the gap between where you are now and where you want to be) – was the key to unlocking strategy.

The book also brought the concept of **synergy** to a wide audience for the first time. Today, the word is overused and much abused. In Ansoff's original creation it was simply summed up as "the 2+2=5" effect. In his later books, Ansoff refined his definition of synergy to any "effect which can produce a combined return on the firm's resources greater than the sum of its parts."[5]

While *Corporate Strategy* was a notable book for its time, it produced what Ansoff himself labeled "paralysis by analysis": repeatedly making strategic plans which remained unimplemented.

"Strategic planning was a plausible invention, and received an enthusiastic reception from the business community. But subsequent experience with strategic planning led to mixed results. In a minority of firms, strategic planning restored their profitability and became an established part of the management process. However a substantial majority encountered a phenomenon, which was named 'paralysis by analysis': strategic plans were made but remained unimplemented, and profits/growth continued to stagnate," he recently wrote.[6]

Undaunted, Ansoff looked again at his entire theory. His logic was impressively simple – either strategic planning was a bad idea, or it was part of a broader concept which was not fully developed and needed to be enhanced in order to make strategic planning effective. Characteristically, he sought the answer in extensive research. He examined acquisitions by American companies between 1948 and 1968 and concluded that acquisitions which were based on an articulated strategy fared considerably better than those which were opportunistic decisions.

IGOR ANSOFF   born 1918; consultant & educator

Education: Stevens Institute of Technology, degree in engineering and MS in math and physics; PhD Brown University in applied mathematics; UCLA senior executive program

Career: Rand Corporation; Lockheed; Carnegie-Mellon University; founding Dean School of Management, Vanderbilt University; Professor European Institute for Advanced Studies in Management, Brussels; now Distinguished Professor of Strategic Management, US International University, San Diego.

Reinforced by his conviction that strategy was a valid, if incomplete, concept, Ansoff followed up *Corporate Strategy* with *Strategic Management* (1979) and *Implanting Strategic Management* (1984). In each of which he sought a broader concept which would include strategic planning and would assure effective implementation of strategic plans. In 1972 he published the concept under the name of **strategic management**. The concept embraces a combination of strategy planning, planning of organizational capability and effective management of resistance to change, typically caused by strategic planning. Ansoff says that "strategic management is a comprehensive procedure which starts with a strategic diagnosis and guides a firm through a series of additional steps which culminate in new products, markets and technologies, as well as new capabilities."[7]

ANSOFF's STRATEGIC SUCCESS PARADIGM

Using the concept of strategic management, Ansoff formulated a Strategic Success Paradigm which specifies conditions which optimize a firm's profitability. This paradigm (the result of "fifteen years of sweat, tears and smiles and occasional flashes of creativity") has five key elements:

1. There is no universal success formula for all firms.

2. The driving variable which dictates the strategy required for success of a firm is the level of turbulence in its environment.

3. A firm's success cannot be optimized unless the aggressiveness of its strategy is aligned with the turbulence in its environment.

4. A firm's success cannot be optimized unless management capability is also aligned with the environment.

5. The key internal capability variables which jointly determine a firm's success, are: cognitive, psychological, sociological, political and anthropological.[8]

Being aware of the spotty record of strategic planning, Ansoff (with the assistance of his graduate students) devoted the next 11 years to empirical validation of the Success Paradigm. The paradigm was tested in over 500 firms in the US, Japan, Indonesia, Algeria, Abu Dhabi, Australia, and Ethiopia. The statistical results gave strong support to the paradigm. Ansoff translated the paradigm into a diagnostic instrument, called "Strategic Readiness Diagnosis" and used it in his consulting practice.

Having identified behaviors by firms which optimize their profitability, Ansoff has refocussed his research on management behaviors which cause firms to behave optimally.

Igor Ansoff

Corporate Strategy, McGraw Hill, New York, 1965

Strategic Management, Macmillan, London, 1979

Implanting Strategic Management, (2nd edn), Prentice Hall, London, 1990

The roots of strategy

Of course, strategy was nothing new. It was simply that Ansoff – and the other thinkers who quickly followed – codified and made sense of something which had been going on for centuries.

The word strategy derives from the Greek for generalship, *strategia*, and entered the English vocabulary in 1688 as *strategie*. According to James' 1810 Military Dictionary, it differs from tactics, which are immediate measures in face of an enemy. Strategy concerns something "done out of sight of an enemy." Its origins can be traced back to Sun Tzu's *The Art of War* from 500 BC. Indeed, Sun Tzu has made a surprising return to the bestseller lists in the last decade. His book is full of neat aphorisms which seem to shed light on the mysterious world of strategy. They are reassuring, if not always appropriate.

Watching the implementation of a strategy which is solely based on analysis is like listening to a synthesizer recreate the sound of a Stradivarius.

The fuel for the modern growth in interest in all things strategic has been analysis. While analysis has been the watchword, data has been the password. Managers have assumed that anything which could not be analyzed could not be managed. The last 30 years have seen a ceaseless quest for things, actions, and decisions which can be analyzed. The belief in analysis is part of a search for a logical commercial regime, a system of management which will, under any circumstances, produce a successful result. But, as Ansoff found, effective analysis does not guarantee effective, or even appropriate, implementation.

Indeed, all the analysis in the world can lead to decisions which are plainly wrong. IBM had all the data about its markets, yet reached the wrong conclusions. It is a problem not restricted to business. British Prime Minister Harold Macmillan was once asked what was the most difficult thing about his job. "Events, my dear boy, events," he replied. For all its usefulness, analysis does not dictate events. Things may add up, but they don't necessarily work.

Even so, international management education has been built around the belief that analysis is fundamental to strategic management. It can, after all, be more easily taught than personnel issues which involve such imponderables as human emotions, aspirations and fears. There is also a tendency for strategy to be taught by people who come from a numerate background. In contrast, subjects such as leadership tend to be taught by psychologists. This bias has evolved slowly. Twenty years ago, as part of its MBA program, Harvard ran two strategy courses: one covered analysis, the other implementation. As time progressed, they found it far easier to find material for the analysis course. It was also more straightforward to teach and students preferred it. Gradually the courses became more analytical.

There are two basic problems with the reliance on analysis. First, it is all technique. Watching the implementation of a strategy which is solely based on analysis is like listening to a synthesizer recreate the sound of a Stradivarius. It is hollow and dehumanized. Even in the technological age, dehumanized management remains a contradiction in terms.

The second problem is more fundamental. Analysis produces a self-increasing loop. The belief is that more and more analysis will bring safer and safer decisions. If analysis is insufficient, the manager begins to feel guilty. How can they produce a strategy when the data is nonexistent or insubstantial? To assuage the guilt they carry out some more analysis. The process continues, relentlessly delaying any decision-making. In such cases, strategy is driven by guilt and fueled by analysis. Eventually, enough data is bound to filter through and a strategy of sorts will emerge. The process is, however, time-consuming and tortuous. Before the resulting strategy becomes action it is likely that the self-perpetuating combination of analysis and guilt will continue to interfere with and slow the process.

The traditional view is that strategy is concerned with making predictions based on analysis. Predictions, and the analysis which forms them, lead to security. The bottom line is not expansion, future growth or increased profitability – it is survival. The assumption is that growth and increased profits will naturally follow. If, by using strategy, we can increase our chances of predicting successful methods, then our successful methods will lead us to survival and perhaps even improvement. So, strategy is to do with getting it right or, as the more competitive would say, winning. Of course it is possible to win battles and lose wars and so strategy has also grown up in the context of linking together a series of actions with some longer-term goals or aims.

This was all very well in the 1960s and for much of the 1970s. Predictions and strategies were formed with confidence and optimism (though they were not necessarily implemented with such sureness). Security could be found. The business environment appeared to be reassuringly stable. Objectives could be set and strategies developed to meet them in the knowledge that the overriding objective would not change.

Such an approach, identifying a target and developing strategies to achieve it, became known as **Management by Objectives (MBO)**. Under

MBO, strategy formulation was seen as a conscious, rational process. MBO ensured that the plan was carried out. The overall process was heavily logical and, indeed, any other approach (such as an emotional one) was regarded as distinctly inappropriate. The thought process was backed with hard data. There was a belief that effective analysis produced a single, right answer; a clear plan was possible and, once it was made explicit, would need to be followed through exactly and precisely.

In practice, the MBO approach demanded too much data. It became overly complex and also relied too heavily on the past to predict the future. The entire system was ineffective at handling, encouraging or adapting to change. MBO simplified management to a question of reaching A from B using as direct a route as possible. Under MBO, the ends justified the means. The managerial equivalent of highways were developed in order to reach objectives quickly with the minimum hindrance from outside forces.

> **Under MBO, the ends justified the means. The managerial equivalent of highways were developed in order to reach objectives quickly with the minimum hindrance from outside forces.**

THE CONVENTIONAL VIEW OF STRATEGY

"The confusion of means and ends characterizes our age," Henry Mintzberg observes and, today, the highways are liable to be gridlocked. When the highways are blocked managers are left to negotiate minor country roads to reach their objectives. And then comes the final confusion: the destination is likely to have changed during the journey. Equally, while MBO sought to narrow objectives and ignore all other forces, success (the objective) is now less easy to identify. Today's measurements of success can include everything from environmental performance to meeting equal opportunities targets. Success has expanded beyond the bottom line.

Another fatal flaw in the conventional view of strategy is that it tended to separate the skills required to develop strategy in the first place (analytical) from those needed to achieve its objectives in reality (practical).

The divide between analysis and practice is patently artificial. Strategy does not stop and start, it is a continuous process of redefinition and implementation. In his book, *The Mind of the Strategist*, the Japanese strategic thinker KENICHI OHMAE says: "In strategic thinking, one first seeks a clear understanding of the particular character of each element of a situation and then makes the fullest possible use of human brain power to restructure the elements in the most advantageous way. Phenomena and events in the real world do not always fit a linear model. Hence the most reliable means of dissecting a situation into its constituent parts and reassembling them in the desired pattern is not a step-by-step methodology such as systems analysis. Rather, it is that ultimate non-linear thinking tool, the human brain. True strategic thinking thus contrasts sharply with the conventional mechanical systems approach based on linear thinking. But it also contrasts with the approach that stakes everything on intuition, reaching conclusions without any real breakdown or analysis."

When the future could be expected to follow neat linear patterns, strategy had a clear place in the order of things. Now, the neatness is being upset, new perspectives are necessary. Even attitudes to time are being questioned. Western admiration of the Japanese economic miracle makes Eastern notions of time intriguing – the East tends to use a cyclical conception of time which is not driven by achievement or by short-term objectives. Instead, it is deterministic and fatalistic.

If time can be questioned – or, at least, our perception of time – nothing is sacred and, corporations must constantly wrestle with fundamental issues. While accepting that every company needs a strategy – either explicit or implicit – it is increasingly recognized that expressing a need for strategy does not help to determine what strategy actually is or entails.

MAKING STRATEGY WORK

In an era of constant and unpredictable change, the practical usefulness of strategy is increasingly – and loudly – questioned. The skeptics argue that it is all well and good to come up with a brilliantly formulated strategy, but quite another to implement it. By the time implementation begins, the business environment is liable to have changed and be in the process of changing even further.

The death knell for traditional approaches to strategy is being sounded. "The humane thing to do with most strategic planning processes is to kill them off," concludes a report by OC&C Strategy Consultants. Research by the American Planning Forum found that a mere 25 percent of companies consider their planning processes to be effective. Similarly, in his book *The Rise and Fall of Strategic Planning*, Henry Mintzberg takes on the full might of conventional planning orthodoxy. "Too much analysis gets in our way. The failure of strategic planning is the failure of formalization," says Mintzberg, identifying formalization as the fatal flaw of modern management.

Mintzberg argues the case for what he labels **strategic programing**. His view is that strategy has for too long been housed in ivory towers built from corporate data and analysis. It has become distant from reality, when to have any viable commercial life strategy needs to become completely immersed in reality. "Strategies appear at predetermined times, popping out when expected, full blown, all ready for implementation. It is almost as if they are immaculately conceived," he caustically observes.

While the debate rages, the fundamental questions posed in the formulation of strategy remain as valid now as ever – probably more so. Organizations are increasingly aware that, as they move forward, they are not going to do so in a straight unswerving line. The important ability now is to be able to hold on to a general direction rather than to slavishly follow a predetermined path. Such flexibility demands a broader perspective of the organization's activities and direction. This requires a stronger awareness of the links between strategy, change, teamworking, and learning.

> "Strategies appear at predetermined times, popping out when expected, full blown, all ready for implementation. It is almost as if they are immaculately conceived."
> **HENRY MINTZBERG**

The new emphasis is on the **process** of strategy as well as the output. Strategy is as essential today as it ever was. But, equally, understanding its full richness and complexity remains a formidable task.

The great strategic debate has filled many bookshelves and continues to do so. The truth is summed up by an editorial in the *Economist* which cheerfully concluded that "nobody really knows what strategy is." The trouble is that people rarely admit that this is the case.

WHAT IS STRATEGY?

The confusion over such a well-debated issue can be attributed to a number of factors.

- **Confusion of what strategy actually is.** There is a confusion between what an organization is actually doing, what it says it is doing and what it should be doing. In practice, strategy tends to embrace all three. In *The Financial Times Guide to Management and Strategy*, Richard Koch provides two senses for strategy:

▶

1. " a good strategy is the commercial logic of a business, that defines why a firm can have a competitive advantage and a place in the sun. To be complete, a strategy must include a definition of the domain – the lines of business, types of customer and geographical reach – in which the firm competes. It must also include a definition of the firm's distinctive competences and the competitive advantage that gives the firm a special hold on the chosen business domain.

2. Strategy also means what a company does, how it actually positions itself commercially and conducts the competitive battle. You can always attempt to describe a competitor's strategy, whether or not you think it sound. In this sense a strategy is what a firm does, not what it says or does, or what its strategy documents propound."

- **The sheer profusion of approaches.** In the faddish world of management thinking no single subject has generated so many bright ideas – from strategic intent to core competencies.

- **Confusion with the actual processes of developing and then implementing strategy.** The process remains clouded by verbiage. Does an organization study its marketplace and competitive environment and then change itself to meet perceived opportunities? Indeed, Harvard's Michael Porter defines strategy as the positioning of the company relative to its industry environment. Or, does strategy begin with the the organization, examining what it excels at and then aiming to make the most of those assets in the current environment?

- **The shift from linear thinking to emergent chaos.** In the current business environment where the calls for change and transformation are constant, the traditional methods of formulating and implementing strategy are increasingly questioned. The conventional approach takes as its guiding light the acronym **MOST** (**Mission, Objectives, Strategy, and Tactics**). This offers an orderly progression from creating a mission to making the strategy happen.

Life is no longer so simple. "In practice, the real process of strategy development and direction setting is much more messy, experimental, uncertain, iterative and driven from the bottom upwards," says Andrew Campbell. "There are five reasons for rejecting the MOST framework. First, the competitive economic system in which companies act provides constraints that are often interpreted as objectives. Second, strategy and objectives are intertwined, not linear. Third, it is useless to develop a separation between strategy, tactics and operations – insights about creating value come as often from operating details as from broad strategic concepts. Fourth, academics and consultants differ in their views about how insights can best be developed and captured. Fifth, there are also differences in view about how best to implement strategy in an uncertain world."

● **The battle between analysis and intuition.** From this it would seem that the days of highly analytical, rational, strategy creation are past. But, strategy can neither be purely rational nor purely intuitive. Indeed, one of the core skills of managers is to know when and how to use their intuitive judgement of a particular situation.

Confusion is endemic. But, argues London Business School's Costas Markides, it need not be. "The confusion surrounding strategy manifests itself in a variety of ways. But, in reality, the confusion is unfortunate – and unjustified. Strategy is a very simple thing – at its simplest it is five or six creative ideas that tell us how our company is to fight the competitive battle in its industry. It is not a plan; it is not a hundred-page report; it is not a budget; and it is not a goal. It is just five or six creative ideas. If your company cannot put down its strategy on one sheet of paper then it does not have a strategy." The problem is that managers have been reared on an unhealthy diet of weighty reports.

Michael Porter
Strategy and competitive advantage

Michael Porter of Harvard Business School is probably the world's most successful academic. While other management thinkers have compromised their approach in search of popular appeal, Porter's work is unashamedly academic in tone and content. Seriousness and rationality is all pervasive. "His work is academic almost to a fault," observed the *Economist*. "Mr Porter is about as likely to produce a blockbuster full of anecdotes and boosterish catch-phrases as he is to deliver a lecture dressed in bra and stockings."[9]

His approach is based on surgical precision, the dissection of the vital organs of companies and industrial nations. Porter's books, not surprisingly, have been few in number, but high in their ambition and influence.

"Strategic thinking rarely occurs spontaneously. Without guidelines few managers knew what constituted strategic thinking,"[10] he lamented in a 1987 article. His work has set about constructing the guidelines. This has brought him into conflict with a number of other leading thinkers. Henry Mintzberg, the champion of spontaneity and intuition, has been critical of Porter's "enthusiasm for generic strategies and checklists of all kinds."[11]

MICHAEL PORTER	born 1947; educator and consultant

Education: degree in aeronautical engineering at Princeton; doctorate in economics, Harvard.

Career: Joined Harvard faculty 1973; also now runs a highly successful consultancy business, Monitor.

Porter's first book was *Competitive Strategy* (1980) which instead of tiptoeing round the edges of management theory went straight to the strategic heart. Porter tackled the apparently imponderable question of how organizations can achieve long-term competitive advantage. He sought a middle ground between the two polarized approaches then accepted – on the one hand, that competitive advantage was achieved by organizations adapting to their particular circumstances; and, on the other, that competitive advantage was based on the simple principle that the more in-tune and aware of a market a company is, the more competitive it can be (through lower prices and increased market share).

Porter managed to absorb both these concepts. From analysis of a number of companies, he developed **generic strategies**. This was not an instant template for competitive advantage – Porter insisted that though the "generic strategies" existed, it was up to each organization to carefully select which were most appropriate to them and at which particular time. The four "generic strategies" are backed by five **competitive forces** which are then applied to five "different kinds of industries" (fragmented, emerging, mature, declining, and global).

THE LOGIC BEHIND PORTER's FIVE FORCES FRAMEWORK

- If **customers** have bargaining power over a supplier (no matter what the reason), they will exercise that power and reduce the supplier's profit margins.

- If an organization's **suppliers** have bargaining power over it, they will exercise that power and sell their products at a higher price.

- If there are **substitutes** to an organization's product or service, they will limit the price the organization can charge and, again, limit profits.

- If there is intense **rivalry** in an industry, it will force organizations to engage in price, R&D and advertising wars, all of which are likely to reduce profits.

- Finally, if **new entrants** move into an industry, they bring with them resources and the desire to steal market share from existing companies. Rivalry accelerates and profits decline.

"Given the logic of these five forces, a strategist needs to decide what to do about them," says London Business School's Costas Markides. Traditionally, most people assumed that the way to proceed was to assume these five industry forces as given and then try and position their firm towards these forces. This is fundamentally wrong and this is probably the most serious misconception about strategy that has developed in the 15 years since the five forces framework was developed.

Instead, what the strategist ought to do is to creatively break the established rules of the game by actively changing these five forces in the company's favor. In other words, the essence of strategy formulation is coming up with creative ideas in response to the following five questions:

- *How can I reduce the bargaining power of my customers?*

- *How can I reduce the bargaining power of my suppliers?*

- *How can I reduce substitutes to my product or service?*

- *How can I limit rivalry in my industry?*

- *How can I prevent new entrants from coming into my industry?*[12]

Even so, Porter's "generic strategies" framework is persuasive and highly attractive to managers. It is clear and the logic irrefutable. The trouble is that, while Porter suggests that the model should only be used to stimulate thinking, organizations often regard it as a direct route to competitive advantage. There is considerable irony in companies using the same model to differentiate themselves from each other.

To examine an organization's internal competitiveness, Porter advocates the use of a **value chain** – analysis of a company's internal processes and the interactions between different elements of the organization to determine how and where value is added. Viewing everything a company does in terms of its overall competitiveness, argues Porter, is a crucial step to becoming more competitive.

"In a volume of over 500 pages it is easy to miss Porter's one reference to human resource management. It occupies only two paragraphs," observes the UK management writer and thinker, Philip Sadler, of *Competitive Advantage*.[13] The human element is not often to be found in Porter's work.

GAINING COMPETITIVE ADVANTAGE

In *Competitive Advantage* (1985) Porter contends that there are three ways by which companies can gain competitive advantage:

- by becoming the lowest cost producer in a given market

- by being a differentiated producer (offering something extra or special to charge a premium price)

- or by being a focussed producer (achieving dominance in a niche market).

This is even truer of *The Competitive Advantage of Nations* (1990). Probably Porter's most ambitious project, it is a detailed study of the competitiveness of the world's top eight economies which emerged from Porter's work on the Presidential Commission on Industrial Competitiveness set up by Ronald Reagan. Interestingly, Porter produces a more pragmatic view of the world in this book. He is highly critical of general prescriptions and the worldwide application of management fads such as just-in-time. What works in one country, fails miserably in another, he warns. This runs counter to much of the prevailing wisdom of globalization. Indeed, instead of national differences and characteristics becoming less pronounced, Porter found them to be as important as ever.

"You can boil Porter's magisterial work down to just three words: 'vigorous domestic rivalry'. That is: Firms that engage in the most intensive competition in their home market tend to improve fastest," commented Tom Peters, cheerfully saluting Porter as "an unlikely prince of disorder."[14]

Again, Porter's research produced a tidy checklist. His **national diamond** framework identified four factors which influence the competitiveness of nations: resources, related and supporting industries, demanding home customers, and domestic rivalry.

While Porter has attracted some criticism for his willingness to boil his mass of theories and ideas down to all-embracing bullet-points, without them it is unlikely that his complex ideas would either be accessible or understood. That they are so influential is a triumph for Porter's abilities of dissection and logic.

Michael Porter

Competitive Strategy, Free Press, New York, 1980

Competitive Advantage, Free Press, New York, 1985

The Competitive Advantage of Nations, Macmillan, London, 1990

Henry Mintzberg
Strategy as craft

The work of Canadian, Henry Mintzberg counters much of the detailed rationalism of other major thinkers of recent decades. From his first publication, *The Nature of Managerial Work*, Mintzberg has challenged orthodoxy, arguing the case for a more intuitive and humane approach to strategy formulation and practice, as well as the structure of organizations. *The Nature of Managerial Work* exposed many of the myths surrounding senior managers, revealing them to be creatures of the moment rather than farsighted strategists carefully planning their next move.

Mintzberg has generated a unique reputation, as someone apart from the mainstream able to analyze basic assumptions about managerial behavior. His most recent work tackles head-on the role and process of strategic planning. Mintzberg argues that intuition is "the soft underbelly of management" and that strategy has set out to provide uniformity and formality when none can be created.

> ## "I am sceptical about everything except reality."
> ### HENRY MINTZBERG

Despite a series of highly important and influential books and appointments at two of the world's leading business schools (McGill in Canada and INSEAD in France) Henry Mintzberg remains something of an outsider in the world of management thinking.

While his books are scholarly rather than populist, he emphasizes the creative and spontaneous, the right side of the brain rather than the left side with its predilection for analysis and rationality. He is a wry humanist who carries out his work with academic rigor. "A well published waif" is how he jokingly describes himself; "perhaps the world's premier management thinker," says Tom Peters.[15]

There is a sizeable dose of cynicism in Mintzberg's world view. Though, when asked, he is quick to add the explanatory coda: "I am sceptical about everything except reality." To keep hold of reality, he eschews the management guru merry-go-round. "There is a lot of obnoxious hype about being a 'guru' to the extent that the medium can destroy the message," he says, "I'm in one of the most competitive fields around, but I've never felt competition for a moment. You can compete by competing head-on or by not competing at all. I care about doing things well, not doing them better – that is a low standard."

Mintzberg's name was initially brought to a wider audience with his first book, *The Nature of Managerial Work* (1973). An article in the *Harvard Business Review* ("The Manager's Job: Folklore and Fact")[16]

95

brought Mintzberg's research further into the public eye. Its origins (and those of subsequent books) lie in Mintzberg's grand plan. "In 1968, I set out to write a text called *The Theory of Management Policy*, to draw together the research-based literature that helps to describe the processes of general management." Mintzberg's plan has expanded – each of the three central chapters became books and an early section of the fourth chapter also developed into a book.

At the time of its publication, *The Nature of Managerial Work* was radically alternative and rapidly dispensed with much conventional wisdom. "I had a lot of difficulty getting my first book published," Mintzberg recalls. "One publisher said they were publishing a book just like it – 20 years later, I have yet to see the book." In his research, Mintzberg got close to managers actually managing rather than pontificating from afar. His research involved spending time with five organizations and analyzing how their chief executives spent their time. While this tracking approach is now commonplace, in the early 1970s it was ambitious – previous research had concentrated on the people managed by managers and the structure of organizations rather than the day-to-day reality of managerial behavior and performance.

The Nature of Managerial Work revealed managers to be hostages to interruptions, flitting from subject-to-subject rarely giving undivided attention to anything. "The pressure of the managerial environment does not encourage the development of reflective planners, the classical literature not withstanding," Mintzberg observed. "The job breeds adaptive information-manipulators who prefer the live, concrete situation. The manager works in an environment of stimulus-response, and he develops in his work a clear preference for live action." Instead of being isolated figureheads analyzing and generating carefully thought-out strategy, managers were suddenly exposed as fallible and human. The corollary of Mintzberg's conclusions was that if we don't understand how managers spend their time and what they do, how can management be improved and the skills of managers appropriately developed?

Twenty years on, Mintzberg's style and approach has remained determinedly iconoclastic. "My books succeeded because they were different," he says. "If you think differently and execute it poorly you are dead."

His background in mechanical engineering might explain the root of Mintzberg's techniques and thinking. "Mechanical engineering is not concerned with image or status. It is about reality and requires a certain kind of thinking," he says, recalling a college assignment to design a pump. While all the other students went away and looked at the latest catalogs to copy a design, Mintzberg didn't look at anything and came up with a pump virtually identical to pumps when they were first invented. In his later research, Mintzberg also seeks to re-invent or establish first principles for himself.

"I am not an intellectual. I am a writer and researcher," he says. "I write primarily for myself, to find things out. I never write anything to boost my reputation or image – sometimes it is **appropriate** to publish something in the *Harvard Business Review*. When I am writing the painful stage is getting an outline and then there is joy when things click and integrate."

THE INTUITIVE MANAGEMENT PROCESS

After his initial success, Mintzberg's focus shifted to organizational structure. In *The Structure of Organizations* he identified five types of "ideal" organizational structure: simple structure, machine bureaucracy, professional bureaucracy, divisionalized form, and adhocracy.

Even so, at the core of Mintzberg's work is a belief in the excitement and spontaneity of management and faith in people rather than organizations – "I don't like to be organized – I am a voyeur." He has little time for the formal dictates of the organization. "We have become prisoners of cerebral management. I'm sympathetic to the management process which is intuitive, based on immediate responses," he says. Instead of seeing strategy as the apotheosis of rationalism Mintzberg has famously coined the term "crafting strategy," whereby strategy is created as deliberately, delicately, and dangerously as a potter making a pot. To Mintzberg strategy is more likely to "emerge," through a kind of organizational osmosis, than be produced by a group of strategists sitting round a table believing they can predict the future.

Mintzberg regards full-time MBA programs as perpetuating the obsession with "cerebral management." He no longer teaches on MBA programs and contentiously advises: "Regular MBA programs should be closed down. It's wrong way to train people who weren't managers to become managers. MBA programs are confused between training leaders and specialists. At the moment, we train financial analysts and then expect them to become leaders. If accountants were forbidden to be chief executives it would probably be an enormous benefit."

Mintzberg's most recent work is probably his most controversial: "Strategy is not the consequence of planning but the opposite: its starting point,"[17] he says, countering the carefully wrought arguments of strategists, from Igor Ansoff in the 1960s to the Boston Consulting Group in the 1970s and Michael Porter in the 1980s. *The Rise and Fall of Strategic Planning* is a masterly and painstaking deconstruction of central pillars of management theory.

HENRY MINTZBERG   born 1939; educator

Education: McGill University; MIT

Career: Worked for Canadian National Railways 1961–3; later he was visiting professor at a number of universities and business schools; President of Strategic Management Society 1988–91; consultant to a large number of organizations; visiting professor at INSEAD; director of the Center for Strategy Studies in Organizations at McGill University; professor at McGill since 1968.

THE FALLACIES OF PLANNING

Arguing that "strategy is not the consequence of planning but the opposite: its starting point," Mintzberg exposes the fallacies and failings at the root of planning. These include:

- **processes** – a fascination with elaborate processes creates bureaucracy and strangles innovation

- **data** – Mintzberg argues that "hard" data, the lifeblood of the traditional strategist, is a source of information; "soft" data, however, provides the wisdom. "Hard information can be no better and is often at times far worse than soft information," he writes. In *The Nature of Managerial Work*, Mintzberg similarly observed that managers relied on "soft information" rather than exhaustive written reports.

- **detachment** – Mintzberg refutes the notion of managers creating strategic plans from ivory towers. "Effective strategists are not people who abstract themselves from the daily detail but quite the opposite: they are the ones who *immerse* themselves in it, while being able to abstract the *strategic messages* from it."

Looking at the development of his work, Mintzberg observes: "My perception of what constitutes effective management is not so different as it was. But now there is a lot more ineffective management." In *The Rise and Fall of Strategic Planning*, he produces a typical paragraph (on the role of the effective strategist) which has the air of someone thinking aloud, but perhaps sums up Mintzberg's own approach: "Perceiving the forest from the trees is not the right metaphor at all ... because opportunities tend to be hidden under the leaves. A better one may be to detect a diamond in the rough in a seam of ore. Or to mix the metaphors, no one ever found a diamond by flying over a forest. From the air, a forest looks like a simple carpet of green, not the complex living system it really is."

Henry Mintzberg

The Nature of Managerial Work, Harper & Row, New York, 1973

The Structuring of Organizations, Prentice-Hall, Englewood Cliffs, NJ, 1979

Structures In Fives: Designing Effective Organizations, Prentice-Hall, Englewood Cliffs, NJ, 1983 (This is an expurgated version of the above.)

Power In and Around Organizations, Prentice-Hall, Englewood Cliffs, NJ, 1983

Mintzberg on Management: Inside Our Strange World of Organizations, The Free Press, New York, 1989 (Collier Macmillan, London)

The Strategy Process: Concepts, Contexts, Cases (with JB Quinn), 2nd edn, Prentice-Hall, Englewood Cliffs, NJ, 1991

The Rise and Fall of Strategic Planning, Prentice-Hall International, Hemel Hempstead, 1994

The route from strategy to action

"The starting point is moving nearer towards solutions – and the implementation of strategy – must be a solid understanding of where you are starting from and the dilemmas you face. If organizations are not in touch with the reality of their situation – however depressing this may seem – they have no hope of moving forward," says Howell Schroeder of Ashridge Management College.

Where do you want to be?

In the process of simplifying strategy, the starting point must be to determine an organization's overall goals or objectives. If you don't know where you want to be you are unlikely to get there.

In pursuit of this starting point organizations throughout the world have developed **mission statements**. "Most companies do have a mission statement. About 99.9 percent are useless," says Costas Markides. Mission statements are also, confusingly, known by a variety of other labels (strategic intent, core objectives, visions, etc.) but the end-result is usually remarkably similar.

Mission statements are, or should be, a pithy explanation of why a company is in business, what it intends to achieve and by what methods. The exercise of distilling an organization's *raison d'etre* into less than 100 words is often useful in itself. However, the results are often fatuous in the extreme. Mission statements have become meaningless PR exercises, pinned on noticeboards, printed on corporate keepsakes and generally ignored by the people they aim to influence. "Many managers misunderstand the nature and importance of mission, while others fail to comprehend it at all," concluded Andrew Campbell and his co-authors in *A Sense of Mission*.[18]

MISSIONS IMPOSSIBLE?

Mission statements take on many forms – from bizarre aspirations which are probably illegal, to jargon-infested triumphs of meaninglessness:

Glaxo "is an integrated research-based group of companies whose corporate purpose is to create, discover, develop, manufacture and market throughout the world, safe, effective medicines of the highest quality which will bring benefits to patients through improved longevity and quality of life, and to society through economic value"

Pearson is "a major international provider of media content, renowned for distinctive products that deliver information, education and entertainment in ways that people want them"

Apple Computer: "Our goal has always been to create the world's friendliest, most understandable, most useable computers – computers that empower the individual ... Our mission is to transform the way people do things by focusing on their experience with our computers. We believe the innovative and creativity of a person's work depends directly on the quality of his or her total experience, not just the need of a microprocessor"

Matsushita: "The duty of the manufacturer is to serve the foundation of man's happiness by making man's life affluent with an inexpensive and inexhaustible supply of life's necessities"

What do you want to achieve?

Any statement of intent relies on some knowledge of what it is you wish to achieve. Michael Porter argues that what every company should aim to achieve is competitive advantage. It must be better than its competitors in some way.

MISSION STATEMENTS

Though they might help to encapsulate an organization's goals, mission statements are not strategy. They are more accurately described as the potential end-result of strategy, the objectives of the organization. Indeed, Henry Mintzberg defines strategy as the embodiment of a company's visions.

Mission statements should be bold, but achievable, goals. It sounds straightforward, but the means of identifying these objectives is clouded by controversy.

This has led to the myth of **sustainable competitive advantage**. In reality, any competitive advantage is short-lived. If a company raises its quality standards and increases profits as a result, its competitors will follow. If a company says that it is reengineering , its competitors will claim to be reengineering more successfully. Businesses are quick to copy, mimic, pretend and, even, steal.

The logical and distressing conclusion is that an organization has to be continuously developing new forms of competitive advantage. It must move on all the time. If it stands still, competitive advantage will evaporate before its very eyes and competitors will pass.

The dangers of developing continuously are that it generates, and relies on, a climate of uncertainty. The company also runs the risk of fighting on too many fronts. This is often manifested in a huge number of improvement programs in various parts of the organization which give the impression of moving forward, but are often simply cosmetic.

Constantly evolving and developing strategy is labeled **strategic innovation**. The mistake is to assume that strategic innovation calls for radical and continual major surgery on all corporate arteries. Continuous small changes across an organization make a difference. "We did not seek to be 100 percent better at anything. We seek to be one percent better at 100 things," says SAS's Jan Carlzon.

What are your core competencies?

The phrase "core competencies" has now entered the language of management. In layman's terms, core competencies are what a company excels at.

Gary Hamel and CK Prahalad define core competencies as "the skills that enable a firm to deliver a fundamental customer benefit." They argue that strategic planning is neither radical enough or sufficiently long-term in perspective. Instead its aim remains incremental improvement. In contrast, they advocate **crafting strategic architecture**. The phraseology is unwieldy, but means basically that organizations should concentrate on rewriting the rules of their industry and creating a new competitive industry.

SHARPENING THE COMPETITIVE EDGE

Even major surgery has its compromises. More realistic than most, Kenichi Ohmae, says that a **good business strategy "is one, by which a company can gain significant ground on its competitors at an acceptable cost to itself."** He believes there are four principal ways of doing this:

1. **Focus on the key factors for success (KFSs).** Ohmae argues that certain functional or operating areas within every business are more critical for success in that particular business environment than others. If you concentrate effort into these areas and your competitors do not, this is a source of competitive advantage. The problem, of course, is identifying what these key factors for success are.

2. **Build on relative superiority.** When all competitors are seeking to compete on the KFSs, a company can exploit any differences in competitive conditions. For example, it can make use of technology or sales networks not in direct competition with its rivals.

3. **Pursue aggressive initiatives.** Frequently, the only way to win against a much larger, entrenched competitor is to upset the competitive environment, by undermining the value of its KFSs – changing the rules of the game by introducing new KFSs.

4. **Utilizing strategic degrees of freedom.** By this tautological phrase, Ohmae means that the company can focus on innovation in areas which are "untouched by competitors."

"In each of these four methods, the principal concern is to avoid doing the same thing, on the same battle-ground, as the competition," Ohmae explains.

FINDING THE CORE

A business' activities can be divided into four main categories:

- **Peripheral** Providing no source of competitive advantage; not essential to the core purpose of the business

- **Supportive** An essential but not core activity – failure in this area would cause serious damage to the business

- **Strategic** An actual or potential source of competitive advantage

- **Core** The primary activity(ies) of the business

SPEED, PEOPLE, COST, PRODUCTIVITY

In order to understand their own structures, aspirations and business recipe, any organization needs to consider:

Time competitiveness – how quick are they?

- Are decisions made speedily?
- Can they move heaven and earth to get something important done?
- Are they the fastest in the business at converting orders into completed deliveries?
- Are they the fastest in the business at converting ideas into products?

People competitive – have they the right people with the right training?

- Is training handled in an *ad hoc* manner as an occasional indulgence rather than systematically as a commercial necessity?
- Do people take responsibility for their own development?
- Is everyone trained regularly or are senior managers missed out?
- Does the organization have a clear idea of the competencies required of its staff?
- Are manning levels higher than those of competitors?

Cost competitive – how expensive is running the business, now and tomorrow?

● Is cost control regarded as the responsibility of the finance department and no one else?

● Is controlling costs regarded as more important than satisfying customers?

Productivity – is the organization productive enough?

● Does the organization have any systematic means of measuring productivity?

● How do productivity levels compare with those elsewhere in the industry?

● How is productivity going to be enhanced in the future?

How do core competencies and objectives fit with the overall environment?

Nothing in the corporate world exists in a vacuum. Formulating a mission or any set of objectives must involve a plethora of people, as well as consideration of the broader forces at work in and on the organization.

This process was neatly summed up by Peter Drucker in a 1994 *Harvard Business Review* article. Drucker argues that every organization has a theory of business – the assumptions on which it has been built and is being run. To create a "valid theory of business" requires four elements:

1. The assumptions about environment, mission and core competencies must fit reality
2. The assumptions in all three areas have to fit one another
3. The theory of the business must be known and understood throughout the organization
4. The theory of the business has to be tested constantly.[19]

Along similar lines, Kenichi Ohmae argues that an effective strategic plan takes account of three main players – the company, the customer, and the competition – each exerting their own influence. The strategy that ignores competitive reaction is flawed; so is the strategy that does not take into account sufficiently how the customer will react; and so, of course, is the strategic plan that does not explore fully the organization's capacity to implement it.

How do you achieve your objectives?

Implementation is where most strategies fail. Success relies on matching an organization's resources, culture, structure and people to the strategies which emerge from consideration of an organization's core competencies and the environment it exists in.

If strategy is to make the leap from theory to effective implementation the people behind it must:

- accept uncertainty as a fact of business life
- continually look outside the organization to learn lessons and improve effectiveness
- learn from past mistakes and achievements
- use unconventional images to communicate strategic initiatives
- produce short, highly informative strategy documents
- regard strategy as a business tool
- not allow preconceived ideas to interfere with honest interpretation
- distrust immediate consensus
- put faith in strong feelings and take risks
- assume nothing
- break down barriers
- involve everyone
- look to the future

Strategy

MARKIDES, C, *Diversification, Refocusing and Economic Performance*, MIT Press, Cambridge, MA, 1995

MOORE, J I, *Writers on Strategy and Strategic Management*, Penguin, London, 1992

OHMAE, K, *The Mind of the Strategist*, McGraw Hill, New York, 1982

References

1 LORANGE, P, (editor) *Implementing Strategic Processes*, Blackwell, Oxford, 1993.
2 OHMAE, K, *The Mind of the Strategist*, McGraw Hill, New York, 1982.
3 ANSOFF, HI, "A contingent paradigm for success of complex organizations," in *Milestones in Management Volume 5*, Schaffer Poeschel, Switzerland, 1994.

4 MINTZBERG, H, *The Rise and Fall of Strategic Planning*, Prentice-Hall International, Hemel Hempstead 1994.

5 ANSOFF, HI, *Strategic Management*, Macmillan, London, 1979.

6 ANSOFF, HI, *Milestones in Management Volume 5*, Schaffer Poeschel, Switzerland, 1994.

7 ANSOFF, HI, "A contingent paradigm for success of complex organisations," in *Milestones in Management Volume 5*, Schaffer Poeschel, Switzerland, 1994.

8 ANSOFF, HI, *Milestones in Management Volume 5*, Schaffer Poeschel, Switzerland, 1994.

9 "Professor Porter PhD," *Economist*, Oct. 8, 1994.

10 PORTER, M, "Corporate strategy: the state of strategic thinking," *Economist*, May 23, 1987.

11 MINTZBERG, H, *The Rise and Fall of Strategic Planning*, Prentice-Hall International, Hemel Hempstead, 1994.

12 MARKIDES, C, "Strategic management," *Financial Times Handbook of Management*, FT/Pitman, London, 1995.

13 SADLER, P, "Gold collar workers – making the best of the best," *Directions*, Dec. 1992.

14 PETERS, T, *Liberation Management*, Alfred Knopf, New York, 1992.

15 PETERS, T, "Plans down the drain," *Independent on Sunday*, April 24, 1994.

16 MINTZBERG, H, "The Manager's Job: Folklore and Fact," *Harvard Business Review*, July/Aug. 1975.

17 MINTZBERG, H, *The Rise and Fall of Strategic Planning*, Prentice-Hall International, Hemel Hempstead, 1994.

18 CAMPBELL, A, DEVINE, M & YOUNG, D, *A Sense of Mission*, Hutchinson Business Books, London, 1990.

19 DRUCKER, PF, "The theory of business," *Harvard Business Review*, Sept.–Oct. 1994.

4

New ways of managing people

"As we constantly see, nothing prevents autocratic companies from making money."
RICARDO SEMLER

"By empowering others, a leader does not decrease his power, instead he may increase it – especially if the whole organization performs better."
ROSABETH MOSS KANTER

"The desire to stand well with one's fellows, the so-called human instincts of association, easily outweighs the merely individual interest and the logic of reasoning upon which so many spurious principles of management are based."
ELTON MAYO

FROM PERSONNEL TO HUMAN RESOURCES

In the world of scientific management, people were relegated to second place behind the efficiency and productivity of machinery. Their wants, aspirations and motivations were largely ignored or paid dismissive lip-service. There were lone voices arguing that the fulfilment of individuals was an important prerequisite of any responsible organization, but they remained isolated and unheeded.

The American political scientist MARY PARKER FOLLET (1868–1933), for example, argued that in a democratic society the primary task of management is to create a situation where people readily contribute of their own accord. She repeatedly emphasized the need for managers to learn from their own experience by systematically observing experiences, recording them and relating these experiences to the total situation. She saw the manager as responsible for integrating the contributions of specialists such as marketing, production, cost accountants, and industrial relations so that they contributed effectively for the benefit of all.

Humane approaches to management, however, have in general been notable by their absence. Though companies have been proclaiming for generations that theirs is a people business, in reality this has been as insincere as it is meaningless. There are few exceptions. In the UK, Marks & Spencer has set high standards in its dealings with its employees and customers. It has heeded the observation of one of its founders, Lord Sieff, that "ultimately, whatever the form of economic activity, it is people that count most."[1]

In the US, Levi Strauss & Co has set exceptionally high ethical standards, but there are very few names that can be uncritically added to the list. In recent years, however, there has been a significant change in attitudes. "There is now a common acceptance that competitive advantage may be achieved by firms from the way their employees are managed. This prescription has gained ground over the last fifteen years to the stage where it may be said to be conventional wisdom. While one may wish that this is because working people are

> "The term *human resource management* (HRM) signifies to managers and to employees a new emphasis on the management of people in order to achieve strategic organizational objectives."
> LORD SIEFF

now treated in a considerate, developmental and respectful manner, equally one might also say that employees have come to be regarded in the same category as business assets: to be acquired with care, to be developed and to be utilized effectively," says Shaun Tyson of Cranfield School of Management. "The term *human resource management* (HRM) signifies to managers and to employees a new emphasis on the management of people in order to achieve strategic organizational objectives."

Some may argue that calling people "human resources" rather defeats the point of the exercise from the very start. If people are simply to be resources, like finance and computing, organizations may as well return to the tenets of Frederick Taylor. However, the elevation of people-related issues to the highest executive agenda is an important development, no matter what the terminology.

Recognition of the human side of enterprise can be traced back to a number of influential thinkers. Though their individual impact on the way companies manage themselves is limited, the cumulative effect has proved significant.

The impetus began with the **Hawthorne Studies** into workers' attitudes and behavior conducted between 1927 and 1932 at the Western Electric Plant in Hawthorne, Chicago. The Studies produced the Hawthorne Effect. This has been much debated and questioned. It found that the output of the workers improved when people believed that management was concerned about their well-being. An alternative, but cynical, view is that their performance improved simply because the experiment was underway.

The Hawthorne Studies were important because they showed that views of how managers behaved were a vital aspect of motivation and improved performance. Also, the research revealed the importance of informal work groups.

The most passionate advocate of the Hawthorne Studies was the Australian ELTON MAYO (1880–1949). Mayo argued that self-esteem was vital to effective performance and that management needs to gain the consensus of working groups as well as individuals. "So long as commerce specializes in business methods which take no account of human nature and social motives, so long may we expect strikes and sabotage to be the ordinary accompaniment of industry," he wrote. Mayo believed that the informal groups revealed by Hawthorne could either be utilized to the individual and corporate good or ignored to everyone's detriment. Following on from the conclusion of the Hawthorne Studies, Mayo championed the need for efficient and recognized communication channels between workers and management in order that individuals and groups could identify with corporate goals and objectives.

The work at Hawthorne was not really capitalized on until the 1950s when a group of like-minded thinkers – later christened the **Human Relations School** – emerged in the United States. Its influence has been wide-ranging with its central figures, Douglas Macgregor, Abraham Maslow and Frederick Herzberg coming into contact with and influencing a wide range of later thinkers including Ed Schein, Chris Argyris, and Warren Bennis.

The social psychologist DOUGLAS MACGREGOR (1906-64) produced one of the most long-lasting contributions with his THEORY X and THEORY Y which sought to provide a rational and accessible framework to motivational factors.

Theory X was based on traditional, and instantly recognizable, carrot and stick thinking. It contended that workers were inherently lazy, needed to be supervised and motivated and that, for them, work was a necessary evil to provide money. In the 1970s, Theory X spawned a humorous forebear in Theory W (W for Whiplash) which advocated generous use of the stick.

More optimistically, Macgregor's Theory Y argued that people wanted and needed work and what should be sought was the individual's commitment to the firm's objectives and then means of liberating their abilities.

When Macgregor died in 1964 he was working on Theory Z which aimed to bring together the needs and aspirations of the corporation and the individual. The work was never completed but was picked upon by William Ouchi who took it as the title of a book which sought to extract lessons from Japanese management. Ouchi's Theory Z organization is centered on lifetime employment, concern for employees including their social life, decisions made by concensus, slow promotion, excellent transmission of information, commitment to the firm, and intense concern for quality. If Macgregor had lived to complete Theory Z it may well have contained some similar elements.

In parallel to Macgregor's work was that of ABRAHAM MASLOW (1908-70). Maslow developed a **hierarchy of needs**. This identified an ascending series of human needs – starting with warmth, shelter and food and ending with self-actualization – achievement of personal potential. The hierarchy was based on the idea that once the need is satisfied you are no longer motivated by it. This is a theory which fired debate but bore little relation to the avaricious nature of human kind.

"What Maslow did not see is that a want changes in the act of being satisfied," says Peter Drucker. "As a want approaches satiety, its capacity to reward, and with it its power as an incentive, diminishes fast. But its capacity to deter, to create dissatisfaction and to act as a disincentive, rapidly increases."

Developing from Maslow came FREDERICK HERZBERG (born 1923). His career – much influenced by wartime experiences – has been dominated by impassioned humanity. "Man has two sets of needs. His need as an animal to avoid pain and his need as a human to grow psychologically," he says in *Work and the Nature of Man*.[2]

Herzberg, a clinical psychologist, identified **hygiene factors** (also called maintenance factors) as the basic economic needs; contrasted with **motivation factors** meeting deeper aspirations. Good hygiene is necessary but not enough in itself to provide adequate motivation. His influence was significant – his 1968 *Harvard Business Review* article, "One more time: how do you motivate employees?" sold over one million copies. Herzberg later coined the term **job enrichment**.

Managing people

BEER, M; SPECTOR, B; LAWRENCE, P R; MILLS, D Q; and WALTON, R, *Managing Human Assets*, Free Press, New York, 1984

BLYTON, P, and TURNBULL, P, *Reassessing Human Resource Management*, Sage, London, 1992

HERZBERG, F; MAUSNER, B; and SNYDERMAN, B, *The Motivation to Work*, Wiley, New York, 1959

MACGREGOR, D, *The Human Side of Enterprise*, McGraw Hill, New York, 1960

MASLOW, A, *Motivation and Personality*, Harper & Row, New York, 1954

MAYO, E, *The Human Problems of an Industrial Civilization*, Macmillan, New York, 1933

STOREY, J (editor), *New Perspectives on Human Resource Management*, Routledge, London, 1989

STOREY, J, *Developments in the Management of Human Resources*, Blackwell, Oxford, 1992

TYSON, S, and FELL, A, *Evaluating the Personnel Function*, Hutchinson, London, 1986

Tom Peters
Evangelizing people

Strangely, in the liberating atmosphere of the 1960s, the human side of management experienced a lull. In the 1990s, however, people have been pushed to the center of the organizational and managerial stage. For this, one major contemporary thinker should be attributed with a considerable degree of credit. Tom Peters, undoubtedly the preeminent contemporary management guru, has proved a potent champion of the humanity of sound business. Peters' books sell in their millions, his seminars fill auditoriums and his syndicated newspaper column is avidly read throughout the world. His message is passionately expressed. Describing his presentational style, the *Economist* observed: "Striding urgently back and forth, bellowing and bantering, he nearly achieves the difficult feat of making management seem exciting."[3]

Unquestionably, management *is* exciting to Peters. Even the titles of his books are exhortations (they have been called "charismatic shockers") – *Liberation Management, A Passion for Excellence, Thriving on Chaos* and, most famously, *In Search of Excellence*. The latter book, cowritten with Robert Waterman, is the best-selling management book of all time, having sold over five million copies across the world.

In Search of Excellence marked an important development in management publishing as well as management thinking. Its popularity has fueled a massive increase in the management book market. Its influence on the practice of management, of course, remains immeasurable. Peters has always insisted that the book's massive popularity should not disguise the fact that very few of the buyers actually read the book – and

---

TOM PETERS   born 1942; consultant and writer

Education: Masters in civil engineering from Cornell; MBA at Stanford

Career: Worked in the Pentagon; served in Vietnam; Office of Management and Budget in Washington; consultant with McKinsey & Co.; author and consultant with his own diverse company, the Tom Peters Group.

---

fewer still converted its potpourri of best practice into managerial reality. The book emerged from work carried out by Peters and Waterman with their then employer, the consultancy McKinsey. Their research identified 43 successful companies and went on to identify the characteristics which were common to their success. The selection was based on six financial measurements – 20-year averages of compound asset growth, compound equity growth, ratio of market value to book value, return on capital, return on equity, and return on sales.

There was nothing earth shattering in this technique. Indeed, the conclusion was largely that the excellent companies managed to exercise commonsense, keeping an obsessive eye on the business basics. The book's success was secured by the fact that it accentuated the positive at a time of unmitigated gloom – it was published in 1982. As managers lurched from crisis to crisis, and one bright new management theory to another, Peters and Waterman drew out what made successful companies tick and they did so in an approachable way.

As part of their research, Peters and Waterman (along with Richard Pascale and Anthony Athos) produced the Seven S Framework, a kind of instant guide to issues and topics which occupy managerial minds.

THE SEVEN S FRAMEWORK

Strategy: plan or course of action leading to the allocation of a firm's scarce resources, over time, to reach identified goals.

Structure: salient features of the organization chart (i.e. functional, decentralized, etc.) and how the separate entities of an organization are tied together.

Systems: procedualized reports and routinized processes (such as meeting formats), etc.

Staff: "demographics" description of important personnel categories within the firm (i.e. engineers, entrepreneurs, MBAs, etc.). "Staff" is not meant in line-staff terms.

Style: characterization of how key managers behave in achieving the organizations' goals; also the cultural style of the organization.

Shared values: the significant meanings or guiding concepts that an organization imbues in its members.

Skills: distinctive capabilities of key personnel and the firm as a whole.

COMPANY EXCELLENCE

The distillation of the lengthy research carried out by Peters and Waterman was that excellent companies:

- had a bias for action
- were close to the customer
- had autonomy and entrepreneurship
- believed in productivity through people
- were hands-on and value driven

- stuck to the knitting
- had a simple form and a lean staff
- had simultaneous loose–tight properties.

The messages which emerged from *In Search of Excellence* have now largely entered into the language and practice of management. In one way or another, Peters and Waterman anticipated the future interest in empowerment, core businesses, customer focus, balancing centralization and decentralization, the lean organization, and the dismantling of hierarchies.

Over the years since its publication, *In Search of Excellence*'s reputation has taken a good deal of criticism. In particular, commentators quickly latched on to the fact that the 43 excellent companies did not necessarily remain so. Indeed, the fortunes of some of the chosen few plummeted dramatically – the airline People's Express was a notable casualty, as was the computer company, Wang. IBM, an unquestioned choice at the time, has since experienced an unprecedented period of decline.

THE FAILURE OF EXCELLENT COMPANIES

The failure of "excellent" companies to last the course has encouraged Peters to address the problem of how organizations can sustain success and cope with increasingly competitive and chaotic markets. In *Thriving on Chaos* he begins with the line: "There are no excellent companies." It reiterates many of the central ideas of *In Search of Excellence*. It has five basic themes:

- obsession with responsiveness to customers
- constant innovation in all areas of the firm with risk and some failures encouraged
- partnership
- leadership which loves change and shares an inspiring vision
- control by means of simple support systems aimed at measuring the right things.

In *Thriving on Chaos*, Peters launched a crusade against management hierarchies. He contends that Drucker's suggestion in the 1950s that there should be a maximum of seven layers in an organization is now outdated. "I insist on five layers as the maximum," insisted Peters, pointing somewhat surprisingly to the Catholic church's structure as a good example. "In fact, even the five-layer limit should apply only to very complex organizations such as multi-division firms. Three layers – supervisor (with the job redefined to deal with a span of control no smaller than one supervisor for 25 to 75 people), department head and unit boss – should be tops for any single facility."

Thriving on Chaos proved a stepping stone to the more dramatic vision of Peters' *Liberation Management*. This is a huge sprawling book – "Mr Peters has not extended his passion for downsizing to his own prose," noted the *Economist*.[4] Undoubtedly it is rambling and lacking in focus but, behind its folksy stories of service excellence, it possesses a fervent purpose. It celebrates the death of middle management – "Middle Management, as we have known it since the railroads invented it right after the Civil War, is dead. Therefore, middle managers as we have known them are cooked geese." The phraseology is colorful, but eulogizes about the successes of people in a way few other management books have ever contemplated. Peters seeks to put people, creativity, technology and speed of thought, and action at center stage.

While challenging for readers to negotiate, *Liberation Management* proved highly successful. Once again Peters' timing and ability to iden-tify trends cannot be questioned. *In Search of Excellence* came out as US unemployment headed to 10 percent; *Thriving on Chaos* came out on the day Wall Street fell by 20 percent; *Liberation Management* emerged as the world was coming out of recession and organizations were becoming aware of the need to understand new ways of working which utilize technology more productively.

Liberation Management noted the trend towards what Peters labels as "fashion" – "The definition of every product and service is changing. Going soft, softer, softest. Going fickle, ephemeral, fashion. An explo-sion of new competitors, a rising standard of living in the developed world, and the ever-present ... new technologies are leading the way. No corner of the world is exempt from the frenzy."

Amid the frenzy emerge the "excellent" organizations of the 1990s – companies like CNN, Body Shop, ABB and many others which espouse organizational liberalism through their commitment to speedy decisions, free-flowing organization and individual ability. Unlike its predecessors, *Liberation Management* does not provide a recipe for success. Instead, the recipe is an apparently random, unique stew of best practice. Peters' message is more pragmatic – if it is a good idea, make it work for you.

Skeptics – and there are many – suggest that Peters has a flair for marketing and self-publicity. This is undoubtedly true. Rather like a nineteenth-century travelling preacher, he has a plentiful supply of colorful slogans – "the nano-second nineties," "crazy times call for crazy organizations." But, what is eye-catching about *Liberation Management* is Peters' intimate knowledge of some of the world's most advanced and innovative corporations. He has a knack of getting under organizational skins – he may interview the chief executive but is just as likely to focus on the chief executive's chauffeur. Among others, *Liberation Management* is dedicated to two workers in a heavy manufacturing company who have revolutionized the way they work. Peters' message is that corporate revolution is not simply about doing away with parking spaces for directors, but is real and touches everyone.

It is this willingness to grapple with human nature which goes some way to explaining Peters' popularity. He is interested in what motivates people and the reality of their day-to-day work. Paradoxically, this sort of down-to-earth realism is set against his evangelical idealism.

Peters' work is an antidote to the dry analysis of strategy or the focus on how companies are organized. Yes, he says, these things are important, but people are the driving force. In an effort to understand people his reading and references are increasingly broad ranging – as likely to include Zen Buddhism as baseball. He recently wrote that he would like his epitaph to be: "He was curious to the end."[5]

While Peters has cut an eye-catching swathe, Waterman's career has continued at a more leisurely pace. "Where Peters is the Savonarola of his cause, Waterman is a gentler prophet," observes Robert Heller.[6] His books, *The Renewal Factor, Adhocracy: The Power to Change* and *The Frontiers of Excellence* have fared less well than Peters'. They are, nevertheless, as perceptive.

In *The Frontiers of Excellence*, Waterman argues that companies which succeed pay primary attention to employees and customers rather than shareholders. Waterman provides a four point plan to sustaining excellence: small, fairly autonomous units; "downward" rather than "upward" organization; effective "adhocracy" (groups cutting across functional lines) as well as bureaucracy; "sheer staying power and the will to commit to long-term plans."

Tom Peters and Robert Waterman

TOM PETERS and ROBERT WATERMAN:

In Search of Excellence, Harper & Row, New York & London, 1982

TOM PETERS:

A Passion for Excellence (with Nancy Austin), Collins, London, 1985

Thriving on Chaos, Macmillan, London, 1988

Liberation Management, Alfred Knopf, New York, 1992

ROBERT WATERMAN:

The Renewal Factor, Bantam, New York, 1987

The Frontiers of Excellence, Nicholas Brealey, London, 1994

Human resources

The late 1980s and 1990s have shaken the world of human resources (HR). Accepted practices have been radically rethought as organizations have sought to restructure themselves. Traditional practices have not only been questioned but, in many cases, have been overturned.

With hierarchies decreasing and the emphasis on becoming leaner and fitter, the onus is on corporations extracting the best possible performance from all employees. In (best) practice this means recruiting well qualified and highly skilled people and developing the skills of everyone in the organization. Standards are increasing – at a Chrysler plant, for example, 20 percent of new assembly plant workers are college graduates. "In the past, we put our energy into making sure we had a well-educated management force," says Dennis Pauley, executive vice-president of manufacturing at Chrysler. "Now, we know that assembly line workers are just as important. My workforce needs to be at least as good as that of the Japanese, or I'm out of the game."[7]

The trouble is that in a period of change, people suffer from fear, insecurity and cynicism about the benefits of what they see happening all around them. "Delayering is seen as a cost-cutting exercise which results for the majority in lower morale, more work and few promotion prospects," noted a report by the UK's Roffey Park Management Institute.[8]

Dealing with such issues has pushed human resources forward as a discipline. "What is happening is that human resource management has always been important for companies, but now it is becoming much more visible. As companies have to become more cost effective, they have to learn how to manage their human resources much more cleverly than in the past," says Chris Brewster, director of Cranfield's Centre for European Human Resource Management.[9] Its emerging role is radically different from that of the past when it dealt with the bureaucracy of employing people and little else. From being a caring role, human resources is being realigned as having a strategic role, focussed on the business needs and strategic plans of the corporation.

> ## THE NEW ROLE OF HUMAN RESOURCES
>
> - **A facilitator of change.** To carry people through upheaval requires the true management of human resources.
>
> - **An integrated approach to management.** Rather than being an isolated function, HR is regarded as a core activity, one which shapes a company's values. In particular, this can have an impact on customer service.
>
> - **A mediator.** Establishing and balancing the new and emerging aspirations and requirements of the company and the individual.

While the role of HR as a process is fast developing so, too, is the treatment of those human resources it seeks to manage. Employees throughout the Western world have never been more demanding or so insecure. They have never exercised so much responsibility or felt as much pressure to develop skills and competencies. The pressure is growing as a direct result of the following key ideas.

EMPOWERMENT

Delegation has always been recognized as a key ingredient of successful management and leadership. But, in the 1980s, delegation underwent a crisis of confidence – managers were intent on progressing as quickly as possible up the corporate ladder, working 12 hours a day to succeed rather than delegating so that others could share the glory. In the corporate cut and thrust, delegation appeared to be a sign of weakness.

The 1990s have seen a shift in attitudes. No longer is delegation an occasional managerial indulgence. Instead, it has become a necessity. At Chrysler in the US, there are now 50 workers to every manager; against 20 to every manager a decade ago. The figure is set to increase to around 100.[10] "With organizations becoming flatter and hierarchies disappearing managers now have a far wider span of control than ever before," says John Payne, consultant and author of *Letting Go Without Losing Control*. "In that situation, delegation is vital. The trouble is that delegation is like driving a car – no one admits to being a bad delegator."

It is not only the fact that many managers consider themselves to be competent delegators that causes problems. Good delegation is hard work and requires substantial amounts of confidence and faith – managers, after all, are usually delegating tasks which they are accomplished at carrying out to less experienced people. "Delegation is being prepared to trust people to do a task and achieve results without your interference," says John Payne. "It is easier said than done. Managers who make delegation work for them are those who have eliminated fear. They do not delegate and then sit worrying that the job won't be done well enough and they will be blamed or have to sort it out. They have confidence in their own position and are not fearful that the person will do too good a job and undermine their position and authority. Also, they make time to delegate properly. Initially, delegation does involve committing time, but there are substantial time savings in the near future."

The trouble is that old habits die hard. Organizations may have shrunk, but managers often remain wedded to habits of a lifetime. "Many companies are in a state of transition. They have taken layers of management out but haven't yet changed the processes. The remaining managers still have a lot of pressure on them and are often working very long hours," says Ginny Spittle, a senior human resources manager at ICL. "The role of managers is changing from controlling and planning to coaching, leading and acting as a resource. If they are to achieve this change they need training and support so they learn to delegate and give full responsibility to people who report to them."

The need for training and support is one also identified by Richard Phillips of Ashridge Management College. "Managers have to come to terms with the fact that they can no longer manage people in a hands-on way any more and dumping trivial tasks onto people is not the best way to delegate," he says. "Managers tend to delegate tasks which they are too busy to do themselves or which they don't want to do themselves. They also tend to delegate them to staff who are judged to be already competent to carry them out to minimize the risk of mistakes and reduce the manager's anxiety levels."

In short, delegation is a last resort, a worry to the manager doing the delegating and an unwanted extra burden to the person handed the task. But, Richard Phillips argues, it need not be like that. He has carried out extensive research on managers who act as coaches. By doing so, he says, managers turn conventional wisdom about delegation on its head. "Instead of selecting someone who can already do the work being delegated, coaches deliberately select someone who cannot do it. In addition to setting the goals of the actual work to be done, they add learning goals. They coach the learner to give them the necessary skills and confidence to carry out the task."

The need to combine learning, task-fulfilment and delegation is also seen as essential by ICL's Ginny Spittle: "Managers have to look at more creative approaches. The onus is now on getting the most out of groups and teams of people, but there simply isn't the time to sit down with everyone who reports directly to you. Managers have to delegate successfully so that everyone learns and contributes as the job is done."

DELEGATION TO THE LEARNER

Ashridge's Richard Phillips cites an example from a major electronics company he talked to as part of his research on coaching. "The job of negotiating a large and important maintenance contract was delegated to a senior programer. There were clear goals, learning objectives and the expectations of both sides were thoroughly aired and discussed beforehand. The end-result was that the manager, new to the job, learned more about his own company; gained an external perspective; and developed interpersonal and negotiating skills. Not only that – he met the target of reducing the cost of the contract by 10 percent."

EMPOWERMENT AND DELEGATION

The once simple act of delegation has also been hijacked by management writers. Instead of delegating, managers are currently "empowering," granting new areas of responsibility. Though this is now part of the language of management, genuine examples of empowerment are not always what they may seem. "With the flattening of hierarchies, empowerment has become a fashionable term. In practice, it is often a synonym for delegation," warns Dr Ian Cunningham, author of *The Wisdom of Strategic Learning*. Instead of granting genuine power to their staff, managers remain as likely as ever to make the important decisions and only pass on relatively unimportant tasks to others. It is worth remembering that empowerment and delegation are not one and the same. Delegation starts off as part of a manager's job which he or she then delegates. Empowerment, however, involves removing constraints which prevent someone doing their job as effectively as possible.

The danger is that while empowerment attracts the management theorists and fad-following companies, delegation remains neglected, its full potential unrealized. A persuasive argument to sit up and take notice comes from Richard Phillips: "Managers should remember that when they perform a task which someone else could do, they prevent themself from doing a task which only they could do.) It is a message which appears to be increasingly understood. Examples of empowerment are growing. For example, at Chrsyler's new plant in Dodge City, each worker has the right to halt the assembly line at any time.

Differentiating delegation and empowerment is not easy. Harvard's Quinn Mills provides one solution: "Empowerment describes a management style. The term is very close in meaning to delegation, but if it is strictly defined, empowerment means the authority of subordinates to decide and act. It implies a large degree of discretion and independence for those who are empowered. Generally, empowerment takes place within a context of limitations upon the discretion of those empowered."[11] The nature of these limitations will continue to be debated.

Rosabeth Moss Kanter
Creating empowerment

In the perennial search to pigeon-hole management thinkers under a suitable title or specialism, Rosabeth Moss Kanter has proved determinedly elusive. She is not an evangelist in the Tom Peters mold, but nor is she an unworldly academic. She travels the world consulting and lecturing, but remains a Professor at Harvard Business School (and, from 1989 to 1992, editor of the *Harvard Business Review*). "Seminars are a performance. But I'm not on the circuit; I have a job," she insists. "I am interested in being a player, a participant, not just a bystander; perhaps a bystander close to power."[12] Her books are tightly and rigorously researched, yet have a clear populist element and appeal. Their subject matter evades neat classification, ranging increasingly widely, geographically and theoretically.

Her early work was concerned with Utopian communities, such as the Shakers. ("In the 1970s I compared IBM to a Utopian culture," she now admits.) This interest perhaps can be identified as the thread which runs through her central trilogy of publications – *Men and Women of the Corporation* (1977), *The Change Masters* (1983) and *When Giants Learn to Dance* (1989). "Kanter-the-guru still studies her subject with a sociologist's eye, treating the corporation not so much as a micro-economy, concerned with turning inputs into outputs, but as a mini-society, bent on shaping individuals to collective ends," observed the *Economist*.[13]

"I don't fit easily into different slots. I see myself as a thought leader, a developer of ideas," she says. "I am idealistic and it was the idealistic entrepreneurs of the 1960s and 1970s who changed things so that business became a great arena for experimentation. I am always interested in

121

ROSABETH MOSS KANTER born 1943; educator and consultant

Education: Bryn Mawr, PhD at the University of Michigan.

Career: Associate Professor of sociology, Brandeis University; joined Harvard 1973; 1977–86 taught at Yale and MIT; returned to Harvard as Professor of Business Administration; editor of the Harvard Business Review 1989–92; runs her own consultancy company, Goodmeasure.

---

positive models and positive change. Business became increasingly interesting to me because it is so pivotal. It is the bedrock."

Kanter's idealism has also led her into politics. She was involved in Michael Dukakis' presidential bid – writing a book with him along the way. Dukakis' revival of Massachusetts' economic fortunes briefly appeared to offer an example of idealism, entrepreneurism, and commercialism in partnership. "I learned a lot working with Dukakis," says Kanter. "He was interested in harnessing the entrepreneurial spirit."

Given this strain of idealism, it is ironic that Kanter's first major book, *Men and Women of the Corporation*, proved more likely to dash any idealism than to nurture it. It was an intense examination of a bureaucratic organization and, in effect, marked the demise of comfortable corporate America. Among its generally depressing findings was that the central characteristic expected of a manager was "dependability." Undaunted by her examination of the limitations and restrictions of the contemporary corporation, Kanter turned her mind to creating the new organizational models. The book which forged her reputation was *The Change Masters*.

This book sought out antidotes to the corporate malaise identified in *Men and Women of the Corporation*. It succeeded in propelling empowerment and greater employee involvement onto the corporate agenda. These issues are developed throughout Kanter's work – "By empowering others, a leader does not decrease his power, instead, he may increase it – especially if the whole organization performs better," she says.

Change Masters discovered the corporate world in an awkward state of flux – unwilling to disengage itself from the last vestiges of corporatism and unable or fearful of what to do next. Its vision remained solidly American. Its success, however, allowed Kanter's gaze to move further afield. "*Change Masters* opened doors for me, as a result I've globalized myself in the last decade," she says. "At the same time, however, a lot of the romance with Japanese companies went away. Instead, there emerged a belief that the source of much managerial wisdom emanates from the US."

The wisdom she encountered on her increasing travels was distilled into her next book, *When Giants Learn to Dance*. Describing the process she goes through in writing a book, Kanter says: "Ideas are, to start off, very vague but, gradually things develop. I say things and if people look blank, I continue. Then I become immersed. I am inductive, not deductive. I need data and experience in front of me. As the book progresses there is a lot of back and forth, checking, questioning and developing." She is keen to emphasize that her works are not simply potboilers full of unsubstantiated or unworkable ideas. "I reject the term *guru* because it is associated with pandering to the masses, providing inspiration without substance. There is a little bit of the shaman in a guru. I have scholarly standards. My books are dense and theoretical. They have footnotes."

THE POSTENTREPRENEURIAL CORPORATION

When Giants Learn to Dance marks the corporate transformation from slumbering behemoth to nimble new creation, what Kanter labeled "the post-entrepreneurial firm." *When Giants Learn to Dance* predicts that as companies recognize and focus on their core capabilities, expansion will tend to occur through strategic alliances, and peripheral activities be taken over by specialist service providers. The burgeoning of the service sector in the developed economies is evidence of the kind of structural changes which Kanter describes. On the other hand, global companies harnessing economies of scale will create the need for managers with the ability to manage across cultural boundaries.

"The post-entrepreneurial corporation represents a triumph of process over structure. That is, relationships and communication and the flexibility to temporarily combine resources are more important than the 'formal' channels and reporting relationships represented on an organizational chart," writes Kanter. "The post-entrepreneurial corporation is created by a three-part mix: by the context set at the top, the values and goals emanating from top management; by the channels, forums, programs and relationships designed in the middle to support those values and goals; and by the project ideas bubbling up from below – ideas for new ventures or technological innovations or better ways to serve customers."

Kanter's argument is that businesses need to be flexible but not freewheeling – she points to the fact that small businesses often suffer from too little organization while larger ones suffer from the reverse problem.

The origins of many of her ideas can be traced back to the work of Elton Mayo in the 1930s and Douglas Macgregor in the 1950s. They, too, tried to come to terms with the imponderables of motivation and the relationship between individuals and large corporations.

ESSENTIAL SKILLS FOR MANAGERS

In *When Giants Learn to Dance*, Kanter identifies seven "skills and sensibilities" essential for managers if they are to become what she labels "business athletes." These are:

- learning to operate without the might of the hierarchy behind them

- knowing how to "compete" in a way that enhances rather than undercuts co-operation

- operating with the highest ethical standards

- having a dose of humility

- developing a process focus

- being multifaceted and ambidextrous

- gaining satisfaction from results.

Kanter's work has highlighted people-related issues which were long ignored by the world's top businesses. "I am increasingly encouraged by the progress some organizations are making in areas like empowerment, but wish they were further along," she says. "The real emergent issue is what will people do with their time if they are not working? Job dislocation is now the coming problem."

In an era of relentless cost-cutting and downsizing, the human side of enterprise has been easily neglected. Indeed, Kanter's idealism is now pragmatic. "Consulting is a way to create. It is practical and I learn. My education comes from the application of my academic knowledge on the job.

"I hope that things might happen in organizations which I have helped to create. It is highly satisfying when chief executives use words or phrases, such as 'infrastructure for collaboration', which I introduced them to, sometimes I invented them," she says. "It is a question of continually broadening the context. There is a halo affect. For some audiences what I say has a great deal of credibility. This brings with it a sense of responsibility. But, I am now doing it for myself rather than for a particular audience."

Rosabeth Moss Kanter

Men and Women of the Corporation, Basic Books, New York, 1977

The Change Masters, Allen & Unwin, London, 1984

When Giants Learn to Dance, Simon & Schuster, London, 1989

Ricardo Semler
Practicing empowerment

Every week groups of executives from leading multinationals visit a company based in the outskirts of Sao Paulo, Brazil. The location is not the attraction – a non-descript industrial complex. Nor is the company's technology exciting or its products – pumps and cooling units – the most thrilling in the world. The difference lies in the revolutionary way the company, Semco, is run.

SEMCO's REVOLUTIONARY SUCCESS

When Ricardo Semler took over Semco from his father he spent the first day firing 60 percent of the company's top management. Almost without thinking he had set in motion a revolution from which the rest of the business world is now anxious to learn.

Today, Semco is a unique success story. It has managed to buck Brazilian commercial chaos, hyperinflation and recession to increase productivity nearly sevenfold and profits fivefold.

Walking through the door, visiting executives immediately notice that there is no receptionist. Everyone at Semco is expected to meet their own visitors. There are no secretaries, nor are there any personal assistants. Managers do their own photocopying, send their own faxes and make their own coffee. Semco has no dress code so some people wear jackets and ties, others jeans.

But, the Semco revolution goes far beyond this. "A few years ago, when we wanted to relocate a factory, we closed down for a day and everyone piled into buses to inspect three possible sites," recalls Ricardo Semler. "Their choice hardly thrilled the managers, since it was next to a company that was frequently on strike. But we moved in anyway."

SEMCO's WORKPLACE DEMOCRACY

Semco takes workplace democracy to previously unimagined frontiers. Everyone at the company has access to the books; managers set their own salaries; shopfloor workers set their own productivity targets and schedules; workers make decisions once the preserve of managers; even the distribution of the profit-sharing scheme is determined by employees.

"We've taken a company that was moribund and made it thrive, chiefly by refusing to squander our greatest resource, our people," says Ricardo Semler. Semler does not regard the transformation of Semco as a lesson to be emulated by other companies. Instead, he believes it simply points to the need for companies and organizations to reinvent themselves for the 1990s. "There **are** some companies which are prepared to change the way they work. They realize that nothing can be based on what used to be, that there is a better way. But, 99 per cent of companies are not ready, caught in an industrial Jurassic Park."

The plea for businesses to become more democratic and humane is a familiar one. The trouble, Semler candidly admits, is that listening to people, accepting their decisions and inculcating people with the need for democracy is far from easy. "The era of using people as production tools is coming to an end," he argues. "Participation is infinitely more complex to practise than conventional unilateralism, but it is something which companies can no longer ignore or pay lip-service to."

There is still a substantial amount of skepticism about Semco's approach and achievement which Semler has recorded in an international bestseller entitled *Maverick!* Former BTR chairman Sir Owen Green commented after a public debate that Semler was "not maverick; he's an eccentric."

The mistake people make, says Semler, is assuming that Semco is some kind of role model. "This is just one more version of how companies can organize themselves and succeed. Democracy alone will not solve all business problems. In fact, as we constantly see, nothing prevents autocratic companies from making money."

It is little wonder that traditionalists among the management fraternity find Semler's message unpalatable. Managers are constantly appraised by Semco workers rather than a coterie of fellow executives, and they have to become used to the idea of accepting that their decisions are not sacrosanct. Semler seems to be adept at biting his tongue when decisions don't go his way and admits "there are a lot of people at

Semco whose styles I don't actually like. I wouldn't have recruited them but quite clearly they do their jobs effectively – otherwise people wouldn't support them."

As part of Semco's revolution, Semler has to a large extent become redundant. The chief executive's job rotates between five people. Diminished power is clearly not something which fills him with sadness – instead, it is confirmation that the Semco approach works. "I haven't hired or fired anyone for eight years or signed a company cheque. From an operational side I am no longer necessary, though I still draw a salary because there are many other ways of contributing to the company's success," he says. Indeed, Semler believes that what many consider the core activity of management – decision making – should not be their function at all. "It's only when bosses give up decision-making and let their employees govern themselves that the possibility exists for a business jointly managed by workers and executives. That is true participative management."

Semler's book is already a massive best-seller in South America. Interestingly, it has also found a receptive audience in Japan – so much so that Semler's advance was the largest ever paid for a business book in Japan. More than 6,500 readers have written to him to find out more. But, the sceptics remain, and Semler admits that it is too early to make cut and dried judgements about Semco's apparent revolution. "Really the work is only 30 per cent completed," he estimates. "In the long-term, success will come when the system forgets me and becomes self-perpetuating."

Ricardo Semler

Maverick!, Century, London, 1993

CAREER MANAGEMENT

When jobs were for life and the corporate apron strings were rarely abandoned, careers took care of themselves. The thought of actually managing your career never occurred to the vast majority of managers. It didn't have to for them to succeed. "The way managers manage their careers is intrinsically linked to the way organizations behave, shape themselves and regard their managers. To ignore this basic truism is to risk misunderstanding the complex nature of career management in the 1990s," say career management experts Carole Pemberton and Peter Herriot.[14]

In those halcyon days there was what ED SCHEIN of MIT has labeled a **psychological contract** – an implicit agreement between an individual and an organization about the way they should be treated and the extent of their obligations to the organization. Clearly, however implicit, if such a contract is to work it must be consistently observed by both sides.

As a corollary to the psychological contract, Schein coined the term **career anchor**, describing the perceptions individuals have about themselves and their worth and role in an organization which encourage them to stay in it. It makes clear that the aspirations, motivations and goals of individuals differ considerably.

SCHEIN's CAREER ANCHORS[15]

Technical/Functional
- exercising particular skills
- reluctant to give up expertise
- management *per se* of little interest

Managerial
- being accountable for total results
- willing to abandon technical for generalist role
- integrating the efforts of others

Autonomy/independence
- freedom from organizational restrictions
- control of how, when and what to work on

Security/stability
- geographic, financial, organizational security
- performs well in certain types of organizational only
- sees career management as the organization's responsibility

Service/dedication
- achieving something of personal value/concern
- would change organization to be able to do so
- would leave organization whose values were incompatible

Pure challenge
- the process of winning is central
- problems or opponents are there to be overcome
- search for novelty and variety

Lifestyle integration
- identity is tied to total life rather than to organization or occupation
- balance sought between home and work

Entrepreneurship
- building something new
- accepting risk.

The other highly influential model of career motivation comes from another American academic, **John Holland**. The logic behind Holland's identification of occupational interests is that at the beginning of their career, or at some time during it, people are drawn to a particular occupation because of some sort of interest in it.

Today, the very nature of this psychological contract is being questioned and reinvented. Managers are questioning why they should stay with corporations; what is in it for them in the short-term and their long-term careers? This takes a variety of forms.

HOLLAND's SIX INTEREST CATEGORIES

1. **Realistic** – a preference for activities that entail the explicit ordered or systematic manipulation of objects, tools, machines, animals; and an aversion to educational or therapeutic activities.

2. **Investigative** – a preference for activities that entail the observational, symbolic, systematic, and creative investigation of physical, biological, and cultural phenomena in order to understand and control such phenomena; and an aversion to persuasive, social, and repetitive activities.

3. **Artistic** – a preference for ambiguous, free, unsystematized activities that entail the manipulation of physical, verbal or human materials to create art forms or products; and an aversion to explicit, systematic and ordered activities.

4. **Social** – a preference for activities that entail the manipulation of others to inform, train, develop, cure or enlighten; and an aversion to explicit, ordered, systematic activities involving materials, tools or machines.

5. **Enterprising** – a preference for activities that entail the manipulation of others to attain organizational goals or economic gain; and an aversion to observational, symbolic, and systematic activities.

6. **Conventional** – a preference for activities that entail the explicit, ordered, systematic manipulation of data, such as keeping records; and an aversion to ambiguous, free, exploratory or unsystematized activities.[16]

The changing psychological contract between managers and the organization[17]

	Traditional	*Future*
Duration of tenure	long-standing	time-limited
Certainty of tenure	safer	less certain
Management development	planned by the company via promotion	opportunistic, self-determined via company changes
Motivational drivers	loyalty	enhancing future employability
Salaries	lower, incremental, predictable	higher, offset by risk, less predictable

The nature and pattern of careers has changed. "We now have the mosaic career, sometimes called the portfolio career, made up of a variety of roles performed either simultaneously by working part-time, or being both employed and self-employed, or sequentially or working on temporary assignments," says Shaun Tyson of Cranfield School of Management. "Although graduate recruitment continues and blue chip corporations still express a strong desire to find the best possible candidates to enter fast track schemes, the days when most managers could expect to spend a whole working life with one company are long since gone. Even if they are not forced to leave and find work elsewhere, the company itself may be taken over, bought out by management, merged, or go into some other type of collaborative venture."[18]

In the empowered, delayered, and hierarchy-free 1990s, career management is an increasingly personal and powerful force – and it is the individual manager who is now doing the work.

"The new pressure on the manager is to take ownership of his or her own career, to ensure that success in business and in learning is documented in a way which has transferable value to a new employment situation, and to invest time and money in personal development. In effect, managers must ensure that their personal profile of achievement holds value in the alien territory of a different corporation," says Theresa Barnett of the UK banking group, TSB.

"The hierarchy of responsibility and loyalty has changed. A few years ago, a manager's loyalty was primarily to the company. Now, loyalty is to the team first, the individual second and the company third," says Robin Linnecar, partner with KPMG Career Consulting. He believes that the company's role has been distilled down to **managing a core group of employees with key skills** (rather than managing large numbers of employees with multifarious specialist functional skills). As a result, the onus is on individual managers to ensure that their skills are the ones the organization requires. "Managers have to realize that they may not be able to move across or up the organization, but they can move forward through learning a new technique or expanding their role," says Linnecar. "The onus is now on having a broad range of experience rather than a simple and restricted functional background."

Inevitably, examining the current status of your career and your aspirations is harder than it seems. Managing the future is secondary when managing the present is so demanding. But, managers have to make the time. Even so, John Dunn, director of organization and management development at Guinness, argues that it is not simply a case of finding the time. "Objectivity is the key. We are working hard at developing and sharing objective assessments of people to aid development," he says. "This can't be done in isolation. Management is all about communicating with others and giving and receiving feedback. The challenge is that we are dealing with complex human skills and, as a consequence, achieving feedback from all sides is not easy."

Taking control of your career involves two basic skills, says psychologist Robert Sharrock. "The first skill is insight. People have to have a realistic view of their own strengths and limitations. This is something managers are often particularly poor at – they don't know what their strengths are and where they would be best used," he says. "The second element is being proactive. Managers have to actively seek out opportunities and be prepared to take personal risks. In fact, talented managers have always taken their development seriously. They know their strengths and where they would be best utilized."

Of course, coming to terms with your strengths also involves accepting gaps in your knowledge and experience. "A lot of executives are more interested in papering over the cracks rather than harnessing their capabilities," observes Robert Sharrock. "Managers aren't comfortable with failure and regard admitting to development needs as a sign of weakness."

Managers need to develop humility. Self-awareness is key to successful career management. They need to realize that they have to learn. For many this means that they have to learn how to learn. In addition, managers must become more efficient users of their networks. KPMG encourages managers to make a basic list of their network. Managers are expected to come up with over 100 names.

With managers seeking out their skills and mapping out their own careers, the cosy corporation of the past also has to find a new role. "Organizations need to commit themselves to the development of their people. Mobility will also need to be valued by the individual and the organization. For individuals it helps broaden experience and sharpen skills; from the organization's view it will enfuse new blood into the body corporate," says Robert Sharrock.

Guinness' John Dunn provides the organizational perspective: "We have to attract and retain the best people. Both sides need to share in the development of the individual so that joint decisions are made which are mutually beneficial." The trouble comes when corporate priorities and those of individual managers collide rather than coincide.

The skeptical might suggest that this is an abdication of a company's responsibility. Companies can't simply abandon managers to plough their own furrow. Effectively managing your own career and development revolves around relationships with a wide range of people – from colleagues on courses to mentors and coaches; from the manager's boss to family and friends. The key relationship, however, must be with the organization.

To some extent, despite the all-pervasive atmosphere of change, the bottom line remains the same. Organizations need to find and keep the most talented managers. And the people most likely to succeed are managers who take the initiative and develop themselves and their careers in tandem with the direction of the organization. "We may not be able to offer long-term employment, but we should try to offer long-term employability," says Sir Brian Corby, former chairman of the Prudential.[19]

CREATIVE CAREERS

Mitch McCrimmon, a consultant with PA Consulting Group, provides a list of action points for organizations adopting a more innovative approach to career management. McCrimmon says they should:

- **share employees with strategic partner organizations** (customers or suppliers) in lieu of internal moves

- **encourage independence:** employees may go elsewhere for career development, possibly to return in a few years

- **fund groups of employees to set up as suppliers outside the organization**

- **encourage employees to think of themselves as a business** and of the organization's various departments as customers

- **encourage employees to develop customers outside the organization**

- **help employees develop self-marketing, networking, and consultancy skills** to enable them to search out, recognize or create new opportunities for both themselves and the organization

- **identify skilled individuals in other organizations** who can contribute on a temporary/project basis or part-time

- **regularly expose employees to new people and new ideas to stimulate innovation**

- **balance external recruitment at all levels against internal promotion to encourage open competition,** "competitive tendering" for jobs to discourage seeing positions as someone's territory – which causes self-protective conformity

- **foster more cross-functional team work for self-development**

- **eliminate the culture of valuing positions as career goals** in favor of portraying a career as a succession of bigger projects, achievements, and new skills learned. The concept of "position" is part of the outdated static concept of the organization. Positions are out. Processes and projects are in.

- **abandon top-down performance appraisal** in favor of self-appraisal based on internal customer satisfaction surveys and assessing people as you would suppliers

- **replace top-down assessment processes with self-assessment techniques** and measure performance in terms of results.[20]

Career management

BECK, N, *Shifting Gears: Thriving in the New Economy*, HarperCollins, Toronto, 1992

BRIDGES, W, *Jobshift*, Nicholas Brealey, London, 1995

TOFFLER, A, *The Third Wave*, Bantam, New York, 1984

ZUBOFF, S, *In the Age of the Smart Machine*, Basic Books, New York, 1988

TEAMWORKING

Teamworking is not a skill traditionally associated with managers. Indeed, the assumption has usually been that teamworking is the preserve of the factory floor rather than the office. In the 1990s, however, teamworking has become highly fashionable.

It is a side effect of the increasing concentration on working across functional divides and fits neatly with the trend towards empowerment. A project team may draw in people from throughout the organization to achieve the best results. Instead of passing reports and paperwork from one department to another, teams provide a dynamic meeting place where ideas can be shared and expertise more carefully targeted on important business issues.

THE GROWTH IN TEAMWORKING

That teamworking is growing cannot be doubted. A survey by the Industrial Society of 500 personnel managers found that 40 percent worked in organizations with self-managed teams. The average team in this survey had around eight people and the main reasons cited for their use were improved customer service, increased staff motivation, and quality of output.[21]

Despite the extensive literature about teams and teamworking the basic dynamics of teamworking often remain clouded and uncertain. What is a team? Is a team simply a fancy word for a group of people? What is the difference between a team and a task force? What is the difference between a team and a committee? Is a team simply a group of people with different skills aiming for the same goal?

THE TEAM EFFORT

Teams occur when a number of people have a common goal and recognize that their personal success is dependent on the success of others. They are all interdependent. In practice, this means that in most teams people will contribute individual skills many of which will be different. It also means that the full tensions and counterbalance of human behavior will need to be demonstrated in the team.

It is not enough to have a ragbag collection of individual skills. The various behaviors of the team members must mesh together in order to achieve objectives. For people to work successfully in teams, you need people to behave in certain ways. You need some people to concentrate on the task at hand (**doers**). You need some people to provide specialist knowledge (**knowers**) and some to solve problems as they arise (**solvers**). You need some people to make sure that it is going as well as it can and that the whole team is contributing fully (**checkers**). And you need some people to make sure that the team is operating as a cohesive social unit (**carers**).

TEAMWORKING: WHO's WHO?[22]

Solver

Role: helps the team to solve problems by coming up with ideas or finding resources from outside the team. Can see another way forward.

Characterized by: innovation, ideas generation, imagination, unorthodox, good networking skills, negotiates for resources.

Doer

Role: concentrates on the task, getting it started, keeping it going, getting it done or making sure it is finished. Some may focus on only one aspect of the task. Making sure it is finished is the most rare.

Characterized by: high energy, high motivation, pushing others into action, assertiveness, practical, self-control, discipline, systematic approach, attention to detail, follow through.

Checker

Role: concern for the whole process, tries to ensure full participation while providing a balanced view of quality, time, and realism.

Characterized by: prudence, reflection, critical thinking, shrewd judgements, causing others to work toward shared goals, use of individual talents.

Carer

Role: concern for the individuals in the team and how they are developing and getting along.

Characterized by: supportive, sociable, concerned about others, democratic, flexibility.

Knower

Role: provider of specialist knowledge or experience

Characterized by: dedication, standards, focus.

Modern management thinking suggests that organizations need a balance of behaviors for any change management activity – they may have to slightly unbalance the team in favor of the type of change they are trying to undertake.

It is also worth noting that for all the research into effective team-working, teams remain a law unto themselves. Managers who sit down and play at human engineering by trying to select exactly the right sort of combination usually end up in a state of confusion. Effective teams often come about spontaneously or include an unusual combination of specialists. The key to success does not appear to lie in the selection of team members – you only have to look briefly at team sports to find examples of talented individuals working poorly as a team. Instead, success is often characterized by the genuine granting of power and responsibility to teams so they can solve their own problems.

References

1 SIEFF, LORD, *On Management: Marks & Spencer Way*, Weidenfeld & Nicolson, London, 1990.
2 HERZBERG, F, *Work and the Nature of Man*, World Publishing, 1966.
3 "Take me to your leader," *Economist*, December 25-Jan. 7, 1994.
4 "Tom Peters, performance artist," *Economist*, Sept. 24, 1994.
5 PETERS, T, "Foreword" to Bennis, W, *An Invented Life*, Addison-Wesley, Reading, MA, 1993.
6 HELLER, R, "In pursuit of paragons," *Management Today*, May 1994

7 Quoted in Griffith, V, "Blue-collar team, white-collar wise," *Financial Times*, 11 May 1994.
8 *Career Development in Flatter Structures*, Roffey Park, Horsham, 1995.
9 "Human planning seeks boardroom recognition," *Financial Times*, October 14, 1993.
10 GRIFFITH, V, "Blue-collar team, white-collar wise," *Financial Times*, May 11, 1994.
11 MILLS, DQ, and FRIESEN, B, "Empowerment" in *Financial Times Handbook of Management*, FT/Pitman, London, 1995.
12 Interview with Stuart Crainer, April 20, 1994.
13 "Moss Kanter, corporate sociologist," *Economist*, Oct. 15, 1994
14 PEMBERTON, C and HERRIOT, P, "Career management," *Financial Times Handbook of Management*, FT/Pitman, London, 1995.
15 SCHEIN, EH, *Career Anchors: Discovering Your Real Values*, Pfeiffer, San Diego, 1990.
16 HOLLAND, JL, *Making Vocational Choices* (2nd edition), Prentice-Hall, Englewood Cliffs, NJ, 1985.
17 SHARROCK, R, "Developing top managers," *Financial Times Handbook of Management*, FT/Pitman, London, 1995.
18 TYSON, S, *Financial Times Handbook of Management*, FT/Pitman, London, 1995.
19 Quoted in Houlder, V, "Shift in loyalties," *Financial Times*, July 26, 1995.
20 McCrimmon, M, "Goodbye to careers?", *Human Resources*, Spring 1994.
21 *Self-Managed Teams*, Industrial Society, London, 1995.
22 Obeng, EDA, *All change!*, FT/Pitman, London, 1994.

The quality revolution

"Good management techniques are enduring. Quality control, for instance, was treated as a fad here, but it's been part of the Japanese business philosophy for decades. That's why they laugh at us."
PETER SENGE[1]

"Total Quality is a world movement. Regardless of country or industry, the laggards are at risk; conversely, the leaders acquire insulation against failure."
RICHARD SCHONBERGER[2]

THE DISCOVERY OF QUALITY

Following the Second World War Japan's industry was devastated. Not only was its industry in tatters, but the goods it produced were known for their indifferent quality. Indeed, this stereotype proved a lingering legacy – in the 1950s and 1960s Japanese cars were virtually impossible to sell in the United States or Europe.

Yet, within two decades Japan was the world's leading industrial power-house, renowned for the quality of its products and the long-sighted nature of its management. Japanese cars became the industry leaders, renowned for their quality and reliability. No one now laughs at a Mitsubishi or a Toyota. The turnaround was as dramatic as it was unexpected.

Ironically for the West, Japan's resurgence owed a great deal to Western thinking. In fact, the Japanese have repeatedly proved themselves masters at magpie-like taking of the best of Western ideas and reinterpreting them to fit their own culture and circumstances.

For example, the Japanese businessman Konosuke Matsushita – the founder of one of the world's largest electronics groups – was greatly influenced by the work of Henry Ford. His interpretation of Ford's work, however, marks one of the seminal differences between Western and Japanese management during the twentieth century.

The logic is simple – one company's success is reliant on the support of others; if there is an effective partnership all sides win and society benefits from the prosperity generated.

From Ford, Matsushita was inspired by the prospect of mass production and also took on board Ford's passion for using price reductions to generate more sales. Matsushita took as his creed the very Ford-like objective of producing "an inexhaustible supply of goods." But, to this he added "thus creating peace and prosperity throughout the land." The conjunction between these two inspirations is something managers in the West have little understanding of. Ford was obsessed with production and forgot the broader view (though he did take a brief stab at achieving world peace). Matsushita looked to the future and beyond the confines of the factory or the marketplace. He saw the company as having a role in society.

This broader view is manifested in many ways. Employees are important – not mere functionaries ensuring a steady stream of products are produced. And, so too, are customers and suppliers. Matsushita was visiting the factories of his suppliers in the 1930s and giving them advice on how to produce their products more effectively. The logic is simple – one company's success is reliant on the support of others; if there is an effective partnership all sides win and society benefits from the prosperity generated. In the 1990s such approaches are only now being contemplated in many Western organizations.

W Edwards Deming and Joseph Juran
The quality gospel

Matsushita was not alone. Other Japanese managers and their organizations seized the initiative. They were guided in the decades after the war by two Americans, W EDWARDS DEMING (1900–93) and JOSEPH JURAN (born 1904).

W EDWARDS DEMING

Having earned a doctorate in mathematical physics in 1928 Deming, in the depressed America of the thirties, became interested in the pioneering work of Walter A Shewhart who was seeking to apply statistical methods to the control of variation in industrial production. With the impetus of World War Two, Deming and Shewhart's innovative systems were introduced to American manufacturing in 1942. They resulted in marked improvements to performance in the organizations where they were instituted. However, following the Allied victory in 1945, American industry, which was suddenly enjoying booming markets, reverted to procedures based around product inspection.

The failure of American corporations to listen to Deming and Juran has often been commented on. In retrospect it appears to be one of the century's most profound errors. At the time, however, it was understandable. In terms of quality, American products were as good as European ones and far better than those produced in Japan. The American preoccupation was on lowering prices and the vehicle for achieving this was generally recognized to be lowering labor costs.

Making things to a specific design and then inspecting them for defects was something the Egyptians had mastered 5,000 years previously when building the pyramids.

In a 1993 *Harvard Business Review* article, Juran also made much of the fact that his Japanese audiences in the early 1950s were the chief executives of major corporations, whereas his North American listeners were primarily engineers and quality inspectors. Juran's message was not, he admitted, new or revolutionary. Making things to a specific design and then inspecting them for defects was something the Egyptians had mastered 5,000 years previously when building the pyramids. The American engineers weren't ready for history lessons.

JOSEPH JURAN

Juran's influential Quality Control Handbook was published in 1951 and his work in Japan got underway in 1953. More original was Juran's insistence that measurement and testing need not simply be restricted to production. This idea had been originally inspired by Juran's own analysis in the mid-1920s of the large number of tiny circuit breakers routinely scrapped by his then employer Western Electric. By scrutinizing the manufacturing process rather than simply waiting at the end of a production line to count the defective products, Juran solved the problem and worked out how the company could substantially reduce the level of waste. His diagnosis was not, however, translated into practice – it was decided that quality was not Juran's problem. This proved Juran's point.

Juran developed a concept called **Company-Wide Quality Management** (CWQM) – the first of many quality-inspired acronyms. His aim was to create a systematic means of disseminating quality throughout an organization. Though his approach sounds dry, it was more humane than Deming's. Indeed, Juran's insistence on the responsibility of each and every employee for quality was a precursor of today's fashion for empowerment.

Deming was similarly well received in Japan and, in 1950, he told Japanese business people: "Don't just make it and try to sell it, but redesign it, and then again bring the process under control ... with ever-increasing quality ... The consumer is the most important part of the production line." In 1951, the first award ceremony for the now prestigious Deming Prize was held.

The timing of Juran and Deming was impeccable. But, it was not only a question of arriving at a time when the Japanese were striving to rebuild their economy. Their ideas struck a chord in the East. Their emphasis on groups rather than individuals was attractive to the Japanese, while it simply failed to ignite a spark in the United States. The Western preoccupation with individual achievement meant that sublimating individual aspirations to group consciousness was a quantum leap rather than a logical progression.

Culture is key to understanding and implementing the lessons preached by both Deming and Juran. Deming appreciated that no matter how powerful the tool of mathematical statistics might be it would be ineffective unless used in the correct cultural context. This combination of culture and measurement eventually evolved into what is now labeled **Total Quality Management.**

Commenting on Deming's work management writer Robert Heller observed: "His work bridges the gap between science-based application and humanistic philosophy. Statistical quality control is as arid as it sounds. But results so spectacular as to be almost romantic flow from using these tools to improve processes in ways that minimize defects and eliminate the deadly trio of rejects, rework and recalls."[3]

The arid world of statistics is the coping stone of Deming's approach (and led to criticism from Juran). Every business generates overwhelming masses of numbers. But, data is not information. Deming sought a means of providing a continuous supply of the data which drives decisions. Generating the right statistics and interpreting and acting on them were crucial elements in his philosophy. Unfortunately, this has in many cases generated a bureaucracy of quality which concentrates on measurement above all else. Deming's philosophy was distilled into fourteen points.

DEMING's FOURTEEN POINTS

1. Create constancy of purpose toward improvement of product and service, with the aim to become competitive and to stay in business, and to provide jobs.

2. Adopt the new philosophy. We are in a new economic age, created by Japan. Transformation of Western management style is necessary to halt the continued decline of industry.

3. Cease dependence on inspection to achieve quality. Eliminate the need for inspection on a mass basis by building quality into the product in the first place.

4. End the practice of awarding business on the basis of price tag. Purchasing must be combined with design of product, manufacturing, and sales to work with the chosen suppliers: the aim is to minimize total cost, not merely initial cost.

5. Improve constantly and forever every activity in the company, to improve quality and productivity and thus constantly decrease costs.

6. Institute training and education on the job, including management.

7. Institute supervision. The aim of supervision should be to help people and machines to do a better job.

8. Drive out fear, so that everyone may work effectively for the company.

9. Break down barriers between departments. People in research, design, sales and production must work as a team to tackle usage and production problems that may be encountered with the product or service.

10. Eliminate slogans, exhortations, and targets for the workforce asking for zero defects and new levels of productivity. Such exhortations only create adversarial relationships; the bulk of the causes of low quality and low productivity belong to the system and thus lie beyond the power of the workforce.

11. Eliminate work standards that prescribe numerical quotas for the day. Substitute aids and helpful supervision, using the methods to be described.

12a. Remove the barriers that rob the hourly worker of the right to pride of workmanship. The responsibility of supervisors must be changed from sheer numbers to quality.

12b. Remove the barriers that rob people in management and in engineering of their right to pride of workmanship. This means, *inter alia*, abolition of the annual or merit rating and of management by objective.

13. Institute a vigorous program of education and retraining. New skills are required for changes in techniques, materials and service.

14. Put everybody in the company to work in teams to accomplish the transformation.

While distilling his ideas down to the "fourteen points," Deming insisted that effective implementation could only be achieved by a full understanding of the underlying theory. "Experience, without theory, teaches management nothing about what to do to improve quality and competitive position," he argued.

In practice, many organizations have claimed to have taken on Deming's philosophy. Often, however, their attempts at implementation come to an abrupt halt because of basic misinterpretations. The "fourteen points" should not be interpreted as tablets of stone, but require subtle interpretations. Quality is not, according to Deming, a matter of setting a standard of how many defects are acceptable. A manager once told Deming: "I need to know the minimum level of quality necessary to satisfy a customer." Deming commented: "So much misunderstanding was conveyed in a few words."

Also, Deming's philosophy revolves around fundamental changes in the way businesses deal with figures and statistics. Instead of setting aspirational profit targets, Deming argues the emphasis should be on providing quality products and services for customers. By working at constantly improving all processes within a business, customer satisfaction will increase and, inevitably, so too will profits.

Deming continued preaching his message until shortly before his death in 1993. Companies such as Ford, Rothmans, and Bosch are among those which have adopted his philosophy. A prophet without honor in his own country for so long, Deming's last years were spent traveling the world. "I'm desperate. There's not enough time left," he is reported to have told a colleague. "For companies that haven't fully adopted the ideas and practices that Deming, as much as any man, made universal, those last five words will be their epitaph, not his," concluded Robert Heller.

W Edwards Deming

Aquayo, R, *Dr Deming: The Man Who Taught the Japanese About Quality*, Mercury, London, 1990

Deming, WE, *Quality, Productivity and Competitive Position*, MIT Centre for Advanced Engineering Study, MIT, Boston, MA, 1982

Deming, WE, *Out of the Crisis*, Cambridge University Press, Cambridge, 1988

Price, F, *Right Every Time*, Gower, Aldershot, 1990

Quality for the masses

It is staggering that Deming and Juran remained largely ignored in the West until as late as the 1980s, and then it took a TV program to bring their ideas and experiences to a wider Western audience. The television documentary, "If Japan can, why can't we?" examined the rapidly increasing performance of Japanese companies and the role of the quality gurus in making it happen.

Propelled into the consciousness of the world's managers, Deming and Juran's messages are now corporate truisms. Organizations routinely accept that inspection is not the route to improved quality; that functions should work together rather than in competition; and that improved processes and systems are more effective than exhortations.

The basics have become part of the every day life of management. But, that does not mean that quality is universally practised or has proved to be a universal panacea for corporate ills. Indeed, the very basic nature of quality leads to a host of misinterpretations and bastardized versions.

"One of the criticisms levelled at Total Quality (TQ) is that it is merely a veneer covering what everyone recognizes as good management and commonsense. Although this criticism has some foundation, it is overly simplistic. A brief spell of managerial experience quickly reveals that not everyone – if anyone – agrees about what actually constitutes good management or commonsense," says KPMG quality consultant, Owen Bull. "TQ can be seen as a complex blend of many different components and techniques. But, it can also be viewed as the way you would run an organization if you started from scratch on a new site and used your own money. This description seems to appeal to people because it brings a real challenge home very sharply – given the right conditions and with all to play for and everything to lose, isn't TQ the way you would run your own business?"

Quality is not revolutionary. In fact, it is anything but revolutionary. Quintessentially it is simple – "Quality is free" argues Philip Crosby, one of the host of gurus who emerged in the wake of Deming and Juran providing their own insight into how to achieve quality; "Quality is a way of life," says Philips chief, Jan Timmer. The aphorisms are platitudinous. But, they are true.

The failure of practice

After the euphoria of the 1980s when quality was *discovered*, there has been a return to the disappointment of reality. Quality has failed to revolutionize the business world though it has revolutionized many individual businesses. Many organizations across the world have brought in external experts to launch their own version of quality management. But, too often, quality initiatives have bitten the corporate dust or reaped isolated or negligible rewards. Juran now estimates that fewer than 50 of the top 500 US companies have "attained world class quality," a meagre reward for so much investment.[4]

Commonly, quality initiatives lead to a single division or function recording a significant quality improvement. Rarely is this experienced throughout an organization. Similarly, the ideal of continuous improvement has proved to be fatally flawed. Indeed, the service economy and those service elements of industry which now dominate product costs have failed to respond to continuous improvement initiatives, evidenced by a reduction in pre-tax profits of 50 percent over the last ten years.

Juran, still preaching his quality gospel, is dismissive of the attempts by the West to take on his quality philosophy. He believes there are a number of reasons for this failure. First, Juran argues that senior managers have often failed to fully understand what achieving quality involves. Instead of being regarded as important in itself, it was seen by many US corporations as a way of competing with imported products. If you can't beat them; copy them.

Juran's chief gripe is that quality is simply not regarded as important enough. Chief executives, as a result, fail to give personal leadership to quality initiatives and do not realize that you need "to manage and measure quality as seriously as one would for profitability."

> **Juran now estimates that fewer than 50 of the top 500 US companies have "attained world class quality," a meagre reward for so much investment.**

In other respects the response has been half-hearted: benchmarking, for example, often sets unattainable goals or is calculated on financial measures. Reward systems fail to be related to quality and people are trained indiscriminately or inconsistently. While the importance of quality is widely accepted, Juran laments that its implementation remains as imprecise and unfocussed as ever.[5]

There are, of course, a myriad of books and manifestos which promise instant quality. Most are worthless. Perhaps the most realistic and practical insight comes from pan-European research by consultant George Binney.[6] He identifies four key characteristics among companies which have gained some measure of success in becoming quality organizations.

BINNEY's FOUR CHARACTERISTICS OF SUCCESSFUL QUALITY ORGANIZATIONS

1. Forthright, listening leadership

Charismatic leadership, contrary to popular belief, is not one of the features of successful companies. Instead the common factor is leadership which is both forthright and listening. It is very assertive about standards and objectives, making clear that quality is non-negotiable and that customer service is genuinely and consistently the number one priority. At the same time the leadership not only encourages

▶

employees to give their views about how to improve quality, it actively listens to those views, acts on them, and draws on the knowledge and experience of staff at all levels.

2. Provoking, not imposing change

The successful companies involve people at all levels at a very early stage in their quality initiatives. This real involvement ensures that those participating have a strong sense of ownership of the new ways of working. Some senior managers resist the temptation to impose ready-made solutions drawn from their previous experience, investing time instead in helping their staff to find their own solution. A clear and compelling vision is created and managers make every effort to ensure that their own behavior and decisions reinforce the vision.

3. Integrating quality into the fabric of the business

Continuous improvement is part of the way the business is run. In these companies quality is the responsibility of everyone, not of a special department or team. Structures and processes support the drive for quality, they do not cut across it. Measurement systems use indicators that matter to customers. Appraisal procedures emphasize customer satisfaction and development of self and of staff in addition to financial results. The selection criteria for recruitment stress attitudes to quality.

4. Learning by doing

In the successful companies time and space are allowed – and respected – for learning and experimentation. There is an emphasis on action and results and on appreciation of the need for regular reviews in order to learn how to improve, Feedback is encouraged; people are able to try out new ideas without fear of pointless retribution or blame if things go wrong.

With the importance of quality now – almost – universally accepted, the debate has moved on. The emphasis is increasingly on involving the customer in the organization. Indeed, for all their eulogizing, Juran and Deming have a tendency to overlook the role of the customer. The most notable and persuasive champion of **customer service** is Tom Peters. Others are now following suit, describing ways in which organizations can become customer friendly. In *The Only Thing That Matters*,[7] for example, American consultant Karl Albrecht argues that quality can only work if customers are brought into the centre of the business. He describes what he calls "fifth dimension organizations," ones which have made service into an art form. They have moved beyond the stage of making a serious effort to improve quality. Their closeness to their customers has made them peak performers.

FOCUS ON THE CUSTOMER

Albrecht believes "fifth dimension organizations' have seven key characteristics:

- leadership which is mentally and behaviorally flexible
- an understanding of and special insight into the needs of their customers
- the ability to redefine the playing field and deliver in ways that separate them from the competition
- commitment to changing themselves in directions that are consistent with evolving customer needs and expectations
- they recognize that human energy is the greatest untapped resource in an organization and that participation from customers, owners and employees is critical
- a caring and sharing culture
- a drive to be the best and a commitment to continuous improvement in all aspects of their organization

The quality revolution

CROSBY, P, *Quality is Free*, McGraw Hill, New York, 1979

FEIGENBAUM, A V, *Total Quality Control*, McGraw Hill, New York, 1983

JURAN, J, *Managerial Breakthrough*, McGraw Hill, New York, 1964

JURAN, J, *Juran on Planning for Quality*, The Free Press, New York, 1988

SCHONBERGER, R, *Building a Chain of Customers*, The Free Press, New York, 1990

REENGINEERING

Twenty years ago, corporate crystal ball gazers predicted an age of leisure. The days of working nine-to-five would, at some time in the not so distant future, be consigned to history. Our lives would be miraculously transformed by technology. At the time, the imagined machines appeared to belong to the world of science fiction. We knew computers existed, but their impact on our lives was minimal, often nonexistent. Computers filled rooms rather than laps.

In fact, the leisure age has not yet dawned. People continue to organize their working lives in much the same way as 20 years ago. But the technological miracle has taken place – and continues at breakneck speed.

The paradox is an apparently simple one. Technology has revolutionized our lives and opened up huge new vistas of untapped human potential. At the same time, the way we work and, more vitally, the way modern corporations are organized have failed to keep pace.

This is not a unique phenomenon. A close parallel can be seen in the way product innovation always precedes process innovation. In the case of the organization of the 1990s, high-tech products are there in abundance. Processes, however, are only gradually being evolved as the business world makes tentative steps forward to end the debilitating paradox.

> "We tend to meet any new situation by re-organizing; and a wonderful method it can be for creating the illusion of progress while producing confusion, ineffectiveness and demoralization."
> GAIUS PETRONIUS

Appearances are deceptive. On the surface companies often appear to be highly proactive. Since the leisure age dream, there have been many changes in the way companies organize their activities and personnel. They are continually refining themselves, introducing subtle variations and adaptations. But, in virtually every case, they are tinkering with an accepted and well-established formula. Change is closed – incremental and evolutionary, rather than dramatic and revolutionary. Change, conventional wisdom dictates, comes in steps rather than quantum leaps.

Organizations cannot really be criticized for their relentless urge to subtly re-structure the way they operate. They are creatures of consensus and, anyway, would quickly point to their financial results as the ultimate arbiter of whether constant reorganization has been successful or not.

An alternative insight can be gleaned from an unlikely source. Writing at a time of rapid change in the Roman Empire, Gaius Petronius succinctly captured the frustration that reorganization brings in its wake: "We trained hard to meet our challenges but it seemed as if every time we were beginning to form into teams we would be re-organized. I was to learn later in life that we tend to meet any new situation by re-organizing; and a wonderful method it can be for creating the illusion of progress while producing confusion, ineffectiveness and demoralization."

While companies have wrestled with various organizational models, they have also recognized the fundamental need to take part and drive forward the technological revolution. Companies don't shirk from making massive investments in IT and other new technologies. They realize that future success depends on technological competence and excellence and recognize that corporate failure can often be attributed to two factors: failure to learn and adapt as rapidly as competitors and/or failure to come to terms with technological innovation.

Technology has often disappointed. But it is not only technology which has provided disappointing returns on investment for the business world. Other initiatives have also singularly failed to transform organizations into leaner, fitter and more efficient bodies. In many companies, the most obvious by-product of increased use of technology has been a strident management commitment to quality. As with investment in IT, the intention cannot be criticized. The equation that more efficient and accurate technology enables companies to achieve higher and more consistent quality levels is clear.

Fundamental problems clearly remain. Organizations appear unable to translate technology into coherent strategy and best practice or to convert quality from an attractive theory into consistent implementation across all their activities. Attempting to buy simple products and services quickly reveals the inadequacies which have survived the quality revolution and various management fads and fashions. A high-tech factory can produce cars more efficiently and more quickly than ever before – yet you can wait a few months for the specific model you require to be delivered. Make a claim to your insurance company and you may well spend three months waiting for the cheque; try to take out a mortgage and the building society can take 28 days to process the paperwork.

The deficiencies in service quality and speed are self-evident in many businesses we come across. It is not only external customers who suffer. Internally, organizations remain prone to functional fiefdoms and silos. Divisions, functions and departments often fail to communicate or blithely continue to exist in their own self-created worlds. Here, too, we would have expected technology to have worked to create more effective organizations. Technology should – and can – bring people closer together.

What is reengineering?

In the 1990s, reengineering has emerged as the latest in the long line of organizational saviours. The interest in reengineering reflects a growing realization that although the continuous improvements of total quality programs are critical, they are not enough to deliver productivity gains from massive investment in IT. To do so calls for periodic and radical changes in key business processes and the way business is organized. This fundamentally perturbs any quality system and runs counter to the philosophy of quality management which seeks and is centered on continuous improvement.

"It is not products, but the processes that create products that bring companies long-term success. Good products don't make winners; winners make good products," contend the reengineering gurus, James Champy and Michael Hammer.[8]

Reengineering is about stripping away what a company does, analyzing the core processes which make up its business and then reassembling them more efficiently in a way which is free of functional divides and needless bottlenecks. Reengineering returns organizations to first principles.

A common image associated with reengineering is that it takes a blank piece of paper and starts again. "Business reengineering isn't about fixing anything. Business reengineering means starting all over, starting from scratch," argue Champy and Hammer in their book *Reengineering the Corporation*.[9] The duo have proved to be masters of

> **"It is not products, but the processes that create products that bring companies long-term success. Good products don't make winners; winners make good products."**
> JAMES CHAMPY & MICHAEL HAMMER

hyperbole. Modesty is not on the agenda – "When people ask me what I do for a living, I tell them that what I really do is I'm reversing the Industrial Revolution," Hammer engagingly reveals.

In reality, the process of reengineering has to be a great deal more pragmatic and flexible. There is unlikely to be a corporate call of "Eureka!" There are no blank pieces of paper. But, even so, if it is to work reengineering involves revolution. It finds out what is getting in the way of the whole organization and attempts to remove the blockage. Reengineering asks basic questions and seeks to re-create organizations designed around the needs of customers, owners, employees, suppliers, and regulators. These are the core constituencies of any business. None can be overlooked if reengineering is to be achieved or even contemplated.

Reengineering treats nothing as sacred and any process, resource or idea that stands in the way of satisfying the customer is eliminated. Old job titles are dispensed with; organizational arrangements and structures are not merely tinkered with, but radically realigned; the methods of mass production, revered and habitual procedures are rigorously scrutinized and abandoned.

> **The methods of mass production, revered and habitual procedures are rigorously scrutinized and abandoned.**

At this point the manager in the real world of pragmatism and compromise is likely to shake his or her head. How can modern, highly complex organizations start again as if the past never happened?

The managers are right to be skeptical. Instead of accepting certain tasks as inevitable, reengineering requires managers to ask why they are doing a particular task so they can dispense with work that does not contribute to goals, or simply does not need to be done.

The fuel behind reengineering is not simply the need to fulfil technology's potential. It is also driven by international competition and the relentless quest for increased quality at lower cost. The demand for reengineering or, indeed, any solution to the problem at the foundations of business, is substantial.

Reengineering in practice

The trouble is that though many corporations have embraced the concept of reengineering few have succeeded in making it work and a large number appear not to have fully understood its meaning or intent. Reengineering guru, James Champy, estimates that 50 percent of large US companies now claim to be reengineering, but only five to ten percent are doing it properly or with sufficient vigor to reap long-term benefits across their organization.[10] Managers and organizations are not natural revolutionaries.

Reaping the benefits

Even so, as the reengineering bandwagon has gained momentum some companies have claimed substantial benefits from their reengineering initiatives. IBM estimates that it has saved £1.8 million a year through reengineering – this has been achieved mainly through automation. Gateway Foodmarkets in the US piloted a more efficient and focussed merchandising process in six of its stores and increased sales by 50 percent and the margin on sales by 30 percent.[11] One insurance company claimed impressive results within two years of implementing a reengineering program – administration costs went down by 40 percent; staff turnover was reduced by 58 percent; productivity increased by 100 percent; claims handling time went down from 28 to four days; and customer call-backs fell by 80 percent.[12]

GTE, the US's largest local telecommunications company, claims that its reengineering program will cut its customer service centers from 171 to 11; revenue collection centers from five to one; and regional centers from 19 to one. These changes will involve the loss of 17,000 jobs over three years and an investment of $680 million to upgrade customer service, administrative systems and software; $410 million for

> **"My objective is to change fundamentally the way we run the company. We need to create discontinuous change; incremental changes will not get us to our vision."**
> **PAUL ALLAIRE**

"employee separation" costs and $160 million to consolidate facilities. GTE estimates the potential annual cost savings to be $1 billion.[13]

The activities of Xerox, one of the world leaders in reengineering, illustrate its broad ranging nature and the size of the investment – and the risks – involved. "My objective is to change fundamentally the way we run the company. We need to create discontinuous change; incremental changes will not get us to our vision," Paul Allaire, chairman and chief executive of Xerox Corporation, has stated.[14]

At Xerox, Allaire has been a prime mover in an attempt to achieve truly revolutionary change. His aims are to increase productivity, lower the company's cost base, be more responsive to customers and improve financial results. This is the managerial equivalent of squaring the circle. To do so requires a sizeable investment – in late 1993 Xerox announced a plan to shed ten percent of its workforce, 10,000 people, over the following two to three years and set aside $700 million to cover the restructuring. Explaining the restructuring in the company's document processing division, Allaire said it was "not a function of any change in the current business environment, but rather it accelerates numerous productivity initiatives that have been under careful consideration for some time."[15] The change is proactive and attempts to integrate a large number of performance improvement initiatives.

Reengineering takes on the sacred cows of an organization *en masse*. Xerox's change program covers four main areas:

- the group's organizational structure
- people and skills
- informal networks, behavior and culture
- redesign of work processes.

In the UK, Rank Xerox which has been the champion of reengineering within Xerox worldwide is aiming to cut around $200 million from its annual overheads. "We need dramatic improvements in performance which will be achieved through reengineering of our business processes," says Rank Xerox managing director, Bernard Fournier. Two teams have been appointed to calculate the value added by every activity in the company and place it within seven "basic processes."[16]

While reengineering first came to prominence in the United States, European companies like Rank Xerox are fast coming to terms with the concept. The Swedish food cooperative ICA Handlarnas linked all of its 3,359 retail stores to a single mainframe database. As a result, it has been able to close a third of its warehouses and distribution centers and has halved its overall costs. Its wholesaling workforce has been cut by 30 percent over three years even though revenue grew by more than 15 percent during the same period.[17]

As James Champy has observed, only a handful of companies seem to have fully understood the full potential of reengineering. All too often reengineering is equated with and inextricably linked to cost reduction. In contrast, full understanding of reengineering goes far beyond financial parameters – it allows the organization to assess its ability to meet its primary business goals.

Obstacles to reengineering

TWO PITFALLS

In practice, though awareness of the need to change apparently remains high, practical implementation of reengineering concepts has been held back by two central pitfalls:

- the human implications are often ignored, overlooked or underestimated

- the revolution does not affect the attitudes and behavior of managers. This, in turn, exacerbates problems caused by underestimating the human implications of the reengineering process.

Reengineering involves more than analyzing processes and restructuring organizations. Many reengineering programs find the changing of culture and people too demanding a challenge. Instead, only processes and systems are changed. It is, after all, easier to redesign procedures and invest in technology which breaks down functional barriers, than to begin to change people's attitudes, beliefs, and values. Reengineering, like any program of change, must involve and alter the perceptions and behavior of people.

The key difference between reengineering and other change programs is that in reengineering change often appears to be illogical. By its very nature, proactive change is harder to rationalize and communicate than reactive change where you can point to specific events which have already occurred and are having a clear effect on the business. Indeed, initial responses to reengineering are emotional – anger, fear, insecurity – though, over time, they may become accepted as logical.

The initial concentration of reengineering programs has been on tackling the "hard" issues – such as processes and systems. The "soft" issues – people, skills, behavior, culture, and values – are at least as critical, often more so, but have tended to be relegated in importance. Indeed, reengineering is often preceded by the words "business process" to suggest that processes are the beginning and end of the program. They are, it is increasingly apparent, only part of the battle.

> **Reengineering does, by its very nature, involve cultural change. It emphasizes how organizations are as well as what they do.**

At the centre of this discussion is the common belief that a changed organizational structure or more radical reorganization naturally leads to a change in corporate culture. Though this may be the case, changing organizational cultures is a lengthy, time-consuming and delicate process. Reengineering does, by its very nature, involve cultural change. It emphasizes how organizations **are** as well as what they **do**.

It is unlikely that successful cultural change can be made in a wholesale way. The past is not easily dismissed – nor should organizations want to totally dispense with some of the more positive and established ways of thinking and working. Marrying the old and new cultures is a formidable balancing act.

Having analyzed processes and removed repetitious or needless activities, organizations have a clear view of the processes necessary to satisfy their core stakeholders. But, by its very definition, this requires flexible and variable inputs from people.

It is here that the second basic flaw in the practice of reengineering has emerged. Managers are loath to reengineer their own activities. Too often they espouse revolution and practice conservatism. "The practice of management has largely escaped demolition. If their jobs and styles are left largely intact, managers will eventually undermine the very structure of their rebuilt enterprises," James Champy observed in an article entitled "Time to re-engineer the manager." He went on to observe that "the work of managers in a reengineered organization must change as much as the work of workers.[18]

MAKING REENGINEERING DELIVER

Given this it is little wonder that there are few examples of comprehensive reengineering programs which have actually delivered what they promised. "The failure rate is probably as high as 65 to 70 percent," says Brett Walsh of Hay Management Consultants. "The trouble is that reengineering is now an abused term. Companies often don't know whether they are simply trying to improve a number of processes or take a quantum leap with the whole business." Success, according to Brett Walsh, demands a number of factors:

- clear business direction and vision
- top management commitment and involvement
- a clear planning and implementation process
- recognition that structural changes will bring changes in people's roles
- changes in HR processes to meet the needs of the new organization.

In reality, making reengineering happen involves a complex combination of skills. For example, process owners, to use the language of reengineering, have to be able to manage the boundaries between different processes (which are deeply rooted in vagueness); understand who are the stakeholders in the process; and help establish and monitor appropriate process performance measurements. They also need to be able to operate confidently up, down and across the organization's structure. This ability, to manage chameleon-like across the organization, is especially important during the early stages of reengineering when many of the functional vestiges of old processes remain in place.

In the majority of process-based companies, managers are required to refine and improve their business processes on an on-going basis. They need to be able to use the tools of process simplification and redesign, which include benchmarking, process mapping tools (such as systems dynamics, flowcharting, and activity diagrams) and require understanding of the potential business benefits of IT applications.

Managers who fail to develop such skills – and organizations which fail to develop their managers – are likely to be stepping from the unknown into nowhere when they begin reengineering. Those that understand and recognize their current recipe, and develop appropriate skills, are liable to make a leap forward.

Reengineering

Hardaker, M, *Total Competitiveness*, McGraw Hill, Maidenhead, 1995

McHugh, P, Merli, G, and Wheeler, WA, *Beyond Business Process Reengineering*, John Wiley, New York, 1995

Obeng, E, and Crainer, S, *Making Re-engineering Happen*, FT/Pitman, London, 1994

Regan, J, *Crunch Time: How to Reengineer Your Organization*, Century, London, 1995

References

1 Quoted in GRIFFITH, V, "Corporate fashion victim," *Financial Times*, April 12, 1995.
2 SCHONBERGER, R, *Building a Chain of Customers*, The Free Press, New York 1990.
3 HELLER, R, "Fourteen points that the West ignores at its peril," *Management Today*, March 1994.
4 JURAN, J M, "Why quality initiatives fail," *Journal of Business Strategy*, July–Aug. 1993 Vol. 14, No. 4.
5 JURAN, J M "Why quality initiatives fail," *Journal of Business Strategy*, Vol. 14, No. 4, July-Aug. 1993.
6 BINNEY, G, *Making Quality Work - Lessons from Europe's Leading Companies*, Economist Intelligence Unit, London, 1993.
7 Albrecht, K, *The Only Thing That Matters*, Harper Business, New York, 1993.
8 CHAMPY, J, and HAMMER, M, *Reengineering the Corporation*, Nicholas Brealey, London, 1993.
9 CHAMPY, J, and HAMMER, M, *Reengineering the Corporation*, Nicholas Brealey, London, 1993.
10 LORENZ, C, "Uphill struggle to become horizontal," Financial Times, Nov. 5, 1993.
11 DEVINE, M, "Radical re-engineering," *Directions*, Sept. 1993.
12 SKINNER, C, "Business process re-engineering," *Internal Communication Focus*, Dec. 1993/Jan. 1994.
13 DICKSON, M, "GTE to reduce staff by 17,000," *Financial Times*, Jan. 14, 1994.
14 DEVINE, M, "Radical re-engineering," *Directions*, Sept. 1993.
15 DICKSON, M, "Xerox to cut workforce by 10% over next three years," *Financial Times*, Dec. 9, 1993.
16 LORENZ, C, "Time to get serious," *Financial Times*, June 24, 1993.
17 "The technology pay-off," *Business Week*, June 14, 1993.
18 CHAMPY, J, "Time to re-engineer the manager," *Financial Times*, Jan. 14, 1994.

Reinventing marketing

"Markets are not created by God, nature or by economic forces, but by businessmen."
PETER DRUCKER[1]

"The marketing view of the business process requires that all innovations be thought of as intended to help get and keep customers, in short, to make the firm more competitive."
TED LEVITT[2]

HARD SELLING – THE RISE OF MARKETING

Few would question that marketing is a core activity of any organization. Its role is critical to success. Marketing involves planning and executing all customer-related activities (apart from the actual process of selling). Marketing identifies customer needs, suggests products to satisfy the demand and then operates a follow-up support system to ensure consumer satisfaction. The marketing department is the mouthpiece of the customer in the organization.

The origins of modern marketing can be traced back to the early 1960s. Until that time the vast majority of Western companies were production-led. They concentrated on producing goods as efficiently as they could. With the produced goods piled in the warehouse they could then turn their attention to actually selling them in the marketplace. The trouble was that often the marketplace was disinterested. Undeterred, the company carried on manufacturing in the hope and expectation that the market's interest would, sooner or later, be captivated by one means or another.

It was only in the 1980s that marketing was rediscovered and companies began to shift their emphasis from production to marketing.

The end-result was labeled **marketing myopia** by Harvard Business School's marketing guru TED LEVITT (born 1925). In a 1960 *Harvard Business Review* article, Levitt propelled marketing to center stage. Levitt argued that instead of concentrating on production, companies should become "customer-satisfying," marketing-led. Levitt's argument marked an important turning point. Inspired by the success of Henry Ford, businesses had remained intent on giving customers what they thought they needed and wanted. Ford had succeeded in creating a market for his cars, but it was a strategy which was inappropriate to the vast majority of products and services. As Levitt pointed out, Ford was soon outstripped by General Motors which gave customers what they actually wanted – more choice, more colors, regularly changing models.

Levitt's message still holds considerable attraction for the modern business. He preempted the current fascination with customers by over 30 years. The only drawback of his popular article was its examples – Levitt castigated railroad companies for not moving into the airline business, a move which would have undoubtedly ended in disaster for both.

160

While Levitt's message was avidly consumed, its effect was minimal. It was only in the 1980s that marketing was rediscovered and companies began to shift their emphasis from production to marketing. They did so with commendable enthusiasm. So much so, that the 1980s saw the apotheosis of marketing. Its importance was more widely recognized than ever before. Companies championed themselves as being market-driven. Budgets swelled and senior marketing managers were given a place on the board of many organizations.

A great deal of this was a case of throwing money at a problem with little overall change in emphasis or behavior. Investing in a marketing department proved far easier than changing a company from being production to marketing-led.

MARKET-DRIVEN OR MARKETING DRIVEN?

Harvard Business School's Benson Shapiro argues that truly market-driven companies have three characteristics:

- information on all important buying influences permeates every corporate function
- strategic and tactical decisions are made interfunctionally and inter-divisionally
- divisions and functions make well coordinated decisions and execute them with a sense of commitment.[3]

Shapiro gets to the nub of the problem. To work, marketing must truly permeate an organization's values and practice. It is not an isolated function, but a *raison d'être*. The beginning of the 1990s saw a shift in attitudes and practice. Some organizations have realized that, despite their talk of being market-driven and market-focussed, they have instead become *marketing-driven* and *marketing-focussed*. Marketing is not any less important but, instead of dispensing blank cheques to marketing departments, companies are beginning to question and examine the role and achievement of marketing managers in attaining their objectives. No resource is an island and organizations want to establish how marketing best fits and relates to the rest of the organization and, most importantly, how effective it is in meeting the needs of customers. There is no point in having a corporate lubricant if all it does is support cyclical motion in a narrowly defined area.

Financial services company Allied Dunbar is an archetypal example of an organization which flourished in the 1980s, thanks to effective marketing, and lost its way in the early 1990s. In 1991, a new chief executive began a radical process of assessment. It was discovered that the company had a distorted view of its marketplace relying on a "market segmentation" model which had little connection with the changing demographics of reality. Allied Dunbar set about finding out what clients thought of the company and what they expected from it. As a result, it hopes to be able to measure the relationship between client satisfaction and profitability – this will enable marketing to be properly directed and be more responsive to customer needs.

Other organizations have come to similar realizations. The malaise now identified in the marketing operation of many organizations is a functional one. Often, marketing departments have not only failed to build close relationships with customers, but have isolated themselves within their own organizations. A 1993 survey of 100 UK companies by management consultants Coopers & Lybrand[4] found huge disparities between what marketing departments think they contribute and what everyone else feels. A third of marketing directors think they are entirely or mainly responsible for strategic planning; but only one fifth of managing directors agree.

> **"Make your business competitive by making the businesses of your customers more competitive"**
> **MACK HANAN**

MEASURING MARKETING EFFECTIVENESS

The Coopers & Lybrand report also demonstrated that most procedures for measuring the effectiveness of marketing activity are irrelevant and result in a lack of accountability. A total of 57 percent of companies used sales revenue to measure effectiveness; 53 percent used market share; 39 percent used net profit to measure marketing effectiveness. It concluded that the effective marketing department of the future will:

- have within its remit all the processes that contribute to managing the customer and consumer interface
- have clear and defined responsibility for these processes
- focus on activities that demonstrably add value
- be measured, and judged against these measures.[5]

Some companies are already reorganizing their marketing resources so that they become more truly aligned to the needs of customers; interact more effectively with the rest of the organization and are treated as a process rather than as an unwieldy and often isolated department. Marketing needs to redefine its role and organization for the future. In *Tomorrow's Competition*, Mack Hanan sums up this challenge. The modern marketing challenge, writes Hanan, is to "make your business competitive by making the businesses of your customers more competitive."[6]

PHILIP KOTLER PROVIDES THREE KEY APHORISMS FOR SHAPING THE FUTURE.

- **Invest in the future** – "Companies pay too much attention to the cost of doing something. They should worry more about the cost of not doing it."

- **Move fast** – "Every company should work hard to obsolete its own product line ... before its competitors do"

- **Excel at everything you do** – "Your company does not belong in any market where it can't be the best."

ELIDA GIBBS

One company tackling these issues is Elida Gibbs, the UK personal products subsidiary of Unilever. Its brands include Fabergé, Brut, Pears, Signal, and Timotei. In a revolutionary move, Elida Gibbs abolished the post of brand manager and reinvented the sales team as the "customer development process." Brands are now the responsibility of brand development managers.

The changes at Elida Gibbs stem from criticisms of its performance in the late 1980s. Poor delivery standards and an old fashioned ordering system were a source of irritation to customers. As a result, Elida Gibbs introduced teamworking at one of its factories in 1988. Responsibility for each production line was transferred to those working on it. As well as these changes, Elida Gibbs reduced the number of its suppliers and gave suppliers more responsibility for quality control, testing, and development. The roles of the company's managers were also redefined on the basis of processes. Functional divisions were replaced by "seamless teams." Many of the day-to-day contacts with retailers which used up brand managers' time have been passed on to customer development managers.

Over the last three years change-over time on one production line has been reduced to less than four hours, when it previously took an entire day. In addition, 90 percent of orders are now correctly completed – against 72 percent in the past. Between 1989 and 1991 the company's pre-tax profits rose by 73 percent and margins widened from 6.5 percent to 10 percent. In April 1993 Elida Gibbs launched its first major product since its internal changes. It involved a development process of less than six months – half as much time as development had previously taken.

Similarly, SmithKline Beecham has overhauled its marketing activities. It believed it had been hampered by the company being divided into geographic units. SmithKline Beecham studied other companies, including Procter and Gamble and Unilever, and then set up six teams – each responsible for a product category. The teams were given free rein to co-opt managers from national subsidiaries. Sales in consumer brands rose by 11 percent in 1993 and product development cycles have been accelerated – a new toothbrush was developed in 40 percent of the previous time.[7]

The message is that marketing must become part of the mainstream of all an organization's activities. The word "marketing" is notably absent from Tom Peters' exhortations for organizations to become customer-oriented. The reason is simple – everyone must be involved in marketing in the same way as everyone must be dedicated to quality. In the best organizations marketing is left unsaid, but not undone.

Reinventing marketing

KOTLER, P, *Marketing Management: Analysis, Planning and Control*, Prentice-Hall, Englewood Cliffs, NJ, 1993

LEVITT, T, *Thinking About Management*, The Free Press, New York, 1991

WEBSTER, F E, *Market-Driven Management*, John Wiley, New York, 1994

RELATIONSHIP MARKETING

Everyone in business has been told that success is all about attracting and retaining customers. It sounds reassuringly simple and achievable. But, in reality, words of wisdom are soon forgotten. Once companies have attracted customers they often overlook the second half of the equation. In the excitement of beating off the competition, negotiating prices, securing orders, and delivering the product, managers tend to become carried away. They forget what they regard as the humdrum side of business – ensuring that the customer remains a customer.

Failing to concentrate on retaining as well as attracting customers costs businesses huge amounts of money annually. It has been estimated that the average company loses between 10 and 30 percent of its customers every year. In constantly changing markets this is not surprising – what is surprising is the fact that few companies have any idea how many customers they have lost.

> **Increasingly the emphasis is on building relationships with customers to create loyalty so they return time and time again.**

Only now are organizations beginning to wake up to these lost opportunities and calculate the financial implications. Cutting down the number of customers a company loses can make a radical difference in its performance. Research in the US found that a five percent decrease in the number of defecting customers led to profit increases of between 25 and 85 percent.

THE REGULAR CUSTOMER

Rank Xerox takes the question of retaining customers so seriously that it forms a key part of the company's bonus scheme. In the US, Domino's Pizzas estimates that a regular customer is worth more than $5,000 over ten years. A customer who receives a poor quality product or service on their first visit and as a result never returns, is losing the company thousands of dollars in potential revenue (more if you consider how many people they are liable to tell about their bad experience).

Creating customer loyalty

Increasingly the emphasis is on building relationships with customers to create loyalty so they return time and time again. Creating customer loyalty can appear relatively simple. Everyone who buys a Land Rover Discovery, Defender or Range Rover receives a telephone call or a postal questionnaire checking what they think about the product they have just bought. This is hardly earth shattering, but gives customers an opportunity to voice their opinion and makes it clear that there is more to the customer–supplier relationship than a simple purchase.

In the car market, customer loyalty has long been recognized as a vital ingredient in long-term success. Research in the US showed that a satisfied customer usually stays with the same car-manufacturer for 12 years, buying another four cars within that time. Not surprisingly, buying a car now guarantees a steady deluge of information and sales literature from the car-maker as they try to ensure that you are not tempted elsewhere.

Once on the road customer loyalty programs can be seen at every petrol station. The simple purchase of petrol is not really affected by price – left to their own devices, customers would stop at the nearest petrol station and fill up. Customer loyalty programs make it a more complex matter. Customers must choose between them.

The logic behind nurturing customer loyalty is impossible to refute. "In practice most companies' marketing effort is focused on getting customers with little attention paid to keeping them," says Adrian Payne of Cranfield University's School of Management and author of *The Essence of Services Marketing.* "Research suggests that there is a high degree of correlation between customer retention and profitability. Established customers tend to buy more, are predictable and usually cost less to service than new customers. Furthermore, they tend to be less price sensitive and may provide free word-of-mouth advertising and referrals. Retaining customers also makes it difficult for competitors to enter a market or increase their share of a market."

> **"In practice most companies' marketing effort is focused on getting customers with little attention paid to keeping them."**
> **ADRIAN PAYNE**

Payne points to a ladder of customer loyalty. On the first rung, there is a prospect. They are then turned into a customer, then a client, then a supporter and finally, if the relationship is successful, into an advocate persuading others to become customers. Developing customers so they travel up the ladder demands thought, long-term commitment and investment.

CUSTOMER LOYALTY PROGRAMS

Customer loyalty programs cover a multitude of activities from customer magazines to vouchers and gifts. Basically, a customer loyalty program aims to persuade a person to use a preferred vendor in order to take advantage of the benefits on offer, whether a trip to Acapulco or a price-reduction voucher for a calorie-controlled canned drink. Skeptics may mutter that there is nothing new in this. Indeed, businesses have been giving long-standing customers discounts and inducements since time immemorial. What is now different is the highly organized way in which companies are attempting to build relationships and customer loyalty.

The process can begin even before the potential user is born. Diaper manufacturers are a prime example of companies which take a long-term view. Prospective parents are bombarded with sample packs, free information and literature about what will be best for their soon to arrive son or daughter. By the time of the birth, the parents already have some degree of loyalty to a company

> **One company estimates that a sales increase of a single percent would pay for its entire customer loyalty program.**

whose product they have never actually bought. It can seem excessive, but one company estimates that a sales increase of a single percent would pay for its entire customer loyalty program.

FREQUENT FLYER PROGRAMS

Nowhere is customer loyalty more highly thought of than in the airline business. It has become a key differentiating factor. Invented in the early 1980s, frequent flyer programs are now well established and expanding rapidly in Europe where BA established its scheme in 1991. The beauty of the programs is that the concept is simple and relatively cheap to administer. Program members earn "points" or "miles" with every flight which can be redeemed for free tickets or upgrades to business class. Virgin's Freeway program is a little more imaginative and offers hot-air balloon trips, flying lessons and visits to health clubs. The programs mean an airline attracts and retains customers at a marginal cost while filling empty seats. The only downside is for the companies who actually pay for the travel – they get the bill while their employees receive the perks.

> **Technology means that customer loyalty programs are becoming ever more sophisticated. When it comes to creating loyal customers, the database is king.**

Though the idea is simple enough, frenzied competition means that airlines are continually changing rewards and rules to outdo others in the market. Clearly, frequent flyer programs work. One survey estimated that a quarter of Europe's

> business air travelers decide on their carrier because of frequent flyer points. Carlson Marketing Group estimates that there are 32 million frequent flyer members in the US clocking up huge amounts of free travel. American Airlines' AAdvantage scheme claims 16 million members.
>
> From the point of view of the airlines, frequent flyer programs offer the treasure at the end of the marketing rainbow: information. Airlines have historically been starved of information about their customers because only 15 percent book direct with the airlines – the vast majority use travel agents and other sources. Frequent flyer programs give airlines priceless competitive information so they can target their marketing more accurately and really focus on particular market segments.

Technology means that customer loyalty programs are becoming ever more sophisticated. When it comes to creating loyal customers, the database is king. When diaper makers introduced trainer pants to the UK they were relying on the power and accuracy of their databases to steal a march on their rivals. Procter & Gamble, Kimberly-Clark and Peaudouce each has a database which identifies families with children of potty-training age. The families were then deluged with special offers and various other inducements – Procter & Gamble's Pampers brand helped its publicity campaign along with an achievement chart ("I can poo in my potty" being the primary goal).

Databases mean that companies can target audiences more effectively. A DIY chain, for example, has a discount card which entitles holders to an annual payout – which comes in the form of a voucher to be spent at the shop. The details of the cardholders enable the store to send out regular mailings to customers giving them advance warning of special offers and giving them an extra five percent discount on certain days.

Technology also means that one customer loyalty program tends to blend into another. "The cycle is never ending with loyalty to one product or service being bolted on to another," says management consultant and author Tim Foster. "The rapid expansion of customer loyalty programs is proof that if they are well thought-out then they can have a great impact. If they are poorly constructed, the effect can be disastrous."

In fact, putting the simple idea into practice has become increasingly complex. Customers are now more highly demanding and fickle than ever before. They are organized and use their lobbying power more effectively. Expectations are high, but companies are quickly realizing that customers with a conscience create new markets.

Companies are now developing loyalty programs which are directly related to the conscience of their customers. There are a plethora of products which pledge to donate money to help save the rain forests or support medical research, if you buy them. A supermarket chain, for example, gives customers vouchers which they can take to their children's schools to save up for a computer. Such loyalty building creates a situation in which all sides appear to win – though, of course, the supermarket wins the most through creating a loyal customer.

Customer loyalty programs are likely to become ever more ambitious. The potential for mutually beneficial link-ups is never ending. A credit card from General Motors would have been unthinkable a few years ago. Now, it is the tip of an expanding iceberg. Some American supermarkets already give customers a "smart card" which means the company knows the contents of each customer's weekly shopping basket. The dividing line between information and intrusion may soon emerge as an important issue.

Relationship marketing

CHRISTOPHER, M; PAYNE, A F T; and BALLANTYNE, D, *Relationship Marketing*, Butterworth Heinemann, Oxford, 1991

CRAM, T, *The Power of Relationship Marketing*, FT/Pitman, London, 1995

PAYNE, A F T, *The Essence of Services Marketing*, Prentice-Hall, Englewood Cliffs, NJ, 1993

BRAND MANAGEMENT

BRANDING

At its simplest, branding is a statement of ownership. Cows are branded and, in the commercial world, branding can be traced back to trademarks placed on Greek pots in the seventh century BC and, later, to medieval tradesmen who put trademarks on their products to protect themselves and buyers against inferior imitations. (Of course, in the modern world people are adept at copying trademarks – whether they are Lacoste, Sony, Rolex or Le Coq Sportif – and producing imitations, which are often highly accurate.) Trademarks remain highly effective prompts – there are now some 50 million registered worldwide.

In the beginning came the product. Branding was a mark on the product – a signature or symbol – signifying its origin or ownership. The traditional view of what constitutes a brand is summed up by marketing guru Philip Kotler in his classic text book *Marketing*

▶

Management. Kotler writes: "(A brand name is) a name, term, sign, symbol or design, or a combination of these, which is intended to identify the goods or services of one group of sellers and differentiate them from those of competitors."[8]

The trouble with older definitions of brands is that they remain preoccupied with the physical product. The product stands alone; the brand exists within corporate ether. The product comes first and the brand does little more than make it clear which company made the product and where.

A more recent definition comes from Richard Koch in his book *The Dictionary of Financial Management*. Koch defines a brand as: "A visual design and/or name that is given to a product or service by an organization in order to differentiate it from competing products and which assures consumers that the product will be of high and consistent quality." Reflecting the emphasis of our times, Koch stresses differentiation – making your product or service different (or seeming to be different) – and achieving consistent quality.

If we think of brands we inevitably begin with the great American brands – Marlboro, Coca Cola, McDonalds, Budweiser, and many, many more. They are the garish, colorful icons of our times. Many have become cultural touchstones. Often, our image of these great icons often bears little relation to the product or reality. Wearing a pair of Levis does not give you freedom. That the iconic brands of the twentieth century are American owes a great deal to the fact that American businesses have continually developed brands at a faster pace than their European counterparts. This can partly be attributed to geography. American companies had (and have) a huge homogeneous national market; Europe does not. While American companies could launch massive advertising and marketing campaigns across the US and the English-speaking world, European companies learned to adapt (or not) to the cultural nuances of individual countries.

The rise of brands

Trailers once traveled the American countryside laden with every possible known cure, stimulant, medicine or treatment. The medicine jamborees may have had an indifferent medical record, but their contribution to the success of brands cannot be overlooked. They played a small but significant part in the development of national branding during the late nineteenth century. Patent medicines and tobacco set the trend. Though distributed only regionally, they developed recognizable brand names and identities.

The increase of brands on a regional basis provided the foundation for growth on a much greater scale. Instead of being restricted to low quality, regionally distributed products, brands took the great leap forward into the high quality mass market. The conditions were fertile. Efficient pan-American transportation had emerged so that a successful product in Chicago could be sold in St Louis cost-effectively.

But improvements weren't limited to transport – production processes and packaging improved and advertising became almost respectable. There were also changes in trademark laws and increasing industrialization and urbanization. While the brands expanded, their management remained resolutely set in its ways. Company owners and directors took responsibility. The array of tools at their disposal – from premiums and free samples, to mass advertising – grew quickly.

The period after the First World War cemented the place of brands. Advertising became increasingly prevalent and the acquisition of brands became identified with success and development. Consumers wanted Fords not motor cars; they bought from Sears rather than elsewhere.

Success brought complexity. Companies began to own a number of brands which they were able to produce, distribute, and sell *en masse*. In 1931 Procter & Gamble took functional organization a stage further when it created a new function: brand management. With brands like Ivory and Camay bath soaps, P&G believed that the best way to organize itself would be to give responsibility to a single individual: a brand manager.

The system did not transform the world overnight, but gradually brand management became an accepted functional activity, an adjunct to sales and marketing – and often a fairly junior adjunct at that. Its popularity was fueled by the economic boom of the 1950s which brought a plethora of new products and brands. These were supplemented by developments such as shopping centers and the emergence of television advertising. We had never had it so good and never had so much. Brand management provided some hope of order amid the confusion introduced by prosperity.

Brand management provided some hope of order amid the confusion introduced by prosperity.

By 1967, 84 percent of large manufacturers of consumer packaged goods manufacturers in the United States had brand managers. Though titles have changed, this system largely prevails today. It is only in the 1990s that the brand management system has begun to be questioned through trends such as reengineering which seek to break down the long-established functional barriers.

FOOD BRANDS

The development of food brands reveals many of the important stages in the development of brands as a whole. The origins of some of the world's largest food brands lie in the nineteenth century when the likes of Heinz and Nestlé created a vast new market in mass produced food. Heinz set off "to do the common thing uncommonly well." He and his company did so with uncommon success – Heinz's sales were $6.6 billion in 1992.

Having invented the market, the companies realized that its parameters were increasingly evident. In response to the simple fact that there's a limit to how much people can eat, the companies shifted their attention to value-added products to which they could attach premium prices. The emphasis was on prepacked meals, eating healthily, speed, and efficiency. A myriad of different brands and segments emerged. Consumers wanted to eat tasty, healthy food. They wanted it preprepared, ready and easy to cook.

The result was a massive market. In 1992 one estimate put the global sales of packaged food at $2.8 trillion. Huge profits and cash reserves meant that the companies could afford to buy brands from other areas of the foods business. In the 1980s there was a steady stream of mergers and acquisitions. Enormous amounts of money and huge numbers of brands changed hands.

As is always the case, even in the world of booming brand budgets, reality returns. As premium prices increased, budgets mushroomed and the value of brands headed towards the commercial stratosphere, but consumers began to become a little reticent. They looked elsewhere and began to concentrate on value for money and the hard facts beyond the marketing.

Supermarkets quickly moved to take advantage of this change in emphasis through developing their own brands which had grown, but not hugely, in the last decades. From having a 23 percent share of packaged grocery turnover in 1978, own-label goods rose to 34.9 percent in 1991. Indeed, research by the Henley Centre found that "best" brands are now often retailer's own-brands. The leading Dutch supermarket chain Albert Heijn's own-label products were ranked far ahead of Nestlé on all criteria – including trustworthiness, product innovation and packaging, as well as price. The wheel has turned full circle. Indeed, the UK chain Tesco is now contemplating buying directly from farmers in another effort to increase profit margins.

The end result is that the market is now in a state of uncomfortable flux. Competition is intense, in a way that it has never been before when the food companies called the shots. The common link is that the process of change is led and formed by brands.

Branding in the 1990s

The new and emerging issues facing brands are, for many, a matter of life and death:

Fragmentation

Thanks to the likes of Heinz and Nestlé markets have become highly fragmented. This means that there is always the possibility of an interloper stealing a march on bigger rivals by finding a small and lucrative niche.

Targeting

The obvious repercussion of this is that targeting the right market and then the right part of that market is crucial. A large amount of information is now available on buying habits as well as a host of other factors. The only trouble for organizations is how they can plough through all the data to find the right information and at the same time move speedily to fill smaller and smaller niches.

Innovation and speed

The answer in many markets is to develop new products and services more quickly than has ever been done before. This means that development times have to be slashed. The big brands of recent years have been those which deluge the market with new ideas – companies like Compaq, Rubbermaid (which boasts a new product every day), and Swatch.

Cost squeeze

To make matters more challenging organizations have to achieve these things within reduced budgets. Gone are the days when a brand could be pushed to the top simply through an expensive advertising campaign. Consumers are more sophisticated and advertising costs have soared. Even a household name like Unilever's Persil only has around 25 percent of its past amount of television advertising. But, not only have advertising costs soared, but there is now also a profusion of media. Growing numbers of TV and radio stations allow companies unprecedented levels of access to audiences which are becoming progressively smaller and more fragmented.

Margins squeeze

In many businesses and entire sectors profit margins are being squeezed dry. The supermarkets are engaged in a perpetual price war with discounters entering the fray throughout Europe, having already wreaked havoc in the United States. The German discounter Aldi is already blazing a trail throughout Europe. Discounters now have approaching 10,000 German stores, 1,200 in the UK, 1,200 in Spain, and 600 in France. Numbers will almost certainly grow.

With supermarket own-label products making huge gains, once strong brands are taking refuge in price cutting. In the past, price cutting was usually soon followed by a succession of small price increases so that the original premium price was restored. This does not appear to happen any more. Prices go down and stay there – unless they can go lower still.

Performance squeeze

If margins are down and costs reduced the performance of individuals and organizations has to be improved. From being an ostentatious decadent world, branding has become obsessed with leveraging performance everywhere and any how.

Creating value

The end-result is, in the phrase of our times, added-value. Companies must add value throughout every single process they are involved in and then translate this into better value for consumers.

A *Financial Times* editorial on the soap wars between Unilever and Procter & Gamble sums it up: "It does not matter how mundane the product. Consumers are more demanding than ever before – and competitors more ruthless. The manufacturer that fails to appreciate these facts will go to the wall."[9]

Brand management

AAKER, D A, *Managing Brand Equity*, The Free Press, New York, 1991

CRAINER, S, *The Real Power of Brands*, FT/Pitman, London, 1995

HANKINSON, G; and COWKING, P, *Branding in Action*, McGraw Hill, Maidenhead, 1993

KAPFERER, J-N, *Strategic Brand Management*, Kogan Page, London, 1992

References

[1] DRUCKER, P, *The Practice of Management*, Harper & Row, New York, 1954.

[2] LEVITT, T, *Thinking about Management*, The Free Press, New York, 1991.

[3] SHAPIRO, B, "What the hell is market oriented?", *Harvard Business Review*, Nov.–Dec. 1988.

[4] COOPERS & LYBRAND, *Marketing at the Crossroads*, Coopers & Lybrand, 1993.

[5] COOPERS & LYBRAND, *Marketing at the Crossroads*, Coopers & Lybrand, 1993.

[6] HANAN, M, *Tomorrow's Competition*, AMACOM, New York, 1991.

[7] JONQUIERES, G DE, "Buying the Bactroban with the bath oil," *Financial Times*, Jan. 10, 1994.

[8] KOTLER, P, *Marketing Management: Analysis, Planning and Control*, (8th edition) Prentice-Hall, Englewood Cliffs, NJ, 1993.

[9] "Soap and chips," *Financial Times*, Dec. 21, 1994.

Leadership

"Our prevailing leadership myths are still captured by the image of the captain of the cavalry leading the charge to rescue the settlers from the attacking Indians. So long as such myths prevail, they reinforce a focus on short-term events and charismatic heroes rather than on systemic forces and collective learning."
PETER SENGE, MIT[1]

"A leader is a man who has the ability to get other people to do what they don't want to do, and like it."
HARRY TRUMAN[2]

"To survive in the twenty-first century we're going to need a new generation of leaders, not managers."
WARREN BENNIS[3]

THE RISE OF THE NEW MODEL LEADER

Leadership is one of the great intangibles of the business world. It is a skill most people would love to possess, but one which defies close definition. Ask people which leaders they admire and you are as likely to be told Gandhi as John Kennedy, Jack Welch as Richard Branson. Yet, most agree that leadership is a vital ingredient in business success and that great leaders make for great organizations.

"Broadly speaking there are two approaches to leadership. You can theorize about it or you can get on and do it. Theorizing about it is great fun, hugely indulgent and largely useless. Doing it – or doing it better – is demanding, frequently frustrating and of immense value," says Francis Macleod, former chief executive of the Leadership Trust. "Those who want to change an organization must be able to change people and in that process there is only one starting point that makes sense. Learning to lead oneself better is the only way to lead others better."

When considering leadership in the business context most roots lead to the military world. Management, long used to the concept of divide and rule, has perennially sought its leadership role models from the military. The temptation to view the business world as a battle field is, even now, highly appealing. Indeed, the success of Sun Tzu's *The Art of War* as a management text points to the continuing popularity of this idea.

Machiavellian leadership

Another key historical text, and one which is increasingly referred to, is Machiavelli's *The Prince*. Amid the grey-suited pantheon of management greats, NICCOLÒ MACHIAVELLI (1469–1527) holds an unlikely, but undeniable, place. A Florentine diplomat and writer, his career was colorful – punctuated by interludes of indulgence in "petty dissipations," torture on the rack, and farming. His abiding relevance to the world of management rests on a slim volume, *The Prince*.

The Prince is the sixteenth century equivalent of Dale Carnegie's *How to Make Friends and Influence People*. Embedded beneath details of Alexander VI's tribulations lie a ready supply of aphorisms and insights which are, perhaps sadly, as appropriate to many of today's managers and organizations as they were nearly 500 years ago.

"It is unnecessary for a prince to have all the good qualities I have enumerated, but it is very necessary to appear to have them," Machiavelli advises, adding the suggestion that it is useful "to be a great pretender and dissembler." But *The Prince* goes beyond such helpful presentational hints. Like all the great books, it offers something for everyone. Take Machiavelli on managing change: "There is nothing more difficult to take in hand, more perilous to conduct, or more uncertain in its success, than to take the lead in the introduction of a new order of things." Or on sustaining motivation: "He ought above all things to keep his men well-organized and drilled, to follow incessantly the chase."

Above all, Machiavelli is the champion of leadership through cunning and intrigue, the triumph of force over reason. An admirer of Borgia, Machiavelli had a dismal view of human nature. "Empowerment" was not in his vocabulary. Unfortunately, as he sagely points out, history has repeatedly proved that a combination of being armed to the teeth and devious is more likely to allow you to achieve your objectives. It is all very well being good, says Machiavelli, but the leader "should know how to enter into evil when necessity commands."

"Like the leaders Machiavelli sought to defend, some executives tend to see themselves as the natural rulers in whose hands organizations can be safely entrusted," says psychologist Robert Sharrock of consultants YSC. "Theories abound on their motivation. Is it a defensive reaction against failure or a need for predictability through complete control? The effect of the power-driven Machiavellian manager is usually plain to see."

In companies addicted to internal politics, Machiavelli remains the stuff of day-to-day reality. But, warns Robert Sharrock, Machiavellian management may have had its day. "The gentle art of persuasion is finding fashion with managers. The ends no longer justify the means. The means, the subtle management of relationships, are the ends by which future opportunities may be created. Also, most managers now recognize that organizations have purposes other than the maximization of profit. There is a return to the age of reason against which Machiavalli rebelled."

> **"The gentle art of persuasion is finding fashion with managers. The ends no longer justify the means. The means, the subtle management of relationships, are the ends by which future opportunities may be created."**
> **ROBERT SHARROCK**

For many the age of reason has yet to dawn. Managers may not have read *The Prince* but will be able to identify with Machiavelli's observation that "a prince ought to have no other aim or thought, nor select anything else for his study, than war and its rules and discipline." In the corporate trenches, Machiavelli remains useful reading.

Military models

Leadership reemerged on the management agenda in the 1980s after a period of relative neglect. A great many books were produced purporting to offer essential guidance on how to become a leader. These tended to follow military inspirations with the business leader portrayed as a general, inspiring the corporate troops to one more effort.

Even so, there are some useful inspirations in the military world for today's corporate leaders. One of the most persuasive, and under estimated, is Field Marshall William Slim. Slim believed that the leadership lessons he had learned in the army could readily be applied to the business world. In his book, *Defeat Into Victory*, Slim described his thoughts on raising morale:

> Morale is a state of mind. It is that intangible force which will move a whole group of men to give their last ounce to achieve something, without counting the cost to themselves; that makes them feel they are part of something greater than themselves. If they are to feel that, their morale must, if it is to endure – and the essence of morale is that it should endure – have certain foundations. These foundations are spiritual, intellectual, and material, and that is the order of their importance. Spiritual first, because only spiritual foundations can stand real strain. Next intellectual, because men are swayed by reason as well as feeling. Material last – important, but last – because the highest kinds of morale are often met when material conditions are lowest.

The doyen of the military-inspired approach is the UK leadership writer and practitioner, JOHN ADAIR, who was himself in the army (as well as spending time on an Arctic trawler and various other adventures). Adair has identified a list of the basic functions of leadership: planning, initiating, controlling, supporting, informing, and evaluating. Central to Adair's thinking is the belief that leadership is a skill which can be learned like any other. This is one of the fundamentals of the military approach to leadership – leaders are formed in the crucible of action rather than through chance genetics.

> "Successful leadership is not dependent on the possession of a single universal pattern of inborn traits and abilities."
>
> DOUGLAS MACGREGOR

In the management world there is a tendency to fluctuate between the two extremes. On the one hand, managers are sent on leadership development courses to nurture and discover leadership skills. On the other hand, there is still a substantial belief that leaders have innate skills which cannot be learned.

Modern leadership writers tend to suggest that leadership as a skill or characteristic is distributed generously among the population. "Successful leadership is not dependent on the possession of a single universal pattern of inborn traits and abilities. It seems likely that leadership potential (considering the tremendous variety of situations for which leadership is required) is broadly rather than narrowly distributed in the population," wrote Douglas Macgregor in *The Human Side of Enterprise*. The American Warren Bennis, inspired by Macgregor, has studied leadership throughout his career. Bennis also concludes that each of us contains the capacity for leadership and has leadership experience. He does not suggest that actually translating this into becoming an effective leader is straightforward, but that it can be done, given time and application.

While such arguments are impressively optimistic about human potential, they are disappointed by reality. The dearth of great leaders is increasingly apparent. This suggests that either innate skills are not being effectively developed or that the business world simply does not encourage managers to fulfill their potential as leaders.

The evolution of leadership

Leadership thinking has moved rapidly from one theory to another. The main schools of thought can be divided into nine theories.

GREAT MAN THEORY

Great Man theories were the stuff of the late nineteenth and early twentieth centuries, though their residue remains in much popular thinking on the subject. The Great Man theory is based round the idea that the leader is born with innate, unexplainable and, for mere mortals, incomprehensible leadership skills. They are, therefore, elevated as heroes.

TRAIT THEORY

This theory continues to fill numerous volumes. If you know who the Great Men are, you can then examine their personalities and behavior to develop traits of leaders. This is plausible, but deeply flawed. For all the books attempting to identify common traits among leaders there is little correlation.

POWER AND INFLUENCE THEORY

This approach chooses to concentrate on the networks of power and influence generated by the leader. It is, however, based on the assumption that all roads lead to the leader and negates the role of followers and the strength of organizational culture.

BEHAVIORIST THEORY

In some ways the behaviorist school continues to hold sway. It emphasizes what leaders actually do rather than their characteristics. Its advocates include Blake and Mouton (creators of the Managerial Grid) and Rensis Likert.

SITUATIONAL THEORY

Situational Theory views leadership as specific to a situation rather than a particular sort of personality. It is based round the plausible notion that different circumstances require different forms of leadership. Its champions include Kenneth Blanchard and Paul Hersey whose influential book, *Situational Leadership Theory*, remains a situationalist manifesto.

CONTINGENCY THEORY

Developing from Situational Theory, contingency approaches attempt to select situational variables which best indicate the most appropriate leadership style to suit the circumstances.

TRANSACTIONAL THEORY

Increasingly fashionable, Transactional Theory places emphasis on the relationship between leaders and followers. It examines the mutual benefit from an exchange-based relationship with the leader offering certain things, such as resources or rewards, in return for others, such as the followers' commitment or acceptance of the leader's authority.

ATTRIBUTION THEORY

This elevates followership to new importance, concentrating on the factors which lie behind the followers' attribution of leadership to a particular leader.

TRANSFORMATIONAL THEORY

While transactional leadership models are based on the extrinsic motivation of an exchange relationship, transformational leadership is based on intrinsic motivation. As such, the emphasis is on commitment rather than compliance from the followers. The transformational leader is, therefore, a proactive, innovative visionary.

THE NEW LEADER

"Today's leaders understand that you have to give up control to get results – they act as coaches not as 'the boss'," observes Robert Waterman in *The Frontiers of Excellence*.[4]

The increasing emphasis in the 1990s has focussed on leaders as real people managing in a consensus-seeking manner. Instead of seeing leadership as being synonymous with dictatorship, this view sees leadership as a more subtle and humane art. It also breaks down the barrier between leadership and management. Traditionally, in theory at least, the two have been separated. "Men are ripe for intelligent, understanding, personal leadership, they would rather be led than managed," observed Field Marshal Slim. Increasingly, management and leadership are seen as inextricably linked. It is one thing for a leader to propound a grand vision; but

> **"Managers who are not leaders can only be failures."**
> **LEONARD SAYLES**

this is redundant unless the vision is managed into real achievement. While traditional views of leadership tend eventually to concentrate on vision and charisma, the message now seems to be that charisma is no longer enough to carry leaders through. Indeed, leaders with strong personalities are just as likely to bite the corporate dust (as Bob Horton found to his cost at BP). The new model leaders include people like Percy Barnevik at Asea Brown Boveri, Virgin's Richard Branson, and Jack Welch at GE in the United States.

FOUR TYPES OF MANAGEMENT STYLE

The trends of the 1990s were partly anticipated in the work of psychologist and researcher RENSIS LIKERT (1903–81). Likert identified four types of management style:

- **exploitative authoritarian** – management by fear
- **benevolent autocracy** – top-down but with an emphasis on carrots rather than sticks
- **consultative** – communication both up and down, with decisions largely coming from the top
- **participative** – decision-making in working groups which communicate with each other via individuals who are linking pins, team leaders or others who are also members of one or more other groups.

Beyond these four "systems" Likert also anticipated System 5 where all formal authority had disappeared.

The magic which marks such executives has been analyzed by INSEAD leadership expert MANFRED KETS DE VRIES. "They go beyond narrow definitions. They have an ability to excite people in their organizations," he says. "They also work extremely hard – leading by example is not dead – and are highly resistant to stress. Also, leaders like Branson or Barnevik are very aware of what their failings are. They make sure that they find good people who can fill these areas."

LEONARD SAYLES, author of *Leadership: Managing in Real Organizations* and *The Working Leader* is representative of a great deal of the new thinking. Sayles suggests that leadership affects managers at all levels, not simply those in the higher echelons of management. "It is leadership based on work issues, not just people issues, and is very different from the method and style of managing that has evolved from our traditional management principles."

Sayles argues that the leader's role lies in "facilitating coordination and integration in order to get work done." Sayles is dismissive of the perennial concept of the great corporate leader. Instead his emphasis is on the leader as the integrator of corporate systems. The leader is a kind of fulcrum "adapting, modifying, adjusting and rearranging the complex task and function interfaces that keep slipping out of alignment." Instead of being centered around vision and inspiration, Sayles regards the leader's key role as integrating the outputs of his or her work unit with those of the rest of the organization. To Sayles, "managers who are not leaders can only be failures."

Interestingly, and unhelpfully for the practicing manager, leadership attracts such aphorisms rather than hard and fast definitions. Indeed, there are a plethora of definitions on what constitutes a leader and the characteristics of leadership. In practice, none have come to be universally, or even widely, accepted.

The very individualism associated with leadership is now a bone of contention. The people we tend to think of as leaders – from Napoleon to Winston Churchill – are not exactly renowned for their teamworking skills. But, these are exactly the skills management theorists insist are all-important for the 1990s and beyond.

"In some cases, the needs of a situation bring to the fore individuals with unique qualities or values, however, most leaders have to fit their skills, experience and vision to a particular time and place," says psychologist Robert Sharrock. "Today's leaders have to be pragmatic and flexible to survive. Increasingly, this means being people- rather than task-oriented. The "great man" theory about leadership rarely applies – if teams are what make businesses run, then we have to look beyond individual leaders to groups of people with a variety of leadership skills."

Indeed, the pendulum has swung so far that there is growing interest in the study of followers. Once the humble foot soldier was ignored as commentators sought out the commanding officer, now the foot soldiers are encouraged to voice their opinions and shape how the organization works. Today's corporate leaders expend a great deal of effort in communicating directly with their employees. Roger Enrico, vice chairman of PepsiCo, spends half his time "coaching" executives.

> "The new recipe for leadership centers on five key areas: learning, energy, simplicity, focus and inner sense."
> PHIL HODGSON

Body Shop's Anita Roddick has installed bulletin boards, faxes, and video recorders in each of the 700 Body Shops so that staff can communicate more effectively and she can communicate directly with them.

"Followers are becoming more powerful. It is now common for the performance of bosses to be scrutinized and appraised by their corporate followers. This, of course, means that leaders have to actively seek the support of their followers in a way they would have never have previously contemplated," says Robert Sharrock.

185

THE OLD MODELS OF LEADERSHIP

Phil Hodgson of Ashridge Management College has analyzed the behavior of a number of business leaders. His conclusion is that the old models of leadership are no longer appropriate. "Generally, the managers interviewed had outgrown the notion of the individualistic leader. Instead, they regarded leadership as a question of drawing people and disparate parts of the organization together in a way that made

> **"Many executives feel it is good to have control. They become addicted to power – and that is what kills companies."**
> **MANFRED KETS DE VRIES**

individuals and the organization more effective." He concludes that the new leader must add value as a coach, mentor, and problem solver; allow people to accept credit for success and responsibility for failure; and must continually evaluate and enhance their own leadership role. "They don't follow rigid or orthodox role models, but prefer to nurture their own unique leadership style," he says. "And, they don't do people's jobs for them or put their faith in developing a personality cult." The new recipe for leadership centers on five key areas: learning, energy, simplicity, focus, and inner sense.

In the age of empowerment, the ability to delegate effectively is critically important. "Empowerment and leadership are not mutually exclusive," says INSEAD's de Vries. "The trouble is that many executives feel it is good to have control. They become addicted to power – and that is what kills companies."

Warren Bennis provides another link between empowerment and leadership. "Leadership can be felt throughout an organization. It gives pace and energy to the work and empowers the workforce. Empowerment is the collective effect of leadership."[5]

Knowing when to let go has become an integral part of the skills of the modern leader. There are many examples of leaders who stay on in organizations and in governments far beyond their practical usefulness. Manfred Kets de Vries contends that leaders, like products, have a life cycle. De Vries identifies three stages in this: entry and experimentation, consolidation, and decline, and estimates that life cycles for leaders are shortening.[6]

The growing interest and belief in the human side of leadership is, in itself, nothing new. Leadership thinker JAMES MCGREGOR BURNS coined the phrases **transactional** and **transformational** leadership. Transactional leadership involves leaders who are very efficient at giving people something in return for their support or work. Followers are valued, appreciated and rewarded. Transformational leadership is concerned with leaders who create visions and are able to carry people along with them towards the vision.

The ability to create and sustain a credible vision remains critical. Harvard's JOHN KOTTER identifies three central processes in leadership: establishing direction; aligning people; motivating and inspiring. The way in which these core elements are put into practice is continually being refined. But, at its heart, is an appreciation that the leader cannot act alone. Peter Drucker has observed that leaders habitually talk of "we" rather than "I." The great leaders appear to be natural teamworkers, a fact overlooked by heroic models of leadership. In *The Tao of Leadership*, John Heider produces another aphorism – but one which cuts to the heart of modern leadership: "Enlightened leadership is service, not selfishness."[7]

Leadership

ADAIR, J, *Effective Leadership: A Modern Guide to Developing Leadership Skills*, Pan, London, 1988

BASS, B, and AVOLIO, B, *Improving Organizational Effectiveness Through Transformational Leadership*, Sage, London, 1994

BURNS, J M, *Leadership*, Harper & Row, New York, 1978

KOTTER, J, *A Force for Change: How Leadership Differs From Management*, Free Press, New York, 1990

LEAVY, B, and WILSON, D, *Strategy and Leadership*, John Wiley, London, 1994 .

MAUCHER, H, *Leadership in Action: Tough Minded Strategies from the Global Giant*, McGraw Hill, New York, 1994

SYRETT, M, and HOGG, C (editors), *Frontiers of Leadership: An Essential Reader*, Blackwell, Oxford, 1992

WRIGHT, P, and TAYLOR, D, *Improving Leadership Performance: Interpersonal Skills for Effective Leadership*, Prentice-Hall, London, 1994

ZALEZNIK, A, *The Managerial Mystique: Restoring Leadership in Business*, Harper & Row, New York, 1990

Warren Bennis
Doing the right thing

In many ways, Warren Bennis is the epitome of the modern-day management thinker. Now based at the University of Southern California, he has a lengthy academic pedigree – beginning as a protégé of Douglas Macgregor, author of *The Human Side of Enterprise*, to become the *éminence grise* of contemporary leadership, advising four US presidents. His work has become steadily more populist and popular.

VITAL LEADERSHIP QUALITIES

The most widely read of Bennis' numerous publications is *Leaders: The Strategies for Taking Charge* (1985), cowritten with Burt Nanus. This examined the behavior and characteristics of 90 leaders and sought to reach general conclusions. The leaders studied were a truly eclectic – and somewhat eccentric – group, including Neil Armstrong and Karl Wallenda, a tightrope walker. Bennis concluded that the leaders possessed four vital competencies:

- **management of attention** – the vision of the leaders commanded the attention and commitment of those who worked for and with them in attempting to achieve it.

- **management of meaning** – the leaders were skilled communicators, able to cut through complexity to frame issues in simple images and language. They were expert distillers of information.

- **management of trust** – "Trust is essential to all organizations," observes Bennis. For the leaders, trust was expressed through consistency of purpose and in their dealings with colleagues and others. Even though people sometimes disagreed with what they said or did, the leaders were admired for their consistency of purpose.

- **management of self** – the leaders were adept at identifying and fully utilizing their strengths, and accepting and seeking to develop areas of weakness.

LEADERS NOT MANAGERS

To Bennis, leadership is a skill which can be learned by the manager willing to put in substantial effort. It is, however, fundamentally different from management. "To survive in the 21st century we're going to need a new generation of leaders, not managers. The distinction is an important one. Leaders conquer the context – the volatile, turbulent, ambiguous surroundings that sometimes see to conspire against us and will surely suffocate us if we let them – while managers surrender to it." He goes on to list the fundamental differences between the two as:

- **the manager administers**; the leader innovates
- **the manager is a copy**; the leader is an original
- **the manager maintains**; the leader develops
- **the manager focuses on systems and structure**; the leader focuses on people
- **the manager relies on control**; the leader inspires trust
- **the manager has a short-range view**; the leader has a long-range perspective
- **the manager asks how and when**; the leader asks what and why
- **the manager has his eye on the bottom line**; the leader has his eye on the horizon
- **the manager accepts the status quo**; the leader challenges it
- **the manager is the classic good soldier**; the leader is his own person
- **the manager does things right**; the leader does the right thing.[8]

The last element has become something of a catch-phrase, another in a long line of neat aphorisms which don't, in the end, bring the practitioner nearer to how to actually develop leadership skills.

Bennis has to some extent become a victim of pigeon-holing. His work actually covers a far wider span of issues than leadership. In the 1950s, for example, he studied group dynamics and was involved in the team-working experiments at the US's National Training Laboratories. In the 1960s he developed a reputation as a student of the future – in a 1964 *Harvard Business Review* article, Bennis and coauthor Philip Slater accurately predicted the downfall of communism ("Democracy is inevitable," they wrote).

In the mid-1960s, he was predicting the demise of the modern organization – a prediction which has taken 30 years to begin to be fulfilled. "Bureaucracy emerged out of the organization's need for order and precision and the workers' demands for impartial treatment. It was an organization ideally suited to the values and demands of the Victorian era. And just as bureaucracy emerged as a creative response to a radically new age, so today new shapes are surfacing before our eyes."[9]

189

Curiously, Bennis' career actually follows many of the patterns of Douglas Macgregor's. Macgregor was president of Antioch College during the time Bennis was an undergraduate and advised Bennis to move on to MIT. In 1959, when Bennis was teaching at Boston University and Harvard, Macgregor recruited him to MIT to establish the new organization studies department. Macgregor moved from being an academic to an administrator before returning to academic life. Bennis has done similarly – his academic career was interrupted by a spell as provost at the State University of New York at Buffalo and as president of the University of Cincinnati. This proved disappointing. "The very time I had the most power, I felt the greatest sense of powerlessness," Bennis observes in the autobiographical *An Invented Life*. In practice, Bennis found that his ambitious intentions were hamstrung by the very organization he purported to lead. Despite the power attributed to him through his job title, in practice he was powerless.

WARREN BENNIS   born 1925; educator

Education: Antioch College; MIT

Career: Army during World War 2; provost at SUNY, Buffalo 1967–71; President, University of Cincinnati, 1971–78; University of Southern California since 1979.

Bennis then returned to academic life, attempting to understand the lessons learned and to convert them into more general lessons about the nature of leadership and the relationship between the individual leader and the organization. His search has not, however, been for the perfectly formed, one-line summation, but rather an enduring study of the humanity behind leadership.

Warren Bennis

Leaders: The Strategies for Taking Charge (with Burt Nanus), Harper & Row, New York, 1985

On Becoming a Leader, Addison-Wesley, Reading, 1989

Why Leaders Can't Lead, Jossey-Bass, San Francisco, 1989

An Invented Life: Reflections on Leadership and Change, Addison-Wesley, Reading, 1993

References

1 SENGE, P, *The Fifth Discipline*, Doubleday, New York, 1990.
2 Quoted in PRIOR, P, *Leadership is not a Bowler Hat*, David & Charles, Newton Abbot, 1977.
3 BENNIS, W, "Managing the dream," *Training Magazine*, 1990.
4 WATERMAN, R, *The Frontiers of Excellence*, Nicholas Brealey, London, 1994.
5 BENNIS, W, *An Invented Life*, Addison Wesley, Reading, 1993.
6 de Vries, MK, "CEOs also have the blues," *European Management Journal*, Sept. 1994.
7 HEIDER, J, *The Tao of Leadership*, Wildwood House, Aldershot, 1986.
8 BENNIS, W, "Managing the dream," *Training Magazine*, 1990.
9 BENNIS, W, "The coming death of bureaucracy," *Think Magazine*, 1966.

Learning and development

"The days of an MBA degree in general management are over. Our new curriculum says that we think that the best way to get to the top of a company is to start off after business school with a jump on the competition – have a special competence, not just know a little bit about everything."
LESTER THUROW

"The human mind is finite though managers sometimes act as if it wasn't."
CHRIS ARGYRIS

THE GROWTH OF THE LEARNING BUSINESS

In the beginning learning and development simply happened. Executives weren't despatched on expensive courses, they learned by coming through the ranks. The job taught them everything they needed to know.

This view appears to be an artefact of ancient history. It isn't. The process of developing people in organizations remains in its infancy. Though the world is crowded with business schools, management development is a relatively new science.

Indeed, in Europe, France's INSEAD offered an MBA for the first time in 1959. It was not until 1965 that the UK's first two public business schools (at Manchester and London) were opened. Elsewhere, management has been seriously studied (at least in academic terms) for a longer period. In the US, Chicago University's business school was founded in 1898; Amos Tuck at Dartmouth College, New Hampshire – founded in 1900 – was the first graduate school of management in the world; and Harvard offered its first MBA as long ago as 1908 and established its graduate business school in 1919.

Of course, these statistics pale into insignificance when set against the centuries spent educating lawyers, clerics, soldiers, teachers, and doctors in formal, recognized institutions. But, during this century, management has begun to claw back the ground lost during past centuries.

Business schools have generally followed the American model with a traditional emphasis on finance and strategy rather than the "softer" side of management. While business schools have become a massively successful industry, recent years have seen increasingly vociferous criticism of their methods and, more fundamentally, of their role in management development.

The chief gripe against them is that as management is the art of the moment, immediate and spontaneous, how can it be taught distant from the workplace?

Indeed, some suggest that learning and development must be enshrined in day-to-day activities rather than being something you do for two weeks of the year on a marketing course. A much neglected concept in the field of learning and development is that of **action learning**. This is an alternative to classroom-based management learning, presenting managers with real business issues from their own or another organization, and inviting the best solutions.

ACTION LEARNING

Action learning's champion has been the indomitable UK thinker (and former Olympic athlete), REG REVANS. Revans argues that sharing problems with others is a vital part of the learning process. "The central idea of this approach to human development, at all levels, in all cultures and for all purposes, is today that of the set, or small group of comrades in adversity, striving to learn with and from each other as they confess failures and expand on victories," writes Revans in his 1980 book *Action Learning*. Revans is a vehement critic of business schools. He labels academic case studies as "flatulent self-deception" and describes them as "academic Klondyke." Action learning is simple, deceptively so, and Revans has largely fought a losing battle in encouraging organizations to make use of it. In the face of ambivalence, he has worked in Belgium, Egypt, India, and Nigeria. However, with growing emphasis on teamworking and the power of groups to solve their own problems, action learning is undergoing something of a resurgence.

It is not only action learning which is attracting a growing number of admirers. The 1990s have seen the emergence of the **learning organization** or, at least the concept of the learning organization. In the learning organization the act of learning is continuous and affects, and involves, everyone.

The rise in interest in developing people throughout the organization can be attributed to a number of factors. First, in leaner organizations people are taking on broader ranges of responsibility. Managers, in particular, are faced with a completely new environment. They are responsible for more people, often working in a process-oriented organization, and the skills and behaviors which previously served them well no longer work. They have to make fundamental changes or fail.

Second, the growth in numbers of what Peter Drucker labels "knowledge workers" means that there is a premium on possessing high quality skills and expertise. The marketplace is teeming with highly qualified people.

Third, there has been a somewhat belated recognition of the importance of recruiting, retaining, and developing talented people. In a

> In the learning organization the act of learning is continuous and affects, and involves, everyone.

turbulent environment it has never been more important to have the right people for the job – and to keep them, motivate them and develop them. There is a need to constantly develop skills, no matter who you are, what you do, who you do it for, or where you do it.

Chris Argyris
The learning challenge

A superficial look at Chris Argyris' work and career gives an impression of the classic academic. Argyris has spent his entire working life at some of the leading centers of American academic excellence – at Yale in the 1950s and 1960s, at Harvard Business School since 1968. But, the scope of his thinking defies conventional academic strictures. "Working in academia is both exhilarating and infuriating," he admits. His work is driven by high quality academic research, rather than unsubstantiated opinion. It is also, he admits, not highly accessible. "My books are not easy to read. It is the way I think," he says. "I write articles based on anecdotes and books based on research. I don't want to research, raise basic questions and then stop."[1]

Underpinning Argyris' career has been a humane desire to develop and nurture individuals within organizations. "I am interested in social sciences in organizations of any kind," he says. "Discipline-oriented people can feel I'm a traitor." Argyris' intellectual armoury includes a Baccalaureate in psychology, a Masters in economics, and a Doctorate in organizational behavior.

Tracing his *raison d'être* back through his career, Argyris observes: "What drives me now has motivated me for the last 40 years. It sounds corny but I love learning for its own sake and, after serving in World War Two, I wanted to do something when I got back. I am optimistic, believing there can be a better, more just world. Though I am an unabashed romantic, I have always been connected with reality. A true romantic has a vision without it being operational. Being a soft-hearted romantic is deadly. In my case, research and theory provide the quality control. Success has always to be compared with your values."

CHRIS ARGYRIS   born 1923; educator

Education: Baccalaureate in psychology; Masters in economics; Doctorate in organizational behavior

Career: Taught at Yale in 1950s becoming Beach Professor of Administrative Finance in 1965; joined Harvard Business School, and became James Bryant Conant Professor of Education and Organizational Behavior in 1971.

For Argyris research has gone hand in hand with teaching and consultancy. He does not compartmentalize his interests in the way of some other management thinkers. Instead, the three strands support and interrelate with each other. His work is based around the fundamental belief that if organizations allow and encourage individuals to develop to their full potential will be mutually beneficial. Argyris' research constantly challenges his natural optimism. Executives are often poor communicators, unwilling to challenge the status quo or able to learn from their experiences. "Some executives can't cope with changing anything. When new ideas are implemented the old theory of control is left intact. This is a source of continual disappointment, but my disappointment is tempered with a sense of understanding," says Argyris. "I am not angry, but just think, let's face reality. Disappointment is an opportunity for leverage for change."

> "Any company that aspires to succeed in the tougher business environment of the 1990s must first resolve a basic dilemma: success in the marketplace increasingly depends on learning, yet most people don't know how to learn."
> CHRIS ARGYRIS

What Argyris has constantly observed is a mismatch between people and organizations. To fit people into organizational structures, they have been limited rather than developed, constrained and contained. People have, in turn, failed to develop themselves or accept responsibility for their actions. "Responsibility is not a one-way process," he says. "We are personally responsible for our behavior but, unfortunately, many companies change their parking space and not people's sense of responsibility."

SUCCESS DEPENDS ON LEARNING

The origins of the development of the now popular concept of the learning organization can be traced to Argyris. "Any company that aspires to succeed in the tougher business environment of the 1990s must first resolve a basic dilemma: success in the marketplace increasingly depends on learning, yet most people don't know how to learn. What's more, those members of the organization who many assume to be the best at learning are, in fact, not very good at it," he wrote in a 1991 *Harvard Business Review* article. "Because many professionals are almost always successful at what they do, they rarely ▶

experience failure. And because they have rarely failed, they have never learned how to learn from failure."[2]

His pleasure in the growing interest in the role of learning is combined with fears that it might be short-lived. "I am pleased that organizational learning is in vogue but I worry that if we are not careful it will become another fad," he says. "I have little difficulty in talking about organizational learning to chief executives but, as you go down the hierarchy, it is regarded as being a bit dreamy."

> **"IT makes transactions transparent so that behavior is no longer hidden. It creates fundamental truths where none previously existed."**
> **CHRIS ARGYRIS**

Argyris' contribution to the debate was the seminal work, *Organizational Learning* (1978), which he cowrote with MIT's Donald Schon. Together with Schon, Argyris developed the concept of **single-loop** and **double-loop learning**. Argyris later explained the idea: "Learning may be defined as occurring under two conditions. First, learning occurs when an organization achieves what it intended; that is, there is a *match* between its design for action and the actual outcome. Second, learning occurs when a *mismatch* between intention and outcome is identified and corrected; that is, a mismatch is turned into a match ... Single loop learning occurs when matches are created, or when mismatches are corrected by changing actions. Double-loop learning occurs when mismatches are corrected by first examining and altering the governing variables and then the actions."[3]

In short, single-loop learning does not question underlying assumptions while double-loop learning tackles basic assumptions and beliefs. The vast majority of learning falls into the category of single-loop learning, though Argyris believes that double-loop learning is now more widely recognized – "Double-loop learning is gaining credence as a practical thing." Indeed, the preoccupations of the early 1990s suggest that managers are more willing to tackle (or at least to contemplate) the big issues and to question and re-establish first principles.

Argyris believes that IT has a crucial role to play in furthering the acceptance and practice of learning within organizations. "In the past the one-way, top-down approach gained strength from the fact that a lot of behavior is not transparent. IT makes transactions transparent so that behavior is no longer hidden. It creates fundamental truths where none previously existed."

Argyris' ability to dedicate time and energy to getting under the skin of organizations is forcefully demonstrated in *Knowledge for Action* (1993). In this book Argyris examines the behavior of one of his consultancy clients, itself a consultancy group. The consultancy arose when seven successful consultants decided to establish their own company. They hoped that it would be free from the Machiavellian political wrangles they had encountered in other organizations. In practice, their dreams were disappointed. Indeed, by the time Argyris was called in, internal wrangling consumed too many of its productive energies.

The company preferred to remain anonymous. "I have always advocated not naming the companies I carry out research in," says Argyris, recalling, "When I worked with IBM Thomas Watson Junior said name the company – at a stockholder meeting someone asked why the company employed Communist consultants!'

DEFENSIVE AVOIDANCE

The consultants featured in *Knowledge for Action* were, in fact, falling prey to what Argyris calls **defensive routines**. Faced with a personally threatening problem, the executives were adept at covering it up or by-passing it entirely. Board meetings, therefore, concentrated on trivial topics – there was always one person keen to avoid discussion of an important issue. Outside the boardroom the big issues were discussed and blame apportioned so that divisions built up relentlessly between the original founders. This approach affected the behavior of the rest of the organization – others consciously kept information to a minimum so that executives weren't forced to face up to something new.

The fact that Argyris' client is a group of management consultants helps convey the importance of his message. If highly trained, intelligent executives fall into such traps, what chance have ordinary mortals?

Argyris' work forms a bridge between theory and practice in a way few other academics have managed. "In education it is important that students connect what they learn to what they actually do. Executive education goes on every day, not simply by sending executives to a classroom. Too much formal executive education reinforces the status quo of the organization and too many academics are romantic in the pejorative sense. They run away from developing new approaches so you read 600 pages on leadership and it adds up to what? There are academic standards, but theories need to be tested," says Argyris. "Academics and executives have a love–hate relationship. Academics say that executives are too shallow; while executives are interested in the pay-off. What executives now complain about is not the newness of the concepts but that the new concepts don't keep implementation in mind. You get unconnected fads and ideas so that managers can't use them."

While critical of formal processes of executive development, he points out that practicing managers have a negligible record when it comes to developing important ideas. "Practitioners don't come up with the ideas, the great theories which influence and create best practice. There have been people like Sloan and Barnard, but they were exceptional."

Even so, Argyris identifies strongly with managers. "I feel sorry for managers to some extent. There tends to be a fundamental assumption that if anything needs correcting it is management. And they are now being asked to deal with a lot of information. But I don't think they will ever be asked to deal with an amount beyond their competence. The amount is not the issue. The human mind is finite though managers sometimes act as if it wasn't."

> **"Too much formal executive education reinforces the status quo of the organization and too many academics are romantic in the pejorative sense."**
> **CHRIS ARGYRIS**

Chris Argyris

Personality and Organization, Harper & Row, New York, 1957

Overcoming Organizational Defences, Allyn & Bacon, Boston, MA, 1990

Organizational Learning: A Theory of Action Perspective (with Donald Schon), Addison-Wesley, Wokingham, 1978

On Organizational Learning, Blackwell, Cambridge, 1993

Knowledge for Action, Jossey-Bass, San Francisco, 1993

COMPETITIVE WEAPONS FOR LEARNING

With learning and development moving to central stage a number of key issues are emerging as vital competitive weapons for the 1990s and beyond. These are:

- **the learning organization** – this concept argues that to fully utilize all the human resources at its disposal any organization must be geared to learn at every opportunity. Learning must not be seen as an isolated or occasional exercise, or an indulgence, but a competitive and continuous necessity for all in the organization.

- **the changing role of business schools** – with organizations undergoing radical change to become leaner and faster, the providers of management development and training must follow suit. They, too, must provide individually tailored, responsive training which provides people with practical interpretations of leading edge concepts.

- **developing talent** – if people are an organization's greatest assets they must be treated as such. Talented individuals need to be attracted, nurtured and retained to maintain a competitive advantage.

- **self-managed development** – through empowerment, managers are encouraged to take greater responsibility. Increasingly this includes managing their own career development and the acquisition of skills which will enhance their employability.

THE LEARNING ORGANIZATION

With his 1990 book, *The Fifth Discipline*,[4] Peter Senge propelled the term "the learning organization" to the forefront of the corporate – and the conference – agenda. The expression has since gone on to rival excellence, vision, and empowerment as useful phrases that have now been almost completely stripped of any consistent meaning.

RECOGNIZING THREATS AND OPPORTUNITIES

In *The Fifth Discipline*, Senge uses examples drawn from his workshops at MIT to describe how organizations suffer from learning disabilities that prevent them from recognizing threats and opportunities. He then describes the disciplines that individuals and organizations need in order to turn disabled organizations into learning organizations.

The learning disabilities that he describes relate to the inability of individuals and their organizations to see patterns – the "invisible fabric of inter-related actions, which often take years to fully play out their effects on each other." He applies these failures to "think systemically" to specific business situations, for example, showing how systems thinking saved Royal Dutch/Shell and how the failure to think systemically doomed People Express Airlines. "The airlines that will excel in the future will be the organizations that discover how to tap people's commitment and capacity to learn," says Senge.

KEY CONCEPTS

The Fifth Discipline includes five key concepts:

1. **Systems Theory**
   Senge developed the idea of **systems archetypes**. These can help managers to spot repetitive patterns, such as the way certain kinds of problems persist, or the way systems have their own inbuilt limits to growth.

2. **Personal Mastery**
   Senge includes within this spiritual growth – opening oneself up to a progressively deeper reality – and living life from a creative as opposed to reactive viewpoint. This involves continually learning how to see current reality more clearly. The resulting gap between vision and reality produces the creative tension from which learning emerges.

3. **Mental Models**
   These are what Ed Schein calls the "basic assumptions" of the organization. Senge believes managers must recognize the power of patterns of thinking at organizational level and the importance of nondefensive enquiry into the nature of these patterns.

4. **Shared Vision**
   Shared vision can develop from personal vision. Senge argues that shared vision is present when the task that follows from the vision is no longer seen by team members as separate from the self.

5. **Team Learning**
   This demands dialogue and discussion, Dialogue is characterized by its exploratory nature and discussion by the opposite process of narrowing down the best alternatives available. The two complement each other, but only if they are separated in the first place.

Success did not come overnight to Senge. He and his team at the Center for Organizational Learning at MIT's Sloan School of Management have been working on the theme for some time. "For the past 15 years or longer, many of us have been struggling to understand what 'learning organizations' are all about, and how to make progress in moving organizations along this path. Out of these efforts, I believe some insights are emerging," says Senge in the multiauthored sequel, *The Fifth Discipline Fieldbook.*[5]

With around 50 contributors, the *Fieldbook* is a tumbling spree of ideas and suggestions. Enthusiasm and energy is apparent on every page. Their underlying message is simple: learning is positive; learning is good for organizations. Skeptics – and there remain many – will continue to doubt the practical wisdom of such wholeheartedness. Indeed, anyone wanting to hear neatly packaged solutions will find it easy to accuse Senge and others in this field of sounding too philosophical and Eastern, and of not being specific enough.

Perhaps the problem is that although the learning organization sounds as if it is a product, it is actually a process. Processes are not suddenly unveiled for all to see. Academic definitions, no matter how precise, cannot be instantly applied in the real world. Managers need to promote learning so that it gradually emerges as a key part of an organization's culture. Being convinced of the merits of the learning organization is not usually a matter of dramatic conversion.

Obstacles to creating learning organizations

Turning the learning organization into practice has proved immensely difficult. The clearest reasons for this are:

- **managers are unhappy about handing over power.** In the traditional organization managers controlled training budgets and attending courses was often treated as an occasional perk of the job, dispensed by the manager when he or she saw fit. In the learning organization managers surrender a great deal of this power to the individual.

- **learning requires flexibility and a willingness to risk something new and having the authority to try it.** Managers are ill at ease with the entire idea of learning from their mistakes. As Chris Argyris has pointed out, they are more likely to attempt to sweep a mistake under the corporate carpet than take it out into the open and attempt to learn from it.

- **dealing with uncertainty.** The learning organization creates uncertainty and ambiguity in areas which were previously clear. Managers must learn to manage in this more nebulous and less easily understood environment.

- **accepting responsibility.** Individuals must take responsibility for learning. They cannot blame others for a lack of development opportunities, but must pursue and create their own.

- **the learning organization requires new skills.** In particular managers must develop listening skills and be able to act as facilitators. Simply dictating adds no learning value.

- **trust.** Reared on the concept of divide and rule, trusting people does not come easily to many managers.

THE CHANGING ROLE OF BUSINESS SCHOOLS

In the 1980s the world's business schools could do no wrong. Managers sought them out, anxious to arm themselves with MBAs; major corporations invested heavily in developing their executives for the future. Their numbers mushroomed, especially in Europe where there are now 400 business schools.

Times change and, in the 1990s, business schools have come under intensifying scrutiny from managers and their companies. Under the harsh glare of unexpected examination, business schools have been fighting to deliver the kind of training now demanded by businesses – rather than the training business schools think managers should have.

In many ways the challenges now facing business schools mirror those facing the rest of the business world. The 1990s have seen major companies struggling with the twin demons of achieving global presence while being locally responsive. The management development world has been facing a parallel paradox – how to deliver general management education; as well as courses and programs continually tailored to the specific requirements of companies and, increasingly, to the needs of individuals.

The situation is further complicated by the fact that, under pressure to "re-invent" themselves and their organizations, as well as managing constant change, managers can often afford to spend little time on developing vital competencies for the future. "Workloads are substantial and if you are sent away on a course, you do think of the work piling up on your desk," says Sheila Dawson, head of business services at the international banking arm of the Bank of Ireland. "We are going through radical business re-design and process improvement, so training must put things in context and help our managers to deliver core objectives."

Developing new approaches

Changed times, demand new approaches to development, says Roger Shaw of Strategic Training. "People now have to manage multiple strategies. They are dealing with great complexity. Bringing in a consultant who stays for a brief period, offers insight on a small number of issues to a small number of people and then disappears, is not useful."

"While classroom-based and distance learning are clearly valuable, they cannot avoid being formulaic or relying on a "one best way" approach. There is a growing need for local learning – learning which is continuously adapted and fitted around the immediate needs of managers. If access to learning is immediate it becomes a far more valuable managerial currency," says Eddie Obeng of Pentacle, The Virtual Business School.

> **"MBA programs generally attract neither creative nor generous people and the end result is trivial strategists."**
> **HENRY MINTZBERG**

THE TRADITIONAL BUSINESS SCHOOL FORMAT

The standard criticism of business schools tends to repeatedly focus on the same points. Business schools, it is said, are out of touch with the harsh world of recession and hypercompetition. They provide standardized off-the-shelf teaching which is often inappropriate for individual managers and their companies; and they are too narrow in their outlook when companies and managers increasingly demand an international perspective.

One of the most influential critics of the traditional business school format is management thinker, Henry Mintzberg. "Regular full-time MBA programs with inexperienced people should be closed down. It's wrong to train people who aren't managers to become managers," he argues. "MBA programs are confused between training leaders and specialists. At the moment, we train financial analysts and then expect them to become leaders."

Mintzberg believes that the conventional approach is limiting rather than expanding. "To be superbly successful you have to be a visionary – someone with a very novel vision of the world and a real sense of where they are going. If you have that you can get away with the commercial equivalent of murder. Alternatively, success can come if you are a true empowerer of people, are empathetic and sensitive." These, he makes clear, are not qualities which most business schools are likely to nurture. "MBA programs generally attract neither creative nor generous people and the end result is trivial strategists."

Mintzberg is not alone in calling for major changes in the approach of business schools. Time is tight, corporate budgets are even tighter and expectations are growing. Under pressure to "reinvent" themselves and their organizations, as well as managing constant change, managers can often afford to spend little time on developing vital competencies for the future. They look to business schools for practical support.

Not surprisingly, given the regularity of its airing, it is a message which many business schools have taken on board. Change is in the air. Some business schools now claim to be "reengineering" themselves though for some this is more of a question of paying lip-service to change than genuinely transforming themselves.

Even so, a blueprint for the business school of the future is now emerging. Instead of providing set courses, it will tailor programs to the particular needs of companies. It will cater to the development needs of individual executives and be truly international in perspective and practice. It will be at the leading edge of technology, harnessing IT to deliver programs throughout the world. It will be outward looking – in constant contact with real business – rather than inward looking and academic. The list is apparently endless and constantly expanding. But is it achievable?

> **Under pressure to "reinvent" themselves and their organizations, as well as managing constant change, managers can often afford to spend little time on developing vital competencies for the future.**

"We believe companies want flexible, close and long-term relationships with the providers of management development," says Peter Beddowes, dean of the UK's Ashridge Management College. "With modern learning methods it is possible for both open programs and programs customized to a particular organization's needs to be tailored to respond to the development priorities of individual managers."

The findings of an Ashridge survey suggest that organizations also now demand that what their managers learn has practical use – preferably as soon as they return to their offices. "There are now much closer links between organizational objectives and executive development," says Peter Beddowes.

"The entire nature of corporate programs has been transformed over the last decade," says Jane Cranwell-Ward, director of company programs at Henley Management College. "There is now a totally integrated approach

> **"There are now much closer links between organizational objectives and executive development."**
> **PETER BEDDOWES**

206

rather than one which keeps different functions neatly separated. Companies demand practical, skills-oriented learning which does not come to an abrupt end when managers return to work. We have to add value to the organization and show clearly that we are making a major contribution to the future development and success of both the organization and its managers."

The shift to tailored corporate programs is already underway. This is especially the case in the UK and the US. At the US's Wharton and Duke University, tailored work accounts for 65 percent of executive education; at the prestigious Kellogg School it has reached 40 percent.

TAILORING IN PRACTICE

To develop the skills of its international managers, Standard Chartered Bank developed a specially tailored MBA program run with Henley Management College. From the start the Standard Chartered MBA program was developed along firmly global lines. The numbers are comparatively small. The first intake in October 1991 included 18 managers drawn from 12 countries selected from over 100 applicants. Just over 60 managers are currently on the Standard MBA with around 15 to 20 now entering each year. The managers are drawn from 16 different nationalities.

"The program brings a diverse cultural group together and helps them to focus together as a team through common experiences and by working together towards the same deadlines," says course tutor Lynn Thurloway. "Students place a great deal of value on working with people they didn't know before and working with people from other countries."

The three-year course features five weeks of residential elements. While the first and last of these weeks is spent at Henley, the remainder occur throughout the world – from Kenya to Kuala Lumpur. The first participants on the Standard Chartered MBA found themselves in teams on a beach in Singapore attempting to put together a TV news program – a task to be achieved in 12 hours from start to finish. Other groups have found themselves working with Standard Chartered customers, including a sports bag manufacturer in China and Kenya's leading brewery.

While the Standard Chartered MBA covers the traditional ground of MBA programs, crucial for the company it is practically based. "Many MBA programs are good at filling managers with knowledge, but weak at developing management skills and identifying real management challenges," observes Standard Chartered's Geoff Rogers.

"Henley's MBA program is the core, but it is important for us that assignments on the course are all done inside the company and concern real problems and issues. A number of initiatives have emerged from MBA assignments – one involved market analysis on the Asia Pacific region which proved instrumental in Standard Chartered growing its business there."

The emerging business school

In the same way as business schools are having to meet the increased demands of companies, they are also having to cater to the individual requirements and aspirations of managers. Increasingly managers and executives are taking the major development decisions for themselves, seeking out the school which is best for them rather than accepting the nearest or cheapest. Today's managers know what they want and are willing to go and find it – rather than automatically taking what they are offered. In response, business schools have to consider and cater for the development needs of individual managers.

This presents a golden opportunity for business schools – as well as teaching and developing managers, much of their future role is likely to be diagnosing which skills are needed by which organization and which individual manager. To achieve this business schools must return to their roots in the real, and increasingly harsh, world of business.

A survey by the European Foundation for Management Development (EFMD) of business schools and major companies in 18 European countries, found that 65 percent anticipated that the future demand for management education would expand, with 23 percent expecting it to remain stable. Only 10 percent anticipated a decline and, perhaps more significantly, companies were more optimistic than the business schools themselves.

THE BUSINESS SCHOOL OF THE FUTURE

The business school of the future is likely to be characterized by:

● close links with client organizations and industry generally with businesses heavily involved in research projects.

● an emphasis on lifetime and continuous learning with business schools in regular contact throughout a person's career rather than for brief, but intense, periods.

- an emphasis on developing managers into facilitators.

- being learning centers and resources rather than providers of standard business "solutions" taught by resident experts.

- networks. Increasingly, business schools are developing networks among themselves and with businesses. This can be seen in the rise of consortium programs involving a number of companies.

- multicultural and international qualities. They will be truly international in terms of course content and outlook.

- use of the latest technology to facilitate continuous learning.

Four generic themes underpinning the future demand emerged from the EFMD survey – internationalization, changes in technology, changes in corporate structure; and changes in economic conditions. The EFMD survey showed that companies now expect business schools to put greater emphasis on providing tailored or in-company programs. Indeed, this was identified as the top priority in a business school portfolio.

DEVELOPING TALENT

The idea that great organizations rely on talented individuals flies in the face of traditional thinking. People once fitted into an organization, neatly categorized into white collar and blue collar workers. Now, there are "gold collar" workers, the high-fliers identified, reared and protected by the company like prize pedigrees.

"Twenty or thirty years ago companies talked of labor management. Later it was realized that knowledge and skills are important. Now it has gone a stage further," says Philip Sadler, author of *Managing Talent*. "Knowledge is hard to destroy; hard to protect; and hard to measure. But, the true source of competitive advantage is not so much knowledge as talent, which is the only remaining scarce resource."

Sadler's research covered 50 leading international companies and American corporations, such as drugs company Merck and Hewlett Packard lead the way. He found that in some cultures individual success and talent sit uncomfortably with the prevailing culture. "In the UK, although there is still a great deal of admiration for the gifted amateur, we are loath to celebrate and reward exceptionally talented people. You can see this in the way the British treat up and coming sportsmen and women. To some extent this thinking has carried over to business.

In contrast, in the US there is a willingness to recognize and reward talented people. In Germany and France too, professionally qualified people have a much higher standing in society."

It is not a matter of indulgence, argues Sadler, but one of commercial necessity. Staying ahead of the competition is no longer simply a question of finding a neat niche or making things cheaper than anyone else. Such advantages are unlikely to last long anyway, they depend on having people talented enough to spot the opportunities in the first place.

"Some, perhaps most, organizations are totally dependent on identifying, nurturing and retaining talented people in order to survive," says Sadler. "The long-term success of the business in attracting, retaining, developing, motivating and utilizing the best talent in its field is likely to be the biggest single factor in determining its long-term commercial viability."

DEVELOPING TALENT: THE FUNDAMENTALS

The research highlighted ten fundamentals for the successful management of talent:

- provide a clear sense of direction and purpose
- develop an appropriate organizational framework
- understand your culture
- identify future requirements for talent
- develop recruitment and selection strategies
- identify high potential
- retain your talent
- set clear objectives and ensure they are met
- motivate and develop your talent
- evaluate your talent.

Even so, part of the traditional distrust of human resource management has been that talent and knowledge are notoriously difficult to measure. Companies have often preferred to concentrate on logistics and productivity which can be more easily measured. So what is talent?

Given this potpourri of skills, sorting out the talented wheat from the chaff is not easy. To find the right people, BA's recruitment operation handles 72,000 applications a year; 13,000 interviews; 159,000 unsolicited inquiries; as well as 10,000 people who walk in off the street.

IDENTIFYING TALENT

A merchant bank quoted in Sadler's book, describes talented people as "intelligent, bright team players capable of progressing and growing." Another organization defines a talented individual as one who knows the business, products, and the markets; is extremely good at communication; has a winner's mentality; has drive; is able to operate in an ambiguous environment; has not just intelligence but social intelligence, able to understand human, political and bargaining processes; can take initiatives and sensible risks.

Having attracted the talent, companies must then ensure that it is developed – ICL invested £25 million in education and training staff while it was still losing money – and that the talented people are not poached by envious rivals. At ICL there is a mentoring

> **"Talent is one thing, achievement is another."**
> **PHILIP SADLER**

scheme which pairs managers with board directors. Austin Mulinder, ICL European services operations manager, is one manager who believes he has benefited from being mentored. "I was progressing, but was very conscious that I could spend my career in one area of the company," says Mulinder. "Having a mentor steered me in a more challenging direction."

GOLD COLLARS AND MERE MORTALS

While the Renaissance men and women with this array of skills are courted and cultivated, what happens to the mere mortals who keep the place running? "There is a danger of creating a large mass of second class citizens," admits Philip Sadler. "But companies have to identify talent and the importance of teamwork. A mechanic on the Williams racing team does not feel as if he or she is a second class citizen – they are part of a team and part of their success."

ICL's Austin Mulinder believes developing talent is not a case of preferential treatment. "It is not career manipulation. If you are producing results, showing initiative and are ambitious you are pushing on an open door."

▶

211

> The search for gold collar workers is ever more competitive and companies need constantly to be on the lookout. Of course, having enlisted talented individuals there is no guarantee of business success. As Philip Sadler says: "Talent is one thing, achievement is another."

SELF-MANAGED DEVELOPMENT

When it came to management development managers were once pawns in the hands of the organization. If the company thought a manager needed a particular skill they were speedily despatched on a suitable course. As their careers progressed, managers assembled an impressive list of courses they had attended – though what they actually learned was often infrequently measured.

In some companies development is still regarded in these terms. The trouble is that the skills needed by managers in the 1990s are so broad ranging that picking off skills is no longer enough. Managers and their organizations have to be more selective and focussed when it comes to development.

THE PROACTIVE MANAGER

As part of this growing trend, managers – and their companies – now realize that developing managerial skills and techniques is not simply the responsibility of the company. Managers, too, have a role to play in being proactive and identifying areas in which they need to develop. Today, instead of being pawns moved around by corporate might, managers are increasingly encouraged to examine their own strengths and weaknesses to develop the skills necessary for the future. Rather than having their development mapped out for them, managers are managing it for themselves.

The growing awareness of the potential of self-managed development is, to some extent, prompted by companies committing themselves to ideas such as empowerment. There is also growing interest in the entire idea of management competencies – the skills which managers will require to manage successfully in the future.

In the 1990s companies realize that they need to extract more and better work from less people. They are intent on investing responsibility – rather than simply money – in their managers. Major companies such as Guinness are already making significant strides in developing their managers through self-managed development.

"Even though many companies are now expressing an interest in self-managed development, the trouble is that the habits of a generation are hard to break. Managers fed on a diet of conscripted training are uneasy about having the burden of their own development thrust upon them," says Fiona Dent, coauthor of *Signposts for Success*. "Being **sent** on a course is something you can complain about – sometimes with justification. It is completely different when you have to identify your own needs and the best methods of satisfying them."

There are other reasons why self-managed development is a difficult concept for many managers to come to terms with. Some point to a lack of motivation. Why, they say, should they develop themselves when their company offers little or nothing in the way of support or rewards? There is also a strong fear of failure. In some areas, training has traditionally been regarded as a last resort, an admission of inadequacy. Other managers are simply unsure of what to do. They don't know where or how to start the process and, even if they begin, don't know how to maintain momentum. Another disincentive from following self-managed development is simple lack of knowledge. Managers may be unable – or perhaps unwilling – to identify areas in which they need to develop and have little or no knowledge of the myriad of techniques, approaches and activities at their disposal.

> **Managers may be unable – or perhaps unwilling – to identify areas in which they need to develop and have little or no knowledge of the myriad of techniques, approaches and activities at their disposal.**

When they are actually given the time, resources and support to look at their own development, managers quickly become excited, realizing that there are opportunities rather than obstacles. For many it is an entirely new experience. Given two days on a training course to analyze their own development needs, it often takes more than a day for managers to really come to terms with what they are doing. It can be a revelation.

WHY NEW SKILLS?

At an individual level, managers are usually prompted to think about their own development through changes in their job. It could be that taking on a new project motivates them to take a close look at the skills they require. A completely new job often encourages greater self-examination.

▶

Perhaps the most widespread stimulus in the current climate is the disappearance of layers of management from major organizations. While once managers anticipated regular moves up the career ladder and the corporate hierarchy, they are now having to become used to the idea of horizontal rather than vertical moves. As the rungs upwards disappear, managers have to make sure they make the right moves sideways which bring them into contact with important and useful new skills.

The skeptical might suggest that self-managed development is an abdication of a company's responsibility, a means of shifting management development onto the already loaded shoulders of their managers. But if it is to work, self-managed development involves and relies on the participation of the manager's organization. The company has a vital role to play, providing opportunities, support, and resources. Fundamentally, however, it is the individual manager who has to take final responsibility and control.

They can't do this in isolation. Companies can't abandon their managers to plough their own furrow. Also, people need and want to share and test ideas with others. Self-managed development revolves around relationships with a wide range of people – from colleagues on courses to mentors and coaches; from the manager's boss to family and friends. The key relationship, however, must be with the organization.

> **Self-managed development revolves around relationships with a wide range of people.**

Many managers already have and use such networks. The trouble is they often don't realize that they exist or that they use them. If you ask a manager whether they have a mentor, many will quickly reply that they don't. Further questioning often reveals that a senior colleague is and has been instrumental in shaping their career and skills development – they have simply overlooked this or don't recognize it as mentoring.

In fact, self-managed development in many ways fully utilizes relationships and resources which already exist. When managers set out to gather information about a particular topic they often don't know where to start. Yet, given guidance they can quickly uncover information and resources they have previously ignored or been unable to use.

It is also true that many managers have neatly compartmentalized their lives and refuse to acknowledge links between their home and working lives. Self-managed development can remove the barriers which prevent managers learning lessons in their private lives which might be useful in their business roles. It regards development as a continuous process taking all aspects of a person's behavior and outlook rather than simply taking one small aspect of it.

Self-managed development offers a degree of flexibility which traditional management training fails to provide. There is no set timescale or approved way of doing things – self-managed development revolves around managers thinking about how they learn and what they need to know. Traditional courses are based on the idea of moving a manager to a stated destination – knowing more about a particular subject or acquiring a new skill. Once the destination is reached, the process is regarded as complete. Self-managed development emphasizes the journey rather than the destination. After all, the skills and techniques you plan to acquire are constantly changing.

FOUR STAGES

Self-management development expert Fiona Dent believes it contains four fundamental stages:

1. **analysis** – managers can use a variety of methods to help them to identify possible development issues. They might, for example, look at how performance reviews would help them and what form they could take.

2. **review** – they might then move on to reviewing – thinking, in a structured way, about what the data is telling them about their learning needs.

3. **planning** – how you intend to meet your development needs. This covers thinking through what course or other form of learning is most useful; where to go to do it and why it is necessary.

4. **activity** – developing and taking part in the most appropriate vehicle for meeting the development need.

There is nothing cut and dried about these stages. Managers can join the process where they think it is most appropriate for them. Flexibility, combined with responsibility, is the key.

Self-managed development is based on commonsense principles. Put simply, it is a matter of recognizing what you can and can't do and then trying to improve your performance. Experience at many companies suggests that self-managed development is going to be an integral part of developing managers in the future and ensuring that companies retain their best people.

SELF-MANAGED DEVELOPMENT: THE POTENTIAL BENEFITS

Andrew Constable, of Roffey Park Management Institute, points to the potential benefits of self-managed development:

For the individual:
- new knowledge, skills, and abilities
- improved management skills
- strategic thinking
- ability to cope with and manage change
- enhanced interpersonal skills
- greater self-awareness
- better understanding of how they learn
- greater confidence
- self-reliance
- belief that they can, to a large extent, determine their own future

For the organization:
- matches individual and organizational needs and objectives
- more versatile and flexible workforce
- can support broader organizational and cultural change
- can link with other development initiatives
- congruence with project/enterpreneurial/change environment
- "owned" by the organization with a strong emphasis on developing internal resources
- can cascade throughout an organization
- facilitates cross-functional working and networking.

Learning and development

CUNNINGHAM, I, *The Wisdom of Strategic Learning*, McGraw Hill, Maidenhead, 1994

DENT, F; MACGREGOR, R; and WILLS, S, *Signposts for Success*, FT/Pitman, London, 1994

MUMFORD, A, *How Managers Can Develop Managers*, Gower, Aldershot, 1993

PEDLER, M; BURGOYNE, J; and BOYDELL, T, *The Learning Company*, McGraw Hill, Maidenhead, 1991

SENGE, P, *The Fifth Discipline: The Art and Practice of the Learning Organization*, Doubleday, New York, 1990

SENGE, P; ROBERTS, C; ROSS, R; SMITH, B; and KLEINER, A, *The Fifth Discipline Fieldbook: Strategies and Tools for Building a Learning Organization*, Nicholas Brealey, London, 1994

References

1 Interview with Stuart Crainer, May 29, 1994.

2 ARGYRIS, C, "Training smart people how to learn," *Harvard Business Review*, May–June 1991.

3 ARGYRIS, C, "Problems in producing usable knowledge for implementing liberating alternatives," Address to the International Congress of Applied Psychology, July 1982.

4 SENGE, P, *The Fifth Discipline: The Art and Practice of the Learning Organization*, Doubleday, New York, 1990.

5 SENGE, P; Roberts, C; Ross, R; Smith, B; and Kleiner, A, *The Fifth Discipline Fieldbook: Strategies and Tools for Building a Learning Organization*, Nicholas Brealey, London, 1994.

Global management

"A transformation of the international economy is well established. It is a transformation into a system of globally integrated networks controlled by international corporations."
BRUCE MCKERN, CARNEGIE-MELLON

"Almost all our problems, and their solutions, are recognizable all over the world. Internationally-operating managers are in the middle of these dilemmas."
FONS TROMPENAARS

DISCOVERING THE WORLD

Management and business are more international than ever before. The 1990s have seen the rise of the truly global organization. Currently, some 37,000 parent companies control over 200,000 subsidiaries abroad. Some 40 percent of the total assets of the world's 100 largest companies are already located outside their home countries. The UN estimates that the sales of international corporations accounted for one quarter of the world's GDP in 1991 (and a higher proportion of *private sector* output).[1] The sales of these international corporations in 1991 were estimated at $US 5.5 trillion.

Globalization is all-embracing – even for organizations which are not global in their operations. "Their company will now face greater competition from others selling into many different markets, who have an advantage over the national manager in that they have the ability to pick up on new ideas and experience from other markets," says Annik Hogg, coauthor of *The Marketing Challenge*. "Marketing, after all, is all about good ideas, and you shouldn't be constantly reinventing the wheel." The national organization is likely to be fighting off competitive threats from companies which are organized on a global scale.

Key drivers behind globalization

Globalization has been spurred on by a number of forces:

Technology

Harvard's Ted Levitt has argued that technology is the most potent force towards homogenization. Technology is clearly a driving force behind globalization in markets such as drugs and cosmetics. In the 1980s Unilever identified cosmetics as an area of potential growth – it backed its enthusiasm with investment in Elizabeth Arden ($1.5 billion), Chesebrough-Ponds and Calvin Klein Cosmetics ($306 million). P&G also followed this route with the purchase of Max Factor. While learning that cosmetic brands behave in different ways from soap powder, Unilever has rationalized and reorganized distribution so that there is a single distribution point in Europe for Elizabeth Arden products (rather than 12). The products are made in Virginia and a small number of European sites. The global structure of the company matches the global nature of the brand.

Cost savings

Globalization tends, in corporate terms, to be synonymous with rationalization. Economies of scale mean that someone somewhere is out of a job. Typically, companies with extensive brand portfolios have closely examined the cost of running and promoting large numbers of brands. If one brand costs £X to promote and ten brands costs £10X, then surely it makes sense to put all ten under a single corporate umbrella brand and concentrate the marketing expenditure there.

The rise of homogeneous markets

With increased international travel, technology and the mass media, markets are now more similar than ever before. Our spending and consumption habits have an increasing amount in common no matter where we live. The logic is straightforward: homogeneous markets lead inexorably to homogeneous products.

Globalization, it is thought, brings speed, flexibility, and cost savings. The company is in tune with and close to all of its markets no matter where they are located. Says Carnegie-Mellon's Bruce McKern: "Firms evaluate a foreign country for investment in terms of its attractiveness (adjusted for risk) as a *market* for the firm's products or services, as a source of *resources* (such as labor), or as a *center for rationalization* of the firm's worldwide operations in its drive to achieve global efficiency."

THE ATTRACTIONS OF GLOBALIZATION

The attractions of organizing a company's activities on a global basis tend to fall into a number of categories:

- **Research and development**
  If R&D is organized on a global basis and aimed toward global markets this should allow an organization to simplify its product range; move more quickly to meet market needs; and be more efficient through mutual cooperation.

- **Purchasing**
  Global purchasing can allow companies to respond quickly to changes in the markets for their raw materials; to move more quickly to meet customer needs and to flex their purchasing power more effectively (such as in making the most of currency dealings).

- **Production**
  If production is organized on a global basis to better meet the needs of customers it can bring economies of scale and cost reductions.

- **Marketing**
  In theory, global marketing can allow a company to make more cost-effective use of global media; save costs by eliminating duplication and share knowledge and experience more easily.

- **Distribution/sales**
  With systems geared to servicing a global market, a company's range of products and services should be more readily and more quickly available anywhere in the world. In addition, after-sales service should be improved – no more long waits of three months for a spare part – plus IT should enable speedy problem solving.

While there are many convincing arguments pointing to the advantages of globalization, the process also produces a number of paradoxes, which organizations are finding increasingly difficult to come to terms with. Globalization may be fashionable, but it is far from straightforward – "All you need is the best product in the world, the most efficient production in the world and global marketing. The rest takes care of itself," said former Sony chairman, Akio Morita. It is simply as complex as that.

The most often observed complexity is that between being globally and locally responsive. The truly global organization runs the risk of losing its local identity. People are reassured by local presence, products specially tailored for their local tastes. But, they also want a wide range of competitively priced products to choose from. Customers want the best of both worlds and organizations have to meet this apparently paradoxical challenge.

The answer lies in **glocalization**, an unwieldy phrase to describe the ability to reap the benefits of global production, IT, R&D, and marketing resources, while still being locally responsive.

It is a difficult, and commercially dangerous, balance. ABB chief executive, Percy Barnevik is one of the few executives who have taken on the challenge. "You want to be able to optimize a business globally – to specialize in the production of components, to drive economies of scale as far as you can, to rotate managers and technologists around the world to share expertise and solve problems," he says. "But you also want to have deep local roots everywhere you operate – building products in the countries where you sell them, recruiting the best local talent from the universities, working with the local government to increase exports. If you build such an organization, you create a business advantage that is damn difficult to copy."[2]

Making the global company work

OPERATING IN THE GLOBAL LEAGUE

Professor Hans Wüthrich of Munich's Universität der Bundeswehr says that a global company:

- operates with one global strategy in place of diverse strategies oriented to national markets

- acts within a homogeneous or increasingly homogeneous market

- markets a standardized product globally, and makes consistent use of the opportunities offered by the international division of labor with the aim of realizing economies of scale and synergy effects.

The global company does not happen overnight, though many organizations persist in believing that a single acquisition will thrust them into the global league. Indeed, Nancy Adler and her colleagues at McGill University in Canada suggest that companies move through different phases of international evolution and that each phase demands a different strategy and structure, different approaches to cultural interaction, and different kinds of international manager:[3]

THE EVOLUTION PROCESS

1. A **domestic** stance in which the company operates primarily in its home market and is structured as a centralized hierarchy. Here, few managers (if any) are sent abroad, although export skills may be needed when the firm starts to go international.

2. A **multi-domestic** phase where the company has expanded internationally and each country in which it operates is managed separately within the decentralized hierarchy. Here, expatriate managers from the home country need country-specific skills for adapting culturally to a single country abroad.

3. A **multinational** phase where the company integrates domestic and foreign operations into worldwide lines of business but headquarters tightly controls major decisions worldwide through a

▶

223

centralized hierarchy. Here, international management roles are focussed on top managers who are drawn from all parts of the worldwide organization and whose role is to integrate the company. Managers in the international cadre require a greater understanding of the world business environment and the cross-cultural skills needed to deal with a multiplicity of cultures. Cultural differences will be minimized by assimilating them into the dominant organizational culture.

4. A **transnational** stage where companies, structured as non-hierarchical "networks of equals," are both globally integrated and locally responsive and depend on worldwide organizational learning. In companies of this kind the old distinctions between local and expatriate managers become obsolete because people from all over the world must constantly communicate and work with each other and consciously manage their cultural diversity. The overwhelming majority of managers have international responsibilities and require the ability to move between local responsiveness and the global perspective. They need to be able to integrate worldwide diversity and create cultural synergy, collaboration, and learning.

On its emergence into the harsh light of the **transnational stage**, the organization faces challenges on a broad variety of fronts:

- **The global company must deliver benefits to consumers** – it must bridge the paradox of producing standardized products which are customized.

- **The global company must provide customer service** – customers will not accept indifferent service. The global organization has to be responsive.

- **Presence is essential** – being a global company cannot be interpreted as meaning that the company does not require offices or representation in its markets.

- **Market information** – homogeneous markets cannot be assumed to be so in every way. Their nature needs to be continually evaluated and monitored.

- **Constant utilization of global cost efficiency** – while global cost efficiencies are highly attractive, they are in a constant state of flux. This requires that purchasing and employment patterns need to be continually evaluated. The end result can be highly complex – the intermediary products for the Ford Escort car are obtained from 15 countries.

- **Avoidance of repetition and duplication** – global operations can result in activities and information being generated by different parts of the same organization. Mechanisms need to be in place to avoid costly replication, for example, through the use of IT.

- **Management efficiency** – the global company must have a dynamic and flexible management structure which enables information and skills to be shared speedily. This may require a federal structure, as championed by Charles Handy, and demands an excellent system of communications – as well as a willingness to communicate.

"We cannot lose sight of the fact that highly efficient management is the primary factor in achieving global competitiveness," says Hans Wüthrich of Munich's Universität der Bundeswehr. "Decision makers must deal in a meaningful way with objectives that may, as we have seen, involve mutually contradictory elements. How far must, and should, local adaptation go when a company's range of products and services are being designed? In what way can the international division of labor be exploited while ensuring an acceptable degree of environmental pollution? How much autonomy can be granted to decentralized operating units without jeopardising vital group synergies? How can managers succeed in encouraging learning and innovation in a guided way? To come up with effective answers to these and similar questions, an organization must place a premium on learning capability, must draw on specific management qualities to deal with paradoxes and must ultimately be prepared to throw unreflected management myths overboard."

Achieving world class

Work at London Business School provides a ten-point agenda for companies aspiring to become world class:[4]

1. **Think before using the next faddish idea.** Just copying what other companies are doing is inadequate: the aim is to find new ideas to beat competitors, not ape them. Success comes from incorporating the best ideas into distinctly local solutions.

2. **The role of the chief executive in pushing forward change is crucial.** But one person is rarely enough. The chief executive needs to galvanize the people around him so that leadership comes from the whole top team.

3. **Financial measurements are a misleading guide** to a company's strategic health. Nonfinancial measures – customer satisfaction, employee morale, quality – are vital warning signs for problems three or four years ahead.

4. **Set ambitious goals.** Survival is not enough. Unless you are aware of what other companies worldwide are doing and strive to be the best, you will not survive.

5. Most firms put the emphasis on efficiency – cutting costs, improving utilization rates and so on. **More ambitious firms aim to combine efficiency with effectiveness** – improving skills and capabilities relative to competitors.

6. **Strategic innovation is crucial.** Today the only sustainable competitive advantage is a company's ability to achieve continuous improvement. This means freeing up innovation and creativity at all levels, particularly in middle management. To survive, a company must become a moving target.

7. **Becoming world class demands continuous building of capabilities.** Develop long, medium and short-term objectives, identify capabilities needed to reach them, then determine strategies to acquire or develop them.

8. **Good management is a process of balancing dilemmas:** achieving effectiveness and efficiency; differentiation and low cost; financial goals and long-term vision; consistency and flexibility.

9. **Look outward.** The international dimension is vital even for companies which are not striving to be global. Nothing less than the best international standards is sufficient in the increasingly open and competitive home market.

10. **A bias for action.** Effective firms remove the hidden disincentives to risk-taking, allow people to make mistakes and learn from failure.

Global management

Bartlett, C A, and Ghoshal, S, *Managing Across Borders*, Harvard Business School Press, Boston, MA, 1989.

Bennett, S and Wallace, T *World Class Manufacturing*, Oliver Wight, 1994

Robock, S H, and Simmonds, K, *International Business and Multinational Enterprises*, Irwin, Homewood, IL, 1989

Trompenaars, F, R*iding the Waves of Culture*, Nicholas Brealey, London, 1993

THE RISE OF THE GLOBAL BRAND

In terms of globalization brands have, to a large extent, led the way. Their flexibility and increasingly international nature mean that it has been automatically assumed in many quarters that particular brands are ripe for a global approach. Many are. To prove the point, any major international sporting event will feature an array of global brands whether they are Mars, Coke, whiskeys, or cigarettes.

Brands travel well and global brands have now penetrated virtually every country on earth. The last bastions against global brands are gradually falling. Research by Gallup into the brand awareness of the Chinese found that Coke was already the second most popular brand, following Hitachi. While the Chinese don't, as yet, have the money or the opportunity, they have the aspirations. They are also fully aware of the power of brands as the profusion of imitation and copying shows. (In a sign of the times, the Japanese dominated the top ten brands identified by the Chinese and only one European company, Nestlé, managed to get into the top 20.)

HILTON HOTELS

Globalization is nothing new to brand managers. Take the story behind Hilton hotels. The realization of the group's founder Conrad Hilton was that hotels were not just used by vacationers, but were temporary homes and offices for the traveling foot soldiers of the business world. In response, Hiltons offered high quality standardized service. While other hotels crumbled through the competition from motels, Hilton invented a lucrative business. Senior managers still flock to Hiltons. The global and standardized brand remains firmly in place – the Hilton in Miami is the same as that in Rome or elsewhere. Indeed the company's advertising features a taxi in a city with the caption "Take me to the Hilton" – the assumption is that any major city will have a Hilton "where you can be yourself again."

More and more companies are seeking to follow the Hilton's example. The importance of global brands was summed up by Unilever chairman Michael Perry:

> The first question to be asked of any successful brand today anywhere is, will it travel? And how fast will it travel? Because you have no time to take this process slowly but surely. If you don't move that successful brand around the world rapidly you can be sure your competitor will take the idea, lift it and move it ahead of you. Speed to market is of the essence. But the point ... central to all of this is a global brand is simply a local brand reproduced many times.[5]

For some, it is a simple argument of economy of scale. If the same advertisement will work in Italy as it does in Finland, you don't need to make two. A television commercial can cost hundreds of thousands of dollars so making one or two rather than 12 represents a huge saving. Similarly, if the Spanish product can have the same packaging as the French, then there is a substantial cost saving. The only thing the company needs to ensure is that the advertising or packaging works successfully in particular countries and markets. This essential detail is often one which is overlooked by companies intent on cost savings rather than brand development.

While its repercussions are widespread, clearly global branding also comes with an array of potential problems. From a logistical point of view legislative differences are still major factors in global brand management. Broadcasting laws are many and varied throughout the world. What is acceptable in one country may well be anathema elsewhere. In France, for example, supermarket petrol stations cannot advertise on television thanks to a ban on advertising by the distribution sector.

The world of mass customization

The issue of the homogeneous nature of markets is also contentious. In Europe, for example, the entire issue of sovereignty and national identity is deeply political. In a nationally splintered area like Europe most brands inevitably began life as local brands. Local brands either remain thoroughly local or develop outwards. There is no middle ground. Those which choose the latter route are pushing Europe towards a greater degree of homogenization. This process can be contrasted to what has happened in the United States where companies had a huge fairly homogeneous market on their doorstep and were quick to attempt to satisfy it. Often their attempts at developing brands in Europe quickly ran aground as they tried to enforce the same level of homogenization on the diverse European market. Now American companies tend to be more realistic and concentrate on more localized marketing and advertising – typically, the management of Playtex in Europe is now separate from the US and there is a far greater degree of autonomy in European subsidiaries than was previously the case.

BRAND FLEXIBILITY RATHER THAN UNIFORMITY

Global brands can be interpreted as uniform, unbending solutions to the needs of particular markets. But, ultimately, uniformity is not what makes brands succeed. They do have to be consistent, but they also have to be flexible and responsive to local needs. People have different expectations and requirements.

Indeed, the way people use a particular product may fundamentally differ from one country to the next. Schweppes, for example, is used as a mixer in the UK and Ireland, but as a straight drink in France and Spain. Finding a neat approach which suits the needs of both markets is practically impossible.

As Interbrand founder John Murphy says in his book, *Brand Strategy*: "The trend towards international branding of goods and services is likely to continue and indeed strengthen. This, however, by no means precludes the need for sensitive brand positioning to suit local conditions."

Any brand which places uniformity ahead of local responsiveness is taking a substantial risk. Organizations may easily master globally organized mass production, but may find harder to achieve the **mass customization** now required. The customer is king and demanding more and more. At Panasonic Bicycle in Japan, for example, customers can specify the size, shape, and color of their chosen bike. The computer-controlled production line then does the work.

Meeting the growing demands of consumers while benefiting from global production using the latest technology is the new challenge for companies and brands. Customization requires local and personal contact. Brands which are based on contacts with people – such as hotels and retail brands – tend to be the most locally responsive. Ironically, they are also among the pace setters in creating global organizations.

References

1 UNCTAD, Program on Transnational Corporations, *World Investment Report: Transnational Corporations and Integrated International Production*, New York, 1993.

2 TAYLOR, W, "The logic of global business: an interview with ABB's Percy Barnevik," *Harvard Business Review*, March-April 1991.

3 ADLER, N J, and BARTHOLOMEW, S, "Managing globally competent people," *Academy of Management Executive*, Vol. 6, No. 3, 1992; and Adler, NJ, & Ghadar, F, "Strategic human resource management: a global perspective" in Pieper, R, (ed.), *Human Resource Management: an International Comparison*, de Gruyter, Berlin, New York, 1990.

4 STOPFORD, J, et al, *Building Global Excellence*, London Business School, 1994.

5 Quoted in *AdWeek* Dec. 14, 1992.

Glossary of management thinkers

John Adair

The leading UK thinker on the subject of leadership. He has had an interesting career and his books have proved influential. His key phrase is **action-centered leadership**. Susceptible to gung-ho interpretations of leadership, but notable for his persuasive insistence that leadership is a skill which can be developed.

Key Work: *Effective Leadership* (1983)

Igor Ansoff

The doyen of **strategic management**. His books are far from being light reading, indeed they have a tendency to become tortuously academic. His contribution is undoubted. His book *Strategic Management* remains an important stage in the development of strategy. His later work has lacked its impact. He has brought the world the **Ansoff Matrix** and added **synergy** to the management vocabulary.

Key Works: *Corporate Strategy* (1965); *Strategic Management* (1979); *Implanting Strategic Management* (1984).

Chris Argyris

The father of the learning organization though MIT's Peter Senge tends to receive most of the plaudits. Argyris' work has never become populist though it has retained its popularity. He has pursued an admirably independent line, coaxing ideas along rather than detonating them in front of gasping audiences. His best work has a knack of infiltrating the underside of organizations – and, more depressingly, human behavior. A convinced romantic, he believes people's potential can – and should – be fulfilled. Introduced the concept of **single-loop** and **double-loop learning**.

Key Works: *Personality and Organization* (1957); *Organizational Learning* (with Donald Schon, 1978).

Chester Barnard (1886–1961)

Unlike most influential management theorists, Barnard was actually a manager. His books have proved important, despite their inaccessibility.

Key Works: *The Functions of the Executive* (1938); *Organization and Management* (1948).

Percy Barnevik

The chief executive of Asea Brown Boveri deserves mention simply because of the vast amount of management literature he and his company have spawned. ABB is venerated as the way a modern global company should be run. Barnevik has proved that headquarters don't need to be huge buildings filled with staff, but can be small, dynamic and still do the job. He has introduced a complex **matrix structure** which is reaping impressive results. The test will come when Barnevik leaves or when the company encounters difficulties.

Christopher Bartlett

Harvard Business School professor and coauthor, with Sumantra Ghoshal, of *Managing Across Borders* (1989) one of the key books in understanding the new world of the global organization. They argue that there is now an emergent organization form – **the entrepreneurial organization** – taking the place of the multidivisional structure.

Key Work: *Managing Across Borders* (1989)

Warren Bennis

Unfortunately, Bennis is automatically associated with leadership. Yet, his career has been more broad ranging. He brought the world **adhocracy** and has predicted many of the issues which are only now emerging. His best read book is one coauthored with Burt Nanus, *Leaders*. It is not his best, providing idiosyncratic examples of leadership in practice from Neil Armstrong to a tightrope walker.

Key Works: *The Unconscious Conspiracy* (1976); *The Temporary Society* (1968); *Leaders* (with Burt Nanus, 1985)

Robert Blake

The joint creator of the **Managerial Grid** with Jane Mouton. This was fashionable in the 1960s. (see **Jane Mouton**)

Edward de Bono

The Maltese-born creator of **lateral thinking** has forged a brilliant career from an idea which is more intriguing than it is practical. His output numbers 43 books. He now argues that competition is no longer enough and "sureption" (which concerns the creation of value monopolies) is going to be the game of the future. He has his own private island of Tessera in Venice, from which he organizes "creativity projects."

Key Work: *The Use of Lateral Thinking* (1968)

James McGregor Burns

Highly influential leadership theorist. Invented the terms **transactional** (focussed on immediate events) and **transformational leadership** (long-term and visionary).

Key work: *Leadership* (1978)

Andrew Campbell

The UK academic is nothing if not versatile. His books include one on Scottish country dancing as well as others covering topics as weighty as the role of vision and corporate-level strategy. Formerly with McKinsey he is now at the London-based Ashridge Strategic Management Centre. In *Strategies and Styles*, Campbell and co-author Michael Goold identify three approaches a parent company can take to its businesses: financial control; strategic planning and strategic control. In *Corporate-Level Strategy*, Campbell attacks the performance of most parent companies, describing them as "value destroyers" rather than value creators.

Key Works: *Strategies and Styles* (with Michael Goold, 1987); *Corporate Level Strategy* (with Michael Goold and Marcus Alexander, 1994)

James Champy

Coauthor of the highly successful *Reengineering The Corporation* (with Michael Hammer). The book is evangelical and passionate about the need for reengineering. Doubts remain about its long-term impact. Now a consultant, he is cofounder of CSC Index.

Key Work: *Reengineering The Corporation* (with Michael Hammer, 1993)

Alfred Chandler

The economic historian whose work formed a highly effective bridge-head in the examination of strategy and the evolution of strategic management. He championed the decentralized organizational form and was an advocate of Alfred Sloan's strategy at General Motors.

Key Work: *Strategy and Structure* (1962)

Philip Crosby

One of the leading quality consultants. Formerly with ITT, his catch phrase, in a business of catch phrases, is "Quality is free."

W Edwards Deming (1900-93)

Deming's rejection in the US and his success in Japan is one of the great business stories. It took a TV documentary to propel Deming to overnight fame in the world's boardrooms. He spent the last years of his life desperately traveling the world preaching his gospels, built around his famed, almost biblical, 14 points.

Key Work: *Out of the Crisis* (1982)

Peter Drucker

Born in Austria, though he has spent most of his life in California, Drucker is the preeminent management thinker of the twentieth century. His work is all-encompassing and always worth reading. Even in his eighties, he remains a shrewd and perceptive commentator on virtually every aspect of management and business.

Key Works: *The Practice of Management* (1954); *Management: Tasks, Responsibilities, Practices* (1974); *The Age of Discontinuity* (1969).

Henri Fayol (1841-1925)

Sadly, Fayol is now virtually unacknowledged, yet he was Europe's first significant management thinker. A French businessman he distilled the core functions of management down to 14 points.

Key Work: *General and Industrial Management* (1949)

Mary Parker Follett (1868-1933)

The American political scientist has recently been rediscovered. Among the first to describe the importance of teamworking, her work had some impact in Japan but was largely neglected in the United States.

Key Work: *Mary Parker Follett: Prophet of Management* (1995)

Henry Ford (1863-1947)

The first to translate scientific management into practice. He is best known for his achievements in mass production. This tends to overshadow an extraordinary life and his extraordinary business success.

Jay Forrester

MIT academic who invented core memory during the first wave of modern digital computers, also pioneered the field of system dynamics – analysis of the behavior of systems.

Harold Geneen

The legendary leader of ITT during the 1960s. He was the archetypal numbers man, driven by an unquenchable desire for information. Though he expanded ITT rapidly and recorded excellent results, the company floundered after his departure. Among modern managers who acknowledge Geneen as an influence are Sir Colin Marshall, chairman of British Airways.

Sumantra Ghoshal

Now Professor of Strategic Leadership at London Business School after spells at INSEAD and MIT. Working with Harvard's Christopher Bartlett he has become one of the most respected business gurus of the 1990s.

Key Works: *Managing Across Borders: The Transnational Solution* (1988); *Transnational Management* (1990); *Organization Theory and the Multinational Corporation* (1993).

Gary Hamel

Visiting Professor of Strategic Management at London Business School and formerly with the University of Michigan. Author and coauthor of a number of highly influential *Harvard Business Review* articles and, with CK Prahalad, of *Competing for the Future*.

Key Work: *Competing for the Future* (1994)

Michael Hammer

Former MIT and computer science professor and joint author, with James Champy, of the bestselling *Reengineering The Corporation*. Hammer is derisory of companies which take only gradual or cautious steps to improve customer service, when they should be making striking improvements in their basic operations. "We've had the same answer for 40 years, but the questions have changed. If the taxicab engine is broken, I don't care if the driver is friendly," he says.

Key Work: *Reengineering The Corporation* (with James Champy, 1993)

Charles Handy

Irish-born Handy has seen his reputation burgeon in the 1990s. His increasingly bleak perspectives on the nature of work and organizations are essential reading. He developed the concept of the **Shamrock Organization** and continues to argue the case for federalism.

Key Works: *The Age of Unreason* (1989); *The Empty Raincoat* (1994)

Frederick Herzberg

Now based at the University of Utah, Herzberg was a major figure in management thinking during the 1960s. He took Abraham Maslow's work a stage further, identifying **motivator** and **hygiene** factors as the two sides of motivation.

Key Work: *The Motivation to Work* (with Mausner and Snyderman, 1959)

Geert Hofstede

The Dutch-based anthropologist and academic is increasingly recognized for his work on corporate and international cultures.

Key Work: **Cultures and Organizations** (1991)

Joseph Juran

The "other" quality guru. Juran has lived somewhat in Deming's shadow. Their careers followed similar paths and Juran continues to try to get his quality message across. Less statistical in his orientation than Deming, Juran foresaw the rise of empowerment, some 40 years ago.

Key Work: *Juran on Planning for Quality* (1988)

Rosabeth Moss Kanter

Harvard Business School's Moss Kanter possesses a formidable intellect. A former editor of the *Harvard Business Review*, her work is based on humane, liberal premises. She championed empowerment and has contributed some of the best books on managing change.

Key Works: *Change Masters* (1984); *When Giants Learn to Dance* (1989)

Philip Kotler

"Marketing takes a day to learn. Unfortunately it takes a lifetime to master," says Kotler. He is a prolific author and his texts are now seminal reading for anyone wishing to understand the intricacies of modern marketing. *Marketing Management: Analysis, Planning and Control* is widely used in business schools and his many other books are similarly rigorous. Kotler is Professor of International Marketing at the JL Kellogg Graduate School of Management at Northwestern University.

Key Work: *Marketing Management* (1993)

John Kotter

Professor of Organizational Behavior at Harvard Business School and world-renowned expert on leadership, culture and managing change. His published output is prodigious.

Key Work: *A Force for Change* (1990); *Corporate Culture and Performance* (with James Heskett, 1992)

Theodore Levitt

The German-born marketing thinker peaked early in his career with the massively influential *Harvard Business Review* article, "Marketing myopia." It exposed the limitations of conventional thinking on market-

ing and exhorted companies to become marketing-led rather than production-led. Levitt's later work has largely failed to match the impact of
"Marketing myopia." However, his work on globalization has proved
critical in developing an understanding of the forces now at work.

Key Work: *Thinking About Management* (1991)

Jane Mouton (1930–87)

A social scientist who, together with Robert Blake, developed the idea of
the **managerial grid**. This measured management styles on two dimen-
sions – concern for production and concern for people. The concept was
refined and developed over numerous books.

Key Work: *The Managerial Grid* (1964)

Douglas Macgregor (1906–64)

From 1954 until his death Macgregor was a Professor at MIT. He is
best known for his development of **Theories X** and **Y**. Theory X was the
motivational stick (people don't really want to work and need to be
constantly cajoled) and the carrot (give them an incentive and they will
work and enjoy it).

Key Work: *The Human Side of Enterprise* (1960)

Abraham Maslow (1908–70)

Labeled "The father of humanist psychology," Maslow was head of the
psychology department at Brandeis University. He developed the **hierarchy of needs** which proved highly influential on a number of thinkers.

Key Works: *Motivation and Personality* (1954); *Towards a Psychology
of Being* (1962)

Elton Mayo (1880–1949)

Prodigiously talented and perpetually underrated. Mayo received medical training in London and Edinburgh. He moved on to an Adelaide
printing company and then taught moral and mental philosophy at
Queensland University. Along the way he pioneered a new treatment for
victims of shell shock and was the driving force behind the Hawthorne
experiments in Chicago.

Key Works: *The Human Problems of an Industrial Civilization* (1933);
The Social Problems of an Industrial Civilization (1945)

Henry Mintzberg

Mintzberg's work is studiously eccentric. Deeply researched in classic academic style, it takes unusual directions which make it essential reading. His 1973 book, *The Nature of Managerial Work*, encouraged an entirely new perspective on what managers actually do. Since then Mintzberg has cast his intellectual net wide. He works at McGill University in Canada and INSEAD in France; this does not prevent him being one of the most vehement critics of the modern MBA.

Key Works: *The Nature of Managerial Work* (1973); *The Rise and Fall of Strategic Planning* (1994)

Kenichi Ohmae

Formerly head of McKinsey's Tokyo office, Ohmae is a brilliant thinker whose range and aspirations have increasingly expanded – they now embrace politics. His views on strategy embrace the apparent opposites of rational analysis and the irrational world of intuition. His later work covers globalization and, what he labels, the Inter-Linked Economy of the US, Europe, and Japan/Asia.

Key Works: *The Mind of the Strategist* (1982); *The Borderless World* (1990)

C Northcote Parkinson (1909-93)

An academic who spent time at universities in the US, the UK, and Malaysia. He is best known for his cynical, but all too accurate, **Parkinson's Law** which observed that work expanded to fill the time allotted to it.

Key Work: *Parkinson's Law* (1958)

Richard Pascale

Unlike many of his contemporaries, Pascale is not a prolific writer. His books only number two – *The Art of Japanese Management* (with Anthony Athos) and *Managing on the Edge* (1990) – but both were bestsellers. Pascale's approach manages to combine heavyweight theory with clarity. His message, unpalatable to many managers, is that change is not enough. He calls for transformation, discontinuous shifts in financial performance, key industry benchmarks, and company culture. Organizations must reinvent themselves.

Key Work: *Managing on the Edge* (1990)

Tom Peters

Amid Peters' exuberant stage technique and expansive writing style lie many great examples and vital messages which can be overlooked. The former McKinsey consultant champions the customer-focused, responsive, dynamic, fast moving humane organization. Peters believes in people; that people make a difference and that people make things happen. Criticized for the failure of some of the companies featured in *In Search of Excellence*, Peters' achievement is to put the humane into management.

Key Works: *In Search of Excellence* (1982); *Thriving on Chaos* (1987); *Liberation Management* (1992).

Michael Porter

Harvard's Michael Porter is the man who brought the world the concept of **competitive advantage**. A prodigiously talented individual, his books are required but demanding reading. Since his first success with *Competitive Strategy* in 1980, Porter's audience has grown with each new book – as has his ambition. Porter has carried academic rigor and analysis to new extremes which, according to your preference, are exactly what businesses need or a rational leap too far.

Key Works: *Competitive Strategy* (1980); *Competitive Advantage* (1985); *Competition in Global Industries* (1986); *The Competitive Advantage of Nations* (1990).

CK Prahalad

Professor of Corporate Strategy and International Management at the University of Michigan. In partnership with London Business School's Gary Hamel, Prahalad is setting the new agenda for management. Their *Harvard Business Review* articles "Strategic intent" and "Competing with core competencies" proved highly influential and readable. Author of *The Multinational Mission* (with Yves Doz of INSEAD) and author (with Hamel) of *Competing for the Future*, the most compelling business book of the 1990s.

Key Work: *Competing for the Future* (1994)

Reg Revans

The idiosyncratic Reg Revans has ploughed a lonely furrow, taking his concept of **action learning** to a variety of relatively obscure countries. Action learning appears blindingly obvious – it emphasizes learning from doing in groups (though putting it into practice is more demanding than it seems). Its very simplicity appears to have put off other academics from embracing it.

Key Work: *Action Learning* (1979)

Edgar Schein

Schein has been with MIT for nearly forty years and during that time has become a pioneer of organizational development. In *Organizational Culture and Leadership*, he clarified the concept of organizational cultures and showed its relationship to leadership. He is also the inventor of the terms **career anchor** and the **psychological contract** which have attracted increasing attention in the 1990s.

Key Work: *Organizational Culture and Leadership* (1985)

Ricardo Semler

One of the more unlikely gurus, Semler has transformed his family business from a staid and traditional one into a model of empowerment and employee participation. Criticized by some as an eccentric rather than a maverick, Semler is a highly persuasive speaker and writer.

Key Work: *Maverick!* (1993)

Peter Senge

Director of the Center for Organizational Learning at MIT and author of *The Fifth Discipline: The Art and Practice of the Learning Organization*. Senge, almost single-handedly, propelled the concept of the **learning organization** onto the management agenda. Since then there has been something of a backlash with attempts at implementing Senge's theories proving disappointing.

Key Work: *The Fifth Discipline* (1990)

EF Schumacher

Schumacher's *Small is Beautiful* is one of those books which can be found on bookshelves the world over. It has entered into the argot of management as surely as *Catch-22* has penetrated popular consciousness. Yet, few have actually read the book and fewer still have turned Schumacher's theories into reality.

Key Work: *Small is Beautiful* (1973)

Alfred P Sloan (1875–1966)

Highly influential role model of the decentralized organization. His work at General Motors revolutionized the company – allowing it to quickly out-perform Ford – and provided a much emulated organizational model. Only now, says Sumantra Ghoshal, are organizations shaking off Sloan's legacy.

Key Work: *My Years with General Motors* (1963)

Frederick Winslow Taylor (1856–1917)

When he wasn't winning tennis tournaments or developing new ways to throw a baseball, Taylor developed the first coherent theory of management: **Scientific Management**. Now, it is routinely derided for its inhumane attitude to those who carry out the work, but as Peter Drucker points out, Taylor was the first man to actually begin to think about the nature of the work.

Key Work: *The Principles of Scientific Management* (1913)

Fons Trompenaars

Dutch expert on cultural diversity.

Key Works: *Riding the Waves of Culture* (1993); *The Seven Cultures of Capitalism* (with Charles Hampden-Turner, 1994)

Lyndall Urwick (1891–1983)

Chief European champion of Frederick Taylor's scientific management. He fulfilled this role to great effect, creating a classical interpretation of management.

Key Work: *The Making of Scientific Management* (with EFL Brech, 1946)

Manfred Kets de Vries

Leadership expert, based at France's INSEAD. Voted one of Europe's top business school gurus by the *Financial Times*. He has unparalleled access to some of the world's foremost business leaders. His interest lies in the interface between international management, psychoanalysis, and dynamic psychiatry.

Robert Waterman

Most famously, Tom Peters' coauthor for *In Search of Excellence*, Waterman has since faded into the background. His books remain forceful reminders that excellence does exist.

Key Works: *The Renewal Factor* (1987); *Frontiers of Excellence* (1994)

Thomas Watson Sr (1874–1956)

Indomitable man behind the rise of IBM. His lasting legacy was the creation of IBM's corporate culture which stood the test of time, until the disasters of the 1980s.

Max Weber (1864–1920)

Unfortunately saddled with responsibility for the invention of bureaucracy. This is a harsh interpretation of his observation that a "rational–legal" organizational form was the best for the times.

Index